Joseph Hendrickson McCarty

Two thousand miles through the heart of Mexico

Joseph Hendrickson McCarty

Two thousand miles through the heart of Mexico

ISBN/EAN: 9783744745789

Printed in Europe, USA, Canada, Australia, Japan

Cover: Foto ©Andreas Hilbeck / pixelio.de

More available books at **www.hansebooks.com**

TWO THOUSAND MILES

THROUGH

THE HEART OF MEXICO.

BY

REV. J. HENDRICKSON MCCARTY, D.D.,

AUTHOR OF "THE BLACK HORSE AND CARRYALL," "INSIDE THE GATES," ETC.

NEW YORK:
PHILLIPS & HUNT.
CINCINNATI:
CRANSTON & STOWE.
1888.

TO

THE MEMORY OF MY MOTHER.

THE AUTHOR.

INTRODUCTORY.

ABOUT two years ago the author was enabled to make somewhat of an extended tour through the lotus land of Mexico, which is almost as old as time and as quaint as Egypt itself.

Mexico is a marvelous conglomerate of the ancient and the modern—the pathetic and the ludicrous. To gaze upon a country and mingle with a people of whom he had read much in various books had long been a cherished desire of his heart. And to be able to gratify that desire constituted an epoch in his life.

When but a mere lad he had read the glowing accounts of the famous battles of Palo Alto and Resaca de la Palma, the storming of Monterey, and the victory of Buena Vista, where the brave Taylor and his gallant troops won renown. He had also read of the bombardment of Vera Cruz and its capture, along with the Castle of San Juan d' Ulloa, the storming of the heights of Cerro Gordo, the battles of Contreras and Molino del Rey, and the fall of Chapultepec. Little did he then think that his feet would ever press the soil crimsoned with the blood of his countrymen in the far-away land of the Aztecs.

Of course, in a tour through Mexico there were many points of special interest to be visited. In the following pages he has kept in view the history of the stirring events of the war of 1846 and 1847, interwoven alike, as they are, in the annals of our own as well as in those of our sister republic.

There is no other land quite like Mexico. A wonderful charm gathers about the scenery, whether it be mountain or valley, sea-coast or table-land. The story of Mexico is as eventful as it is pathetic. Her people, in many of their characteristics, are unlike any other on the globe. Her history, which runs far back into the past, is a sanguinary one. When the Aztec empire was in its zenith of power her altars were stained perpetually with the blood of human sacrifices. And ever since the conquest her rich plains have been the scenes of innumerable fierce and bloody revolutions. Here truth is, indeed, stranger than fiction. It has been said, " See Naples and die." See Mexico and live!

To be able to do something to redeem that lofty land should be a stimulus to one's life.

The author traveled through the most populous portion of the republic. The trip embraced about two thousand miles within the territory. As far as possible he allowed nothing worth seeing to escape his observation. Yet he does not claim to have seen every thing. That would require years instead of months. He journeyed by diligence, railway, and horseback, traversed several mountain ranges, and courageously walked into the crater of a volcano—an extinct one! He descended into the bosom of the earth and witnessed the miners blasting out the silver ore with cartridges of dynamite. He saw the pure liquid metal running into the molds in the *haciendas de beneficios*, and was compelled to carry in his pocket, in heavy coin, sixteen dollars to the pound, what was needed for temporary use. So that for once in his life he had more solid cash than he wanted. He was on several of the largest ranches, where cattle and horses roam in herds of thousands. He was in scores of huts in the interior, as well as in some of the finest dwellings in Mexico. The route took him through many villages and gave him an opportunity to visit fifteen of the principal cities. He conversed with people of all grades of society, from the ignorant peon, in his rags and filth, up to persons of high social position, including army officers, college professors, bankers and merchants, as well as the governors of three States. He visited a number of the most renowned old Toltec and Aztec remains, had free entry into art galleries, museums, and schools. In short, he saw Mexico from Nuevo Leon, on the extreme north-east, to Yucatan, on the far south, studying every feature of the land-surface, and all the customs and manners, religion and politics, of the people as far as it was possible to do in so short a period of time. That he mastered the subject he does not pretend; he only claims to have improved the time in sight-seeing, and to have gained some knowledge at least of this wonderful land and its people, which will be available in after years. Much has been omitted that might have been written in these pages. The story of Mexico is a long one. If the reader is disposed to find fault with the frequent references to the predominant religion of Mexico, let it be remembered that the Church is the largest thing in Mexico, and that the "play of Hamlet with Hamlet left out" would be a poor play. Even American Catholics, with some of whom he has conversed on the subject, do not uphold the degraded form of their own faith among the Mexicans. Facts are stubborn things.

The author left home in the railway coach "Mayflower," symbol of the nation to be, and returned in a ship bearing the name of the capital of a nation that is, the "City of Washington."

On reaching home he had the satisfaction of having made one of the most profitable as well as enjoyable trips of his life, even if he had to undergo some discomforts on the way. It was a sufficient compensation for these to be able to see the land of the ancient Aztecs, a portion of our own continent so near to us geographically, and yet as remote socially, as if it were on the opposite side of the globe.

If the reader would see Mexico, while the glamour which Prescott's *Conquest* threw over it lingers, he must go quickly, for the "prince, whose name is Young America, is already on the way to awake the Sleeping Beauty from the repose of Centuries."

Mexico, under the new light which is dawning upon her social and civil fabrics, may yet have a future, let us all hope, as brilliant as her past has been thrilling.

THE AUTHOR.

PENN YAN, N. Y., *June* 17, 1886.

CONTENTS.

CHAPTER	PAGE
I. Dreams Realized	11
II. On the Wing	17
III. Gate-ways to the Land of the Aztecs	29
IV. Across the Rio Grande	43
V. Gem of the Mountains	50
VI. Land of the Beautiful View	62
VII. Amid the Sierras	76
VIII. Hut Life among the Aztecs	85
IX. Village Life on the Table Lands	94
X. The Eye of the Sierras	105
XI. The Haunts of the Banditti	117
XII. The Home of Forty Robbers	121
XIII. The Vales of Anahuac	145
XIV. The Adventurer of Miramar	156
XV. The Paris of the Western World	170
XVI. Wanderings along Old Paths	191
XVII. From Toltec to Spaniard	202
XVIII. A Grip of Steel	217
XIX. The March of Scott's Army	241
XX. From Sea-Coast to Mountain-Crest	255
XXI. Songs in the Night	273

TWO THOUSAND MILES THROUGH THE HEART OF MEXICO.

CHAPTER I.

DREAMS REALIZED.

Away from the snows—Short summers and long winters—So near and yet so far—The art of travel—People who can be approached—"All's not gold that glitters"—Oldest of countries—The adjustment—First run—"Mayflower" and "Pilgrim"—Speed and safety—Men die, but man does not—A thousand guards to life—The Zero point of danger—Grumblers—Patience.

MEXICO! In the month of February, 1884, when the winds were moaning dismally through the naked branches of the trees, and all nature, as if asleep, lay in quiet repose beneath a coverlet of snow all over this north-land, I found myself able to realize a pleasure which had long occupied a place only in my dreams—a trip to the sunny land of Mexico.

Out of the cold and away from the snows into a tropical latitude, where I might inhale the aroma of rare flowers and listen to the songs of other birds than those whose warblings greet and cheer us in this northern clime! What a privilege! I knew, from experience, all about the short summers and long winters of the region of the northern lakes, as well as the short winters and long summers of the gulf coast. It was not only a pleasure, but it seemed to be a duty I owed to my "day and generation," that I should at least take a look at our neighbor, whose cities are built and whose fields are cultivated in sight of the Southern Cross. Mexico is a country quite closely related to the United States in form of civil government if not in religion. But taken all in all, owing to its peculiar civilization, it is almost as far removed from us as the antipodes.

This trip grew out of a desire to look upon that strange old country once the home of the Toltecs, a people who came and went away again more than a thousand years ago, leaving many remarkable monuments of their rude civilization scattered over all the land, from the valley of the Rio Bravo del Norte to the southern borders of Yucatan; land of the Aztecs, a people who succeeded the Toltecs, leaving behind them signs of former power, whose children are yet numerous in the land of their forefathers, and whose characteristics, well defined and marked, will be noticed hereafter; land of mountains, whose crested summits are whitened with eternal snows; land of rich valleys burdened with luxurious tropical vegetation, and fertile plains filled with perpetual bloom; land pre-eminent of political revolutions; that old land, that land of superstition and false religion and consequent moral degradation; that richest and at once poorest of all countries. I had long been possessed of a strong desire to look upon it, to mingle with its queer people, and study it from within, even though a closer view should but confirm the impressions made on the mind from reading a few of the many books written upon Mexico by both American and European authors.

I stood, satchel in hand, which contained my entire traveling outfit, conversing with a few friends who had come to the depot to offer their adieus, when "All aboard!" shouted the conductor of the train on the Erie Road, which was to bear me away on that winter evening. "Good-bye!" "Good-bye!" "Safe journey!" "*Bon voyage!*" "Home in May!" were expressions which yet linger in my recollection.

The train was soon in motion and I was really *en route* toward Mexico. The last few hours before starting on a journey one is usually very busy, and consequently very weary. It matters not how early he begins the needed preparation, there are always some last things to be done, and they can only be done at the last.

I threw myself down in my berth, for I was tired, but for two or three hours there was neither "sleep to mine eyes, nor slumber to mine eyelids." It was like a first night on the Atlantic Europeward. It always takes some time to adjust one's self to new conditions. I had just turned my back, not my heart, upon friends and home.

There was no desire to sleep, but rather to think— to think of friends gone, and of friends left behind and living. I just wanted to cast off all cares, as trees drop their leaves in autumn-time. When one departs to rest or sight-see, it is not wise to go like a ship freighted to the water's edge with a multitude of home cares. So, acting on this principle, I shook them off— not the friends, but the cares—and tucking the blankets close about me, on that cold February night, gave rein to my thoughts, which ran over the past somewhat, and out on the present, and then down along the future. "While I was musing the fire burned." The hours sped away until at length all was lost in sleep. "Blessed is the man who invented sleep," said Sancho Panza. With a "conscience void of offense," and a good supper in process of digestion, why shouldn't a weary traveler fall off into pleasant dreams!

The first run was from Elmira, New York, to Cincinnati, Ohio. The particular parlor coach to which I was assigned bore the significant name " Mayflower "—hence I became a " Pilgrim." Onward sped the " Mayflower " toward the first objective point—Cincinnati. What speed! what safety! O the faith we have after all!— not alone in God who keeps the planets in their course, timing them so perfectly that there never can be "a wreck of matter and a crash of worlds" about which poets have dreamed, but in man too.

The Builder and Preserver of worlds is not dead. " In him we live, and move, and have our being." Man is not dead either, and I thought of it as I drew the covering over me.

The train speeds on through the dark, up the grades and down the grades, around the curves, over bridges and through the sleeping valleys, and withal there is not much danger to life or limb. Does the reader ask why? Because man is not dead. Men die, but man does not; he lives on and on forever.

There he stands on the platform of the engine, a master-spirit controlling that monster thing whose heart-throbs keep in motion this long train with its precious freightage. Were he to fail in his duty what sadness might come to scores of homes over all the land!

But he does not fail. His arm is ready to curb the fury of his iron steed, or control its power as easily as a mother governs her child. His hand is on the lever; his eye is on the track; his ear is open to catch every sound, while his own heart possibly is beating its warm pulses for some dear wife and child a hundred miles away. On and still on we fly, trusting all to God and man. Conductors and train-men are awake the night through, guarding the lives and property committed to their keeping. Far out in the darkness lanterns are swinging, lights are revolving, green, red, white. Wheels

Dreams Realized.

are pounded at the stations by men whose trained ears can quickly detect the slightest divergence from soundness. Switchmen are guarding the switches. Telegraph operators are bending over their tables, amid a din of noisy clicks, reading what is worse than Hebrew to the uninitiated.

No, no; man is not dead, and the traveler can lie down knowing that a thousand men between Elmira and Cincinnati are standing guard over his life. Why not feel safe?

After having journeyed much, and in many regions, by railway and steamer, I have never yet seen a railway or steam-ship accident. One may make the circuit of the globe and return in safety, and then, alas! lose his life in going to the nearest town. It is really wonderful that the percentage of lives lost in traveling should be so small. On all seas and over all lands thousands upon thousands are traveling, and only a few comparatively lose their lives by accident.

It is not well when one starts on a journey, long or short, to begin to speculate on the possible disasters that may befall him. "Sufficient unto the day is the evil thereof." But I was going to remark that there is always some danger in traveling. At any moment a train may be wrecked or a boat may sink. Some one has said, "Man thinks all other men mortal but himself." It is true. But if there is a little danger in traveling a distance of ten miles on a railway train anywhere, the danger does not increase ten times that amount in going a hundred miles, nor a hundred times that much in going a thousand miles; else few would start upon long journeys, and so it comes to pass that the danger-point is near Zero.

Our train was a couple of hours late when it reached Cincinnati. When one thinks of this distance, and the possibilities always in travel, it is not at all wonderful that we should be a trifle late ; it would be almost a miracle if we were not. Traveling as much as any thing else brings out human nature. How impatient some are, and how ready to complain! "I will never go to St. Louis again by this line, for it is most wretchedly managed," says one. "I shall miss all my connections for the West, and it will be a most terrible disappointment," mutters another. While a gruff old fellow thought the railroad company might be prosecuted for not fulfilling the contract implied in the purchase of a ticket. As I sat there listening to these grumblers, I thought of the old lady who ascribed her long life and good health to the "obsarvance of that Scriptur' which says, Fret not thy gizzard!"

The best outfit, next to a pure heart and a good conscience, is a happy and contented mind. "Godliness with contentment is great gain," even when one is on a journey by car or boat.

O, traveler, whenever you pack your satchel for a tour of eight thousand miles, more or less, be careful to stow away somewhere a good stock of patience.

CHAPTER II.

ON THE WING.

Cincinnati—Verge of spring—The great flood—Breath of Boreas—The ideal *versus* the actual railway—St. Louis hardness, lime, and wind—The old French power in America—Arkansaw *versus* Arkansas—Coal and gold—Negro and caste—In hot water—Texas and green grass—Extent and varied history—More room wanted—Corner lots—Two lovers.

THE reader must bear with me in what may seem to be a digression from the main subject. If he is in haste to plunge into the middle of this book to know what the author thinks of Mexico and its people, this, and possibly another chapter or two, can be passed over. But one thing is certain, I was as anxious to enter the land of the ancient Aztecs as the reader can well be to read about it from these pages. Will it not be well to move slowly? Patience, therefore, is the word. The time was when Cincinnati was only a frontier town in the then very distant West, almost beyond the abodes of civilization. Now it is a large city in about the center of the population of these United States. The "Mayflower" wheeled into the depot a little after schedule time. The building so called was only a temporary structure, awaiting the erection of a more commodious and beautiful one. I had noticed, as the train drew near Cincinnati, that the snow had all disappeared, and that the grass on sunny southern slopes was commencing to show signs of life. Nature was already beginning to awake. She was in the condition of some people when they first open their eyes in the morning, not quite ready to get up. She wanted " a little more sleep and a little more slumber." It was too early for spring to arise and come forth. The air was, nevertheless, quite balmy, and I began to felicitate myself on at least a speedy escape from snow and ice. If I had caught some severe colds during the winter; I should, doubtless, catch some big warms before I got out of Mexico and Yucatan. Being familiar with Cincinnati, and having to lie over a couple of hours, a good opportunity was afforded to take a stroll and obtain a glimpse of the devastation caused by the great inundation which so recently had come upon that whole region. At this date the waters had retired, and, as in Noah's day, once more the dry land had appeared. But the country wore a strange appearance. It looked as if some giant had gone over it with a broom and given it a mud-wash. The whole landscape had a yellowish tinge. Over all the region around Cincinnati the destruction had been very great. Probably not less than seventy-five square miles of territory, included in the lower part of the corporation and surroundings, had been almost ruined. Hundreds of houses had been carried away bodily. It is true they were mostly cheap and poorly built wooden structures, but they were the homes of hard-working people, and to their owners and occupants were as highly prized as the stately mansions upon Walnut Hills are prized by the rich people who own and live in them. From Columbia, above the city, all the way around to Spring Grove Cemetery, a distance of twenty-five miles, and across to the city of Newport, on the Kentucky side, all had been literally under water. The Ohio was like an inland sea, whose waters rushed and foamed and engulfed. Thousands of people were shut in their upper rooms, above the water-line, to whom fuel and provisions were conveyed by small boats. The gardeners, who raise vegetables for the Cincinnati market on the lowlands, must begin life anew, their buildings and the frames for their hot-beds having been borne away by the flood. The ground has been enriched by a new deposit of fresh sediment, it is true ; but, good as that is, it cannot replace the loss sustained in the destruction of buildings and farm implements. I came in from a walk and took my seat in the dining-room of the substitute for the Grand Central, and called for supper, which was soon served by an intelligent young man of African blood. In speaking of the flood, he said that the water right where I was sitting had been about one foot higher than the top of my head, and that the depot was like a great mud-hole after the waters had subsided. Along the banks of the river were many overturned houses, while hundreds had gone down stream to make kindling wood for the people along the lower Mississippi.

The train pulled out of the Cincinnati station at half past eight o'clock for St. Louis. But a snow-storm was just setting in, and the spring-like appearance of the previous day was all gone. The ground was white with snow, and a westerly wind betokened a "blizzard." St. Louis was reached next day at eleven o'clock instead of seven o'clock, as the time-tables promised. There are two kinds of railroads—the ideal and the actual. The ideal railroad is perfect. The train leaves on the minute and stops on the minute, and there is not a single delay anywhere, nor a break in any piece of machinery. No employee ever makes a mistake. Every thing moves like the sun, and all the passengers are happy. But the actual railroad ever reveals to us human imperfections. No man with the best rule can draw a perfectly straight line, nor with the best compass describe a perfect circle; for nothing human is perfect. Well, these imperfections show themselves occasionally in cold cars, detentions, late trains, and many minor annoyances to the traveler; but in all these things we must learn the art of living contentedly. Let "patience have its perfect work." The actual railroad is for the benefit of the growlers. It gives them an opportunity to show off their dispositions. On this occasion they were not thankful because we had come safely over a road that had been washed out in many places by the recent floods, nor for the fact that there had been no collisions or broken rails or wrecked bridges to send the whole company into eternity. O no! the average man is selfish, unthankful, and wants to have his own way and every body else's way at the same time. Once we were quite content when we traveled six miles an hour—now we must chase through life forty or fifty miles an hour, and, if a train is an hour or two late in reaching its destination, every one finds fault with the railway company. But where is this "sunny South?" During the night Cincinnati softness had become St. Louis hardness, and when our train reached the depot the chill was severe. The mercury was below zero.

St. Louis is built on a limestone formation, and the streets are macadamized or paved with it in many places. The perpetual pounding of myriads of hoofs and the crushing of ten thousand wheels have pulverized the limestone into dust, and when it is dry, as it was on this occasion, and the wind blows fiercely, as it did then, the air becomes laden with dust almost to suffocation. St. Louis is a very large and prosperous city, the rival of Chicago; the latter has the railroads and the lakes, the former the railroads and the Mississippi River. Chicago is the *entrepôt* of the mighty North-west; St. Louis is the *entrepôt* of the mighty South-west. Both will continue to grow; but which will outgrow the other? Let Chicago answer! The name St. Louis tells of the old French power in America, when heroic priests, spurred on by religious zeal, joined with love of adventure, sought foothold in the new world. That history records many of the boldest adventures ever undertaken by man. Think of the distance from Quebec to New Orleans, including the whole of the great lake region which lies between Canada and the United States! France was emulating Spain in those days. Possibly commerce was joined with religion at Quebec; but the spirit of exploration and conquest for the Church of France and Rome sent Peré Marquette and his fellow missionaries traversing these lands and cruising on their waters. Canada then embraced a large country. The legend in regard to its name may or may not be true. Then the Indian said to the adventurous white man in quest of gold, *aca nada*—nothing here—no gold here—and so *aca nada* became Canada. But if there were no gold mines, there were lands whose productions are easily transmuted into gold.

The city of St. Louis is well situated at the junction of the Ohio with the "Father of Waters," but the Mississippi rises far up to the northward. Even Lake Itasca, out of which it rises, bears the stamp of these same old French Jesuit propagandists. The story runs, as I have read somewhere, that when the source of the Mississippi was reached, and a name was needed for it, the old priest said, "What shall we call it?" Various names were suggested; but none suited him. "Let us," said he, "invent a new name. This is the *true head* of the Mississippi; in Latin that would be *veritas caput*. Now cut off the *ver* and the *put*, and you have Itasca."

St. Louis was left behind, and I found myself headed toward the more distant South. It was spring-time in this region, but the snows had fallen over Missouri and Arkansas, and the winds were cold and piercing. This name should be pronounced *Arkansaw*, for a pamphlet was written by a learned Arkansas judge in support of it, and the State Legislature passed an act making it authoritative. The reasoning in the case was largely analogical. For instance, Tensas Parish, in Louisiana, which was settled by Creole French and Acadians, is pronounced Tensaw. Tamaulipas in Mexico is properly pronounced Tamaulipaw; hence Arkansas should be pronounced Arkansaw. But custom, in the pronunciation of names especially, makes law, so say "them literary fellers," as scholarly Congressmen were called by some one. I was once present at a school where a teacher was hearing a class in English analysis. The lesson was from Pope, and a young miss read:

> "Lo! the poor Indian, whose untutored mind
> Sees God in clouds, and hears him in the wind."

"Wynd," said the professor, "not wind." And the pupil so read it until she came to the couplet:

> "And thinks admitted to yon equal sky,
> His faithful dog shall bear him company."

"Correct," remarked the professor. "Why so?" said I, "custom is capricious. If w-i-n-d should be pronounced wynd, why should not company be pronounced compan*eye*?" "But custom makes law, and custom is capricious," said the professor.

Well, this State of Arkansas is a territory three hundred miles across either way, and lying between the hot belt bordered by the Gulf of Mexico and the cold belt bordered by the great lakes, the climate is very mild and equable. The State is traversed by the Blue Mountain range, which at no point rises to an altitude above two thousand feet. The country is quite level. In the northern part it is heavily timbered with a mixture of pine and hard wood. In the southern part not so much so. Coal of good quality is found in some sections in large quantities. Reports are current, too, of gold and silver some distance south of Hot Springs city, but as yet it is not known whether it exists in paying quantities or not. Arkansas is not a wheat State, but raises good corn and cotton. No finer fruit region can be found. In the museum of the Iron Mountain Railroad, at Little Rock, may be seen preserved specimens of apples, pears, peaches, plums, etc., equaling those of California. But much of the territory of the State is very sterile. Even the trees show it in their stunted appearance. The Iron Mountain Railway, which crosses the State from the north-east to the south-west, is doing much toward bringing Arkansas into the notice of the world. The country people whom I chanced to meet in the villages and on the trains were exceedingly rustic in their manners and appearance. The Negroes are not so numerous here as they are in Georgia and Louisiana, though they make up a considerable percentage of the whole population. The old caste spirit seems to have pretty much died out, for I noticed that in the second-class cars blacks and whites rode together promiscuously in entire harmony. That would not have been tolerated a few years ago. It is not allowed even yet in some of the Southern States. The State has a good public-school system for all its children, colored as well as white. But I must pass by Little Rock and the city of Hot Springs, with its numerous hotels, its heated waters, which bubble out of the rocks hot enough to cook an egg, and its strange mixture of people, sick and well.

I must omit any description of the ancient mounds around Malvern, which tell of that strange people, the mound-builders, who once dwelt here, but who have departed to the land of the unknown. I turned into my berth just as the train pulled out of Texarkana Station, on the Texas and Pacific Railway. Texarkana is situated at the junction of the three States, Texas, Arkansas, and Louisiana, each of which forms a part of the name. I regretted to be compelled to pass over three hundred miles of northern Texas in the night-time, but the conductor of the train assured me that any one square mile was a fair sample of the whole region through which we would travel. The weather had been growing warmer as we approached the real South. Now I was in Texas, and at one of the stations actually got out and put my feet on Texas soil. But has the reader any correct idea of the extent of this territory?

Texas extends from Galveston, on the Gulf of Mexico, north-westerly to near the junction of Colorado with Kansas, and from the western boundary of Louisiana to the center of the southern boundary of New Mexico, which any one can see by looking at the map. It is equal in geographical extent to six Englands. If all the cities and villages with all the people of our great United States were taken up and put down upon Texas, it would not be crowded as densely as many portions of the Old World. It has the possibilities of an empire in itself.

What a history Texas has had. Once under the rule of Spanish Mexico—the arena of many a bloody conflict—now independent of Mexican rule, and anon held in the strong grip of Mexican armies. At one period the "Lone Star Republic," and then a member of the American confederation of States. Out of the Union by Confederate action in 1861, back in the Union by the fall of the Confederacy in 1865, and to-day one of the richest and most prosperous States in the Union, one of the brightest stars in the galaxy of the great Republic.

Louisiana was once a vast territory reaching far up into the great North-west. Its purchase from France, at an insignificant price compared with its value to the nation, was a most masterly stroke of good statesmanship. Ben Franklin said: "Never buy what you don't need because it is cheap, for if you do, it will prove to be dear enough in the end;" or at least he said something very much like that.

We purchased Louisiana cheap, and we needed it. Texas once belonged to Mexico, and so did all that vast region north to the Indian Territory—Colorado and California—including New Mexico and Arizona. San Francisco, previous to 1847, was a Mexican port. The war with Mexico really began in 1845, when Gen. Taylor occupied Corpus Christi, and ended in 1847, when Gen. Scott took the capital. That war was fought in the interest of American slavery. Mexican soil was drenched with blood to make room for our then so-called "peculiar institution." A slave market was wanted by Southern statesmen. Texas we had and must have, and they said we must have more than that.

The territory which our government acquired by the treaty of Guadalupe de Hidalgo cost us in cash, for war expenses and purchase money, one hundred and thirty-four millions of dollars, and twenty-five thousand lives, when, it has been said, the whole territory could have been purchased outright for thirty millions without war. By that treaty, inclusive of Texas, the United States came into possession of territory equal to seventeen States as large as the State of New York, or about one half of the land area of the Mexican domain. We needed the territory, not for slavery, but for civilization and freedom, and God permitted us to acquire it, though the motives actuating the breasts of the chief actors in that whole affair cannot be commended from a moral stand-point.

In those days our politicians were speculating in corner lots, and doing it very successfully. Texas has much poor soil, but it has also a vast amount of good and arable land. Almost any thing that grows out of the earth can be produced in some part of Texas. It is especially adapted to grazing, however, and is a great cattle-producing region. Many are the men who have acquired and are acquiring princely fortunes in this line of industry in Texas.

As the train drew near San Antonio the grass was very green. The soil had changed from an ironish or limeish appearance to that of a dark rich loam. The absence of timber is noticeable, and what trees there are scattered over the plains are small and of second growth.

At all the stations where the train stops, even for a minute or two, men and boys, black and white, come running and stand and gape and stare at the passengers, as if they were a lot of imported white elephants. Some stand with their hands thrust down into their pockets—as if to show their emptiness—others have cakes and apples to sell. The store-rooms and saloon buildings have high and square fronts, which rise above the roof of the porches, and cause the structures to resemble Texas steers, with the space between their horns boarded up. The scenery is monotonous, level and rich here, level and poor and stony there. Over the southern part of Texas grows the Nopal cactus, and the mesquite, the latter a beautiful shrub just now very green.

Owing to the good understanding of mankind, a train full of people can come from Boston to San Antonio, or go from New York to San Francisco, without change. The standard gauge permits this. Unity is the word of the hour. Napoleon the First had a dream, and a splendid dream it was, that of unifying all of Europe, giving all a common standard of weights and measures, and a common standard of coin. The American nation must realize this dream of the great Corsican. The standard railroad gauge, standard time, standard bank bills, standard English speech, "standard oil," plus the American eagle, will conquer the continent in the end.

Morning came, my first morning in Texas. A long ride was before me, and the day must be passed in looking out of the window upon the country, chatting with the passengers, and taking an occasional romp with the children for recreation. Just now, to relieve the monotony, there comes into our coach a Texan and Texaness, evidently a bride and groom fresh from Hymen's altar. How do I know? Because they appear a little abashed, a trifle awkward. They have just been made one and are on their way to San Antonio, I imagine. They may be brother and sister, or cousins; but no, he is too attentive to her for that. She is more than sister any way. He is a gaunt, strapping fellow, six feet tall and over twenty-one years old, weighs nearly or quite two hundred pounds, is brown skinned, and wears a broad-brimmed white hat just out of the store. He has on buff-colored pants and a blue coat, with large buttons, is shod with heavy shoes, is without a neck-tie—a slovenly habit common in some sections of the South among many. Every few minutes he looks at a great moon-shaped watch, which he pulls out of his pocket. His mustache, like his hair, is black, and promises well if kept under a good state of cultivation, but is a little sickly yet. It is like an approaching comet, faintly visible to the naked eye. She is rather a bright-looking little lady, plainly but neatly attired in a brown silk. Over her shoulders rests easily a very light white zephyr shawl. She has on a brown straw hat with blue trimmings, which is further ornamented with a crimson rose surmounting a spray of green. It don't look quite right, but what the matter is I cannot tell. The little Texaness has about her neck a very neat fixture held together by a modest pin. What she saw in that great awkward man to attract her attention and win her heart she only knows. She looks up into his face and leans over on his arm very prettily at times, precisely as if she were not a bit afraid of him. Ah, who knows what a great hearted generous soul he may be after all!

CHAPTER III.

GATE-WAYS TO THE LAND OF THE AZTECS.

Routes to select from—Quick and easy—Long and hard—San Antonio, old and quaint plazas and past times—Struggles of early days—The Alamo and its story—Mexican invasion—Bloody scenes—Santa Anna—Genial skies—Davy Crockett, the hero—The old mission ruins—What might be—Springs of Saint Peter—Street-car scene—Mixed—The Spanish mule, etc.

THERE are a number of routes by which the tourist can reach Mexico from the Atlantic side. First, he can purchase tickets over the Texas and Pacific Railway from St. Louis to El Paso. This latter point is two thousand four hundred and fifty-six miles from New York. Thence he can reach the city of Mexico, distant one thousand two hundred miles, by way of the Mexican Central Railroad It will be seen that by this route the distance from the city of New York to the Mexican capital is three thousand six hundred and fifty-six miles.

On the American side the road runs through one of the finest sections of our continent, a region whose future is yet to be. On the Mexican side the country is level, barren, and monotonous. Humboldt described it as a great table-land, which could be traveled in four-wheeled carriages without the advantage of artificially prepared roads. The tourist can take another route, and go by rail to New Orleans, and thence by steamer to Vera Cruz. Or he can take steamer at New York, and sail by way of Havana to Vera Cruz. Thence he can go directly by rail to the city of Mexico, visit a few points of interest in and around the capital, and return home by the same route. I once knew of a gentleman who visited Palestine after that fashion. He went to Rome, and crossed the Mediterranean Sea to Alexandria. There he took ship to Jaffa, and from the latter place went on horseback to Jerusalem, where he remained over night. Then he rode the same horse back to Jaffa the following day, took passage on the same steamer to Alexandria, and came home. He spent the following winter in delivering lectures on "Travels in Palestine!"

The route selected for this trip to Mexico was not the longest, but it was the hardest of any. It was one which would take me over the Sierra Madre—a journey which would involve five or six hundred miles of staging, and would not only enable me to rough it, but it would show me the very heart of Mexico, and that was the end in view. San Antonio and Laredo constitute the gate-ways through which one must pass in taking this route. Both once belonged to Mexico. So I began to get a glimpse of Mexican life while yet in our own country. San Antonio, or the "Alamo city" as it is poetically called, when speaking of the storied past, may well be considered historic. Just when it was founded is not certainly known. But ancient records show that Texas was invaded by the French and Spaniards as far back as the latter part of the sixteenth century. The most definite information given is that in 1714 the old San Antonio road into Mexico was laid out, and a military post established at this point.

In 1733 the city was granted a charter by the King of Spain, which was confirmed by the Texas republic one hundred and four years later. The subsequent events which transpired during the heroic struggle of the brave

Texans for independence are so well known as to need no repetition here. As a resort for the invalid, the historian, or the pleasure-seeker, the "Alamo city" possesses superior charms and advantages. The "San Pedro" springs, the beautiful little San Antonio River, the romantic and picturesque nooks along its banks, the many poitions of this frontier city which have been baptized in human blood, render this locality rich in history and deeds of valor and devotion to principle, causing the thoughts of visitors, as well as of her citizens, to turn naturally to the important events of the past.

San Antonio will, undoubtedly, have a future as remarkable as its past has been interesting. Every stranger who visits this queer old Spanish American city must, of course, see the sights about town, and so I sallied forth first to the plazas—the Plaza Mayor, the Plaza de Armas, and then the Alamo. San Antonio having once been a Mexican city, the plaza is an institution, as we Americans are in the habit of calling things which we regard as very common or necessary. The plaza will be described when Mexico proper is reached.

The most interesting historic point here is the Alamo. The Alamo was one of the "missions" founded by the Catholic Church, more than a century and a half ago, under the name of San Antonio Valero. It was some distance east of the city, but is now almost in its center. It is not the Alamo as a "mission" that is now so full of interest, but the Alamo as a fort, into which it was converted by the necessities of war—the scene of one of the fiercest of struggles, where occurred a sacrifice which made it the Thermopylæ of America, as we shall see. Any one acquainted with the early struggles through which this country has passed cannot fail to be interested in the old Alamo, the scene of the most memorable battle ever fought on the soil of Texas—the altar on which as brave men as ever breathed yielded up their lives in the cause of liberty and popular government. The Alamo,* now, alas! instead of being preserved as a landmark, has been utilized as a grocery warehouse.

Having read of the great struggles in and around the Alamo when the Texans were fighting to free themselves from Mexican rule, its present size' quite disappointed me. The main chapel, now recognized as the Alamo, is only about seventy-five feet long by sixty-five feet in width. The walls are four feet thick, and about twenty-three in height, built of solid masonry. It fronts to the west. In the days of its glory it was much more pretentious. From the north-west corner a wall extended fifty feet to a convent building. The convent was of two stories, one hundred and eighty-six feet in length and eighteen feet in width, with flat roof. From the north-east corner of the chapel a strongly-built stockade extended seventy-five feet to a building called the prison. The latter was a one-story structure, one hundred and fifteen feet in length by seventeen feet in width, and was joined to a'portion of the east wall. The *patio*, or court, inclosed within these various walls was one hundred and fifty-four yards in length by fifty-four in width, and embraced between two and three acres. Here a thousand men could find ample shelter, and defend themselves with arms against an attacking foe. The outer walls were two and a half feet thick and eight feet high.

The Alamo was first used for defense against hostile Indians, and was, consequently, destitute of salient and

---

* The name signifies cotton-wood in Spanish, and was probably given to it by the Mexican troops who came there in the olden times from Fort Alamo de Parras, in the State of Coahuila, to which Texas, as a Mexican province, was attached.

dominant points in case of bombardment. From a local history we are told that—

"At the time of the memorable siege, which resulted in the heroic death of all of its brave defenders, on the 6th of March, 1836, three heavy guns were planted upon the walls of the church—one pointed north toward the old mill, one pointed west toward the city, and one south toward the village of La Villeta, where Santa Anna pitched his chief camp. Two guns protected the stockade between the church and prison, and an eighteen-pounder was planted at the south-west angle of the main square. A twelve-pound carronade protected the center of the west wall, and an eight-pounder protected the north-west angle. Two guns were also planted on the north wall of the plaza, making in all ten guns in position. Over the church building, the present Alamo, floated the flag of the Provisional Government of Texas, as it was called, but at that time the struggle of the Texans was for the re-establishment of the Constitution of 1824 and the securing of the granted rights to the colonists, and against the tyrannical policy of confiscation and annihilation as adopted by the usurper, Santa Anna. The Declaration of Independence of Texas was not passed until nearly a month later. The flag, therefore, consisted of the Mexican tricolor, with the numerals 1824 in the place of the eagle in the white stripe.

"After the battle the Alamo was a ruin. The arched roof was destroyed and the walls were marked by the cannon-balls, and in some places serious breaches had been made in them. For fifteen years there were no repairs attempted, and then the church and the convent were rebuilt on the old walls so as to conform as nearly as possible to the original plan, except in the roof of the church building. That received a pitched roof instead of the original arched roof, and a second story was made within the structure. In its restored condition the church building, which is now known as the Alamo, has been used mainly as a warehouse, and the city of San Antonio has also added a one-story addition on the south side, which is used as a police station."

From the earliest colonial times the struggles in southern Texas were numerous and fierce. It is not to be wondered at that the Mexicans desired to keep a tight grip on that rich belt of territory along the east bank of the Rio Grande. There are some, however, who believe that Spanish Mexico preferred that Texas should not be settled, that thus a wilderness might lie between that land of Catholic superstition and bigotry and the growing Protestant republic of the north. Nor is it remarkable that the people in search of homes under the genial skies of the great South-west should seek to free this beautiful portion of a continent from Spanish rule. The Texans were determined to be free. The slave-holders of the Southern States saw in that region a good outlet for their human chattels. Daring and adventurous men invaded Texas, then of right belonging to Mexico. The standard of revolt was raised, and Mexican armies soon came to maintain the integrity of their national domain. Numerous battles were fought, and they were great in proportion to the population. Texas revolutionists held the sympathies of the people of the United States, and in time were able to throw off the Mexican yoke and stand before the world as an independent nation recognized by our government and also by England. But it is with the fall of the Alamo I have to do as a tourist.

During the early part of this century General Santa Anna had been extending his conquest all over Mexico.

Texas alone had held out against his power and in favor of the republic. This he now determined to conquer. At the head of a considerable army flushed with victories over internal foes — an army trained to long service in the field and amply equipped with arms and munitions of war—he marched into Texas, and at once proceeded to San Antonio. On the morning of the 22d of February, 1836, the people arose to see themselves confronted by this daring chieftain and his army. Their independence must then have seemed a thing of the past. Colonel Travis, with one hundred and forty-five effective men, at once retired to the Alamo to hold the place and await re-enforcements or fight to the bitter end. Santa Anna was a brave man and a skillful general. He at once issued his orders and prepared to capture the Alamo. That lost to the Texans, all would seem to be lost. During the night of March 5, 1836, the Mexican army formed in accordance with the orders given by the general in chief. Thus writes the historian of the times:

"At the first light of dawn on that memorable Sunday morning the Mexican bugles sounded the fatal peal. With a rush like tigers springing on their prey the enemy dashed forward, but the heroic Texans, roused to their last duty by the bugle notes of their requiem, with the sound of the terrible *dequelo* (the Mexican bugle call for 'death, no quarters') ringing in their ears, every man was at his post, and so well did they do their duty that twice the hosts of Santa Anna were hurled back defeated, only to be again forced forward by the sabers of the Mexican cavalry. This time Santa Anna himself urged forward his troops. General Castillion's division, after half an hour's desperate fighting, and after repeated repulses and unheard-of losses, succeeded in effecting an entrance in the upper part of the

Alamo in a sort of outwork. The fighting had only begun. The doors and windows of the Alamo Church were barricaded and guarded by bags of sand heaped up as high as a man's shoulders, and even on the roof were rows of sand-bags, behind which the Texans fought as never men fought before—muzzle to muzzle, hand to hand. Each Texan rifle shot exhausted its force and spent itself in successive bodies of Mexicans packed together like a wall of flesh. Muskets and rifles were clubbed, and bayonets and bowie-knives never before wrought such fearful carnage.

"The ceaseless crash of fire-arms, the shots of the beleaguered, desperate, and defiant Texans, and the shrieks of the dying, made the din infernal and the scene indescribable in its sublime terrors. Each room in the building was the scene of a desperate struggle with fearless men driven to desperation and conscious that escape was impossible. They fought even when stricken down, and when dying, still struggled, not with death, but to slay Mexicans. In the long room, used as a hospital, the sick and wounded fired pistols and rifles from their pallets. A piece of artillery, supposed to be that which Crockett had used during the siege, was shotted with grape and cannister and turned upon the desperate occupants of this apartment. After the explosion the Mexicans entered and found the emaciated bodies of fourteen men, torn and mangled and blackened and bloody. Forty-two dead Mexicans lay at the door. Colonel James Bowie, whose name tells of his fearful knife—the 'Bowie-knife,' of which he was the inventor—lay dead on a cot in this room. He was helpless and in bed when the Alamo was invested, twelve days before, but the bodies of the victims of his unerring aim and invincible courage attested that his death was not accomplished without tenfold loss to the enemy.

"There are several accounts of the death of Colonel Travis, one of which is that he was shot in the head by a rifle ball, but even then had strength enough left to impale on his sword a Mexican officer who was attempting to mutilate him. Another account, derived from a Mexican soldier in the army of Santa Anna, is that Colonel Travis and David Crockett were found lying among the Texan dead, utterly worn out by sleepless nights of watching and long-continued fighting. When discovered, Colonel Travis gave a Mexican soldier some gold, and while conversing with him, General Cos, with whom Colonel Travis had dealt very generously when San Antonio was captured by the Americans, appeared. Cos warmly embraced Travis, and induced other Mexicans, and among them General Castillion, to join with him in asking Santa Anna to spare Travis's life. Then David Crockett also wearily arose to his feet from among the corpses. Santa Anna was terribly enraged at the disobedience of his orders, saying: 'I want no prisoners,' and turning to a file of soldiers ordered them to shoot the heroes. Colonel Travis was first shot in the back. He folded his arms stiffly across his breast and stood erect until a bullet pierced his neck, when he fell headlong among the dead. David Crockett fell at the first fire, his body being completely riddled with bullets. Even a cat, that was soon after seen running through the fort, was shot, the soldiers exclaiming: 'It is not a cat, but an American.' Major Evans was shot while in the act of applying a torch to the magazine in time to prevent an explosion."

One cannot blame the Mexican general for contending bravely to subdue an insurrection or recover a lost province, but the butchery was horrible and needless. The army of Santa Anna could easily have invested the Alamo with a cordon of soldiery and compelled its surrender in a short time. The Mexican general must have delighted in bloodshed. Señor Filison, the Mexican historian, who accompanied the army of Santa Anna, thus concludes his account of the battle of the Alamo:

"Finally, the place remained in the power of the Mexicans, and all its defenders were killed. It is a source of deep regret, that, after the excitement of the combat, many acts of atrocity were allowed, which are unworthy of the gallantry and resolution with which this operation was executed, and stamps it with an indelible stain in the annals of history. These acts were reproved at the time by those who had the sorrow to witness them, and, subsequently, by the whole army, who were certainly not animated by such feelings, and who heard with disgust and horror, as becomes brave and generous Mexicans, breathing none but noble and lofty sentiments, of certain facts which I forbear mentioning, and would wish, for the honor of the republic, had never taken place.

"In our opinion, the blood of our soldiers, as well as that of the enemy, was shed in vain, for the mere gratification of the inconsiderate, puerile, and guilty vanity of reconquering Bexar (San Antonio) by force of arms and through a bloody contest. In fact, as we have already stated, the defenders of the Alamo were disposed to surrender, upon the only condition that their lives would be spared. Let us even admit that they were not so disposed—what could the wretches do, being surrounded by five thousand men, without proper means of resistance, no possibility of retreating, nor any hope of receiving sufficient re-enforcements to compel the Mexicans to raise the siege?"

The fall of the Alamo and this terrible slaughter did not arrest the progress of the Texans. The heroes of the Alamo were put to death, but other defenders of Texan liberties were raised up. At the battle of San Jacinto, a few months later, Santa Anna's army was routed and its commander taken prisoner, and on the first day of March, 1845, Texas was admitted to the American Union. The Alamo has been purchased by the State of Texas from the Catholic Church for $20,000, and is to be restored, renovated, and preserved as a monument of stirring events. Aside from the old Alamo, there are the ruins of five of these old Catholic "missions" in the neighborhood. The Nuestra Señora de la Concepcion, built in 1716; San Jose Aguayo in 1720; San Francisco de la Espada, 1716; Espiritu Santo, 1720; Nuestra Señora del Rosario, 1754; Nuestra Señora del Refugio, 1791.

There are records which tell that the Catholic missionaries began their labors among the Indians of Texas as early as 1554. The royal treasury of Spain contributed millions of dollars toward the spiritual conquest of these savages, and yet the whole six "missions" never contained so many as five hundred souls. It was, indeed, a fruitless effort, as even Spanish Catholic writers themselves testify.

Of course I visited some of these old missions, and was especially interested in the "Nuestra Señora de la Concepcion. They are fortress-like stone structures, built more than a century and a half ago by Spanish gold, under the direction of the fathers of the "Holy Church," designed by Spanish architects, erected by the labors of the Indians embraced in the mission, but whether enforced or remunerated does not appear. They were intended for the Christian culture of these same wild savages, and for their shelter in time of war. There they stand, landmarks of a former age, decorated stone-fronts, which are of the most elaborate workmanship and artistic design, wood-carvings in cedar, almost equal to those in old Chester Cathedral, in England, now crumbling year by year through the beating of rains and the chafing of winds, broken and splintered by audacious visitors, who carry away fragments as souvenirs, now moldy, dirty, and forbidding. The putrid carcass of a dead cow lay on one of the ground floors. Nopal cactus plants grow upon the stony roof, and all, save a single small room, used at present for prayers by a few native Catholics whose huts are near, may be called simply a ruin. ⋎ These old ruins, in all that is romantically antique, equal those of old Conway Castle, in North Wales, and Linlithgow, in Scotland, and remind one of them. Why does not the State of Texas or the city of San Antonio take measures to preserve these relics of a former age, that they may be looked upon a thousand years hence? If the ground were cleared of the accumulated rubbish, and fenced in and shaded with the live oak, the magnolia, and the China-tree, for instance, and then converted into a public park, with walks and drives, doubtless there is no place in the whole Southern country which would present a greater attraction to the tourist than the neighborhood of San Antonio, Texas.

A number of shops were visited, and I also attended a lenten service one evening at the old and famous Church of San Fernando, the church where all resident Mexicans worship. A great many Mexicans are scattered over Southern Texas.

There is old San Antonio and new San Antonio. Over a door-way on the main plaza is a stone, bearing an old Spanish coat of arms, dated 1743. But new buildings by the score are being erected throughout the city, replacing the low one-storied houses of the olden times. Lines of street railways have been extended to all the principal points. I took several rides on them, first to the government military head-quarters, where a few companies of United States troops were stationed. Every thing here betokened the most perfect army arrangements. The next place to visit was the San Pedro springs, a suburb of San Antonio, where water rises up out of the earth in sufficient quantities to drive the wheels of several mills.

In the street car from San Pedro springs, in the evening, I could not help noticing the strangely mixed company. There were probably twenty persons in the car drawn by a Spanish mule. The proportion between the size of the car and the diminutive mule would be very well expressed by harnessing an ordinary sized sheep to a phaeton. They are very small, but very strong, and one of them will draw a car packed with passengers. The mule furnishes the motive power of the street car, and of all other vehicles of burden everywhere in the South.

A certain noted infidel of our time attempts to free himself from moral responsibility by charging that he was not consulted when he was created. In this he is like the mule. The mule, alas! if he has any sensibilities, must feel the pangs of the insults heaped upon him, for every body in the South owns the mule, drives the mule, whips the mule, and hates the mule ; and every body makes fun of the mule, the poor mule, and that is not at all figurative. He is generally lean, shaggy, lank, and dirty. He can't sing, is far from being handsome— I mean the average mule—and is the subject of every body's ridicule on account of his long ears. The mule is never petted by the sentimental young lady, who fairly kisses the noble horse. Poor fellow! he must drag the wagon and the street car through the mud, and carry all the burdens. About the only real recreation or amusement he can ever hope to enjoy in all his life is to kick. Well, let him kick, it is a comfort to him; nature allows him this privilege, and so long as I like to see the poor hod-carrier sit down under the lea of a building and enjoy his noon lunch, just so long will I plead for the posterior liberties of this universal friend of humanity, the mule—only it is always best to keep at a suitable distance, say about four rods, when he indulges this festive nature of his.

But what a mixture! There were in this car several whites of the true Anglo-Saxon blood. Two German gentlemen talked away vigorously about a new contract one had just taken, and by which he hoped to make *viel gelt*—much money. Two young Boston girls, I thought from their speaking of Joseph Cook's last lecture, sat near me. There were three or four Mexicans, judging from their tan-bark complexion and straight black hair and black eyes. Then there were some Negroes, two of whom were very black, others quite light of complexion. All the world seems to have sent its representatives to San Antonio.

CHAPTER IV.

ACROSS THE RIO GRANDE.

Rivers — Sand-bars — Uncertainties — "Down in the mouth"— Boundary line — The Jumping-off place — War clouds — Famous fields — March of "Old Zach"—Poverty and dirt—Strange sights —Mistaken fun—Two forests—Long range—Beauty of scenery— Rocks and railroading—Cooling shadows.

A WRITER, in a popular magazine, speaks of the "majestic rivers of Mexico." I fear he was never in the country about which he writes. When Texas and all that rich belt of territory forming our southern boundary constituted a portion of the Mexican domain there was one river that was entitled to the appellation majestic, known in Spanish as the Rio Bravo del Norte, and to us as the Rio Grande, or, in simple English, Grand River.*

Mexico is not a land of great rivers because of the narrow form of the continent.

Large rivers, like the Mississippi and the Amazon, imply vast interior regions, where great masses of water may collect.

There are some rivers in Mexico which have their origin far back in the mountainous regions, from two hundred to five hundred miles from the sea-coast, as the Rio de Santiago, the longest river in the country, and the Rio de las Balzas. But during the dry season, which lasts through about three fourths of the year, many of these rivers disappear almost entirely, others entirely.

* The Rio Grande has been called the "muddiest, crookedest, and swiftest" river in America.

River navigation in Mexico is almost unknown. Where streams might be navigable for some distance sand-bars near the mouths are constant barriers, and there is not enough enterprise among the people to clear them away.

Mexico has no harbors for shipping. The only one on her great coast-line is at Acapulco, on the Pacific coast. When vessels come into Mexican waters they are compelled to anchor a distance out in the sea, and then both freight and passengers are swung overboard to the lighters, often at the peril of life and risk of property, for these southern waters, far from being placid, are among the roughest in the world. Consequently freight which is shipped to Mexican ports at certain seasons cannot be unloaded, and hence must be carried back and forth for months in succession before an opportunity is presented for its delivery.

Landing in a Mexican port is not the most certain thing in the world. Genuine national enterprise would remove the sand-bars from the rivers and create harbors for the accommodation of those who "do business in great waters." At the time of this tour the famous Rio Grande was quite "down in the mouth;" but in the rainy season, when it reaches high-water mark, as it does generally, it is, indeed, El Grande Rio.

At the close of the Mexican war, in 1847, this river was made a part of the boundary line between the two nations. That line follows westward from the mouth of the Rio Grande north-east to the parallel of 31° 47'. It then continues for one hundred miles to the 111th meridian, there bending to the north-west as far as 32° 29' 45". It runs from this point onward to the dividing line between Upper and Lower California, at the bay of San Diego. Mexico has a northern frontier reaching from the Gulf to the Pacific Ocean, a distance of nearly two thousand miles. My starting-point into Mexico was from Laredo, on the Texas frontier.

When Mexico ceded, at the cannon's mouth, that portion of territory to the United States which now constitutes our great South-west, she lost the exclusive control of this her principal river.

The Rio Grande now belongs to both nations, the boundary being the middle of the stream. It was at Laredo that I passed the last gate-way, and set foot on Mexican soil.

There are two Laredos. Old Laredo is on the Texan side, a town of one-story adobe houses, with very narrow streets. The population is made up of three fourths or more of Mexicans, the balance being Americans; while New Laredo, on the opposite side of the Bravo, is all Mexican, and shows signs of considerable prosperity. This whole region was once the scene of stirring events. The war cloud hung dark over all this border forty years ago. Mexico assembled her warriors on one bank of the Rio Grande, the United States marshaled hers on the other. It was in this section the first battles of that war, waged against inoffensive Mexico, were fought. General Taylor's forces landed from New Orleans, at Corpus Christi, at the mouth of the Nueces River, in August, 1845; then he removed to Point Isabel, established Fort Brown, on the Texas side of the Rio Grande, and in due time bombarded and took Matamoras, besides winning the victories of Palo Alto and Resaca de la Palma, where American troops greatly distinguished themselves.

The battle of Palo Alto—*High Palms*—was scarcely worthy of so dignified a name. It was great only in the fact that it was the beginning of actual war. From the high-colored description at the time one might conclude that it was a great trial of national strength and prowess. It was fought on May 8, 1846, at which ten of General Taylor's troops were killed and forty-four wounded. The Mexicans lost one hundred killed and three hundred wounded. The following day the army of Taylor and the Mexican forces met at Resaca de la Palma—Ravine of the Palms—and another battle ensued, when a few more of his men were killed. The Mexican loss was reported at five hundred killed and wounded.

After fighting these two somewhat celebrated little battles on the lower Rio Grande the American commander marched his forces directly upon Monterey, by way of Mier. The distance from Laredo to Monterey is a trifle less than two hundred miles *via* the Mexican National Railway.

This road may be considered the pioneer in the modern railroad movement in Mexico. Its beginning dates back to 1872. The Mexican Railroad, from Vera Cruz to the city of Mexico, the oldest one in the republic, will be described hereafter. The route by the Mexican National, beginning at Laredo, is about five hundred miles shorter than that by the Central *via* El Paso. For eighty or ninety miles after leaving the Rio Grande at Laredo, the landscape is exceedingly monotonous. Any one mile is a fitting sample of the whole. The soil is very poor. Evidently in some age of the globe, and, geologically speaking, not very long ago, this valley of the Rio Grande was a part of the great gulf into which the river now pours its waters.

The vegetation is peculiar to a semi-tropical latitude. The mesquite grows abundantly every-where. It is a very pretty bright green shrub, a species of the acacia, which yields a sweet edible pulp, used as food to some extent by man and beast. The yucca-tree also grows in this region, the leaves of which furnish a strong fiber, employed in making coarse cloth and cordage for shipping. These, with a few varieties of the cactus, constitute the vegetation one sees in this part of Mexico. At every station on the railway motley groups of men, women, and children, brown-skinned, black-haired, dirty-looking human beings, sadly in need of fine-tooth combs and soap, were gathered around in seemingly listless idleness.

As I gazed upon them it almost seemed as if I had been transported into a new world. If one should go up in a balloon, and drift away into space until he came to a point where "gravitation turns and works the other way," and should then drop down on some distant planet, he would not be likely to find himself surrounded by more unaccustomed scenery or more strangely appearing people than he will meet in crossing the Rio Grande into Mexico.

As the train moved along and came within a hundred miles of Monterey I began to get a view of the eastern range of that great system of mountains, the Sierra Madre.

At first I supposed the black mass banked up in the western skies indicated a coming rain-storm, and was glad, for the day was very hot and the air was filled with dust. Over all this region it had not rained for many months. But the mistake was soon discovered. Instead of clouds I was obtaining a first glimpse of the Sierra Madre, or "Mother Mountains," as the words import.

As we neared them their altitude seemed to increase while their jagged slopes and rocky prominences became more and more visible. They seem, as one views them at long range, to be naked rocks just as the fires left them when they were first formed. But through a field-glass I could discern here and there patches of deep green, having a mossy appearance, which, I was told, were forests of a species of pine in which there were trees from sixty to seventy-five feet in height. If the microscope converts the mold on a piece of stale cheese into a forest growth, the telescope would in the same way reveal the genuine forests of these bold Sierras. Then they seem so near. Yonder I notice, opposite the town of Lampazos, what they call the Mesa de los Cartuhanes, which is a terrace rising above the level plain.

Instead of being five miles away, it is not far from twenty-five. Instead of being three hundred feet high, is two thousand. Instead of being three or four miles in length, is twenty. And on the flat tableland of the Mesa were sixty thousand head of cattle fattening for the foreign market, as their owner, whom I chanced to meet, assured me.

The scenery of the Sierras is the great feature of Mexican travel. Over all the plains you see little else than white sand, out of which grows the vegetation peculiar to this latitude. But the mountain scenery is grand. Mountains on the right of you, mountains on the left of you. Look back, and they tower above you in dim and distant majesty. Cast your eye ahead, and they confront you with what seems an impassable barrier. No pen can accurately portray the beauty of these mountains. Their color varies with the passing hours of the day and night, and they are never seen twice alike. They often present a rosy appearance in the early morning, and then are blue and brown at noonday. At sunset they are arrayed in amethystine robes, and at night they don the purple. Sometimes their tops are lost in clouds which threaten rain, but do not speedily execute their threats, and then they lie distinctly visible in clear, bold outlines against the serenest of skies.

ACROSS THE RIO GRANDE. 49

If any country in the world has tested the skill of the civil engineer, Mexico is that land. Over much of the way between Laredo and Monterey, the ascent is continual, and when the latter city is reached, the traveler has attained an elevation of nearly two thousand feet above the level of the sea.

Having reached the first city of any importance, after leaving the valley of the Rio Grande, weary and dusty, I sat down in the cool shade of the hotel veranda. The thermometer during the day had registered not far from eighty-five degrees. The evening air was balmy, the skies were cloudless. The moon shed her silvery light over all, and I thought of the ice-bound north, the home from which my steps had turned. It was delightful to be in such a place. But I remembered that, after all, the greatest wealth, the highest intellectual and physical vigor, are in the snow belt of the north, and not in the land which boasts of perpetual summer.

CHAPTER V.

THE GEM OF THE MOUNTAINS.

In summer land—Loitering amid bright scenes and sweet odors—The plaza and its delights—Beautiful Monterey—Legend of the miter—A saddle of stone—The ruined palace—Taylor in Monterey—The city a fortress—The surrender—Magnanimity of "Old Rough and Ready"—A visit to the governor—Relics of blood—Legend of the Virgin—Building a bridge on which to die.

IT was in the early part of March, on a Saturday evening, and about eight o'clock, when I reached the city of Monterey—gem of the mountains. I was in summer land. Had I been in my own home at that hour, I should doubtless have retreated from the war of the elements without and sought shelter within doors, but here it was next to impossible to remain in-doors. The moon was throwing her soft light over mountain and valley, the atmosphere came laden with the delicious perfume of tropical flowers. The notes of bewitching, soothing, and most entrancing music fell on the ear. Strange sights were before me, and hence I could not resist the impulse to take a stroll before composing myself to much-needed rest.

It did not require a long walk to find a plaza. The plaza is the point where all the people in a Mexican city, of all classes, and tourists as well, naturally congregate. This particular one is called the Plaza de Zaragoza, and is only a few steps from the principal hotels and city and state buildings.

Why do great rivers always run by large towns? was innocently asked by some one. The rivers first, the towns afterward. In laying out a Mexican city the first thing thought of was the plaza around which the city seemed naturally to crystallize. The plaza first, then the city.

In every Mexican city there are generally a number of these small parks called plazas and alamedas. Some of them are mere "sand lots," where donkeys can roll and dogs play. But the Plaza Mayor, or main plaza, is the fashionable promenade where rich and poor, old and young, meet and enjoy, on equal footing, the evening air. In Monterey, the Plaza de Zaragoza lies in the heart of the city. It is not large, but very attractive. Fine old trees cast a cooling shade during the daytime. A fountain, with spouting dolphins, occupies the center. This is flanked by two smaller fountains, whose artistic designs show that a trained hand had part in their construction. They keep up a perpetual plash. Paths cross and recross each other in all directions. The whole is surrounded by a wide double promenade of some kind of cement, which is as white and smooth as polished marble. It is a weird sort of place, for both the costumes and the customs of the people are purely Mexican. The air is almost burdened with the aroma of orange blossoms, rose, and jasmine.

The conversation you hear is Spanish. The foliage on the trees is quite dense, and consequently the shadows are dark, save where the moonlight percolates between the glossy-leaved sprays, and falls, like molten silver, on the winding pathways. Are you weary? There are seats which lure you to rest. Great white broad-bottomed sofa-shaped benches, made of concrete as hard as stone, more graceful, too, than the stiff iron ones we often see at home, with this advantage, that they can't be whittled away by every loiterer who is rich enough to own a jack-knife. In nearly all of these

Mexican plazas, military bands play two or three evenings in the week for the entertainment of the people who crowd the plazas. The effect can only be wholesome, for music is divine.

All classes meet here, the poor and the rich, the refined and the unrefined. The peon, in his coarse cotton and zarape; his wife and daughters, in their calico and rebosos; the better-to-do, in their silks and broadcloths. The inner circle of the plaza, near the band-stand, is the rendezvous of these common people, who walk and talk and dance to the quicker strains of the music. The outer circles are conceded to the upper-tendom, which moves with slow dignity to the measured strains of cornet and bugle. The scene is, indeed, fascinating, as one sits and views these men with their wives, young ladies with their chaperons, and parents with their children. Ladies, with their male attendants, march in one direction, gentlemen alone move in the opposite, so that they may meet face to face. Acquaintances at the first meeting bow their recognition, and then pass on as strangers through the whole evening. There is no stopping to chat by the way, it is a procession, a gala evening, an hour given to fresh air, music, and life. This plaza at Monterey was the first one I had visited in Mexico, and is a fair sample of all the rest, only that some are larger and more highly embellished than others, all of which depends upon the size and wealth of the city or village, and the disposition of the "city fathers." That night's rest was sweet to me, and when the Sabbath morning came I was early awakened by the clatter of numerous church-bells calling the people to worship. Here is a city where the Church of Rome holds almost absolute sway. A mere handful of Protestants only may be found in it. Monterey is the capital of Nuevo Leon—New Leon—the largest of the frontier

States of the Mexican republic. It is not far from eight hundred miles north of the city of Mexico and two hundred miles south of the Rio Grande. It was once the most important place, from a commercial point of view, in Northern Mexico. Hither came the traders from Durango, Zacatecas, San Luis Potosi, and far-away Chihuahua.

Monterey is so called from one of the mountains at whose foot it nestles. The word means King Mountain. It is a charming little city, that is, for Mexico. The highly salubrious climate makes it a sanitarium, especially for lung diseases, besides mineral medicinal springs bubble up not far from the base of the Saddle Mountain, which are said to possess remarkable curative qualities. The city is situated on the Rio de Santa Catarina—in plain English, St. Catharine's River, and lies in a rich plain tolerably well supplied with water. The population of Monterey is about sixteen thousand souls, though some claim more than twice that number.

Just to the westward, and in plain sight, towers up to a height of about four thousand feet the great Cerro de la Mitra, a king among mountains. Its peak bears a fancied resemblance to a bishop's miter. This the devout Catholic can see quite plainly, but the vision of the Protestant is not quite so keen.

I was told that the faithful here have a belief that within the heart of that Cerro and beneath that miter are concealed untold riches which, at some time in the future, the great Father will bring forth and give to his children.

Alas! if the poor Mexicans ever expect any kind of riches, they will not come from beneath a bishop's miter.

The Church for three hundred years has only impoverished the people of Mexico. A view of the mountain miter called to mind the "old man of the mountains," in

New Hampshire, which is a colossal human face, and so plain as to have attracted the gaze even of the wild Indian, who founded upon it various superstitions. Yet when you climb the hill, in the perspective of whose curves and angles the "old man's" face is formed, lo! it has vanished. Distance lends enchantment to this view. So here, when the tourist ascends the mountain, the miter has vanished.

Directly to the eastward of the city is the Cerro de la Silla, or Saddle Mountain, which also rises about four thousand feet above the plain. The top of the mountain, as its blue outline lies against the sky, appears as if some giant with mighty cleaver had cut the rock into the shape of a saddle. The figure is so plain as to require neither imagination nor field-glass.

Another object of interest in Monterey is an old and massive stone building, on the brow of the Obispada Hill, on the west side, known as the Bishop's Pleasure Palace. It was planned for a magnificent structure, but is now only a ruin. It has stood there for over a hundred and fifty years. The blocks of stone used in its construction were carried on the backs of men from the mountain east of Monterey. It seems almost incredible that such a task could have been performed in that way, but when one has seen the burden-bearers of Mexico at work in mines and along the new railroads, he can easily believe this, as well as the story told by Prescott, of Cortes having transported his fleet of brigantines over the mountains to the waters of Lake Texcuco. The view of Monterey from this hill is charming, and amply repays the effort put forth in the ascent. As I strolled about Monterey, I could not help thinking of the difference between that day and the 20th of September, 1846. Now all is peaceful and quiet and the people are happy. Then these streets were the arena of contending armies.

General Taylor had marched his army, of about six thousand six hundred from the banks of the Rio Grande into the interior, with the city of Mexico as the objective point. Had he been suitably re-enforced, some believe, though it is doubted by others, he could ultimately have reached and taken the capital, *via* San Louis Potosi, saving both blood and treasure. This army, whose artillery comprised a dozen ten-inch mortars, two twenty-four pounder howitzers, four field batteries of four guns each, with brigades of infantry, and regiments of cavalry, flushed with recent victories, and backed by a powerful government, is the attacking party. The city is defended by ten thousand Mexicans, indifferently armed, commanded by General Ampudia, men in whose minds is still fresh the bitter recollection of defeat at Palo Alto and Resaca de la Palma, men who must have been conscious of their inferiority to the foe before them. But their resistance to the invaders through nearly four days of battle is ample proof of their courage.

Taylor's army fought its way through this city house by house and block by block, for every house was an armed citadel and every man a soldier. Muskets flashed from every window and azotea, while shot and shell were poured forth upon the ranks of the invaders from the heights of Obispada, the Bishop's Palace having been converted into a citadel of defense.

But brave as the Mexicans were, they were not equal to our own troops, nor were their arms so good. The Mexican general imagined that the Bishop's Palace would be assaulted from the front. He threw up his breastworks accordingly, and prepared for the assault. But General Taylor only made a feint in that direction sending the main army of attack into the rear, thus capturing the place with comparatively a slight loss.

Then planting his guns in front of the palace, he had entire command of Monterey. There was nothing left for the Mexicans to do but to surrender, and this they did.*

Like General Grant at Appomattox, General Taylor was a generous conqueror. The defeated Mexicans were allowed to retain their arms and accouterments. The artillery were granted a field battery of six guns with twenty-one rounds of ammunition. When the troops evacuated the city, the brave Taylor stipulated that when the Mexicans struck their colors they might salute with their own battery.

After the city was captured General Taylor sent a squad of soldiers to plant the stars and stripes on the summit of Saddle Mountain. The difficult task required a number of days in its accomplishment. That banner floated in the Sierra winds until it was wasted to shreds. Forty years have passed away since that siege, all traces of which are gone, save a few old rust-eaten Mexican cannon spiked by Taylor's men, which lie yet on the declivity of the Obispada heights.

One of the places of much interest was the state building, the Capitol of Nuevo Leon. I had the good fortune to have a note of introduction to Señor Bernandez de la Vega, son of General de la Vega, a brave Mexican, who was made prisoner at the battle of Resaca de la Palma by General Taylor's forces. This son was at that date a pupil in a Boston high school. He speaks several languages well. It was through him I was introduced to his Excellency, Canuto Garcia, Governor of the State of Nuevo Leon. The governor is a lawyer by profession, under forty, very dark complexioned, about five feet nine inches tall, and a

* At the capture of Monterey, the Americans lost in killed, 126, including 18 officers; wounded, 363, including 26 officers. The Mexicans lost in killed, 500; the number of wounded unknown.

thorough gentleman. I talked quite a good deal with him through Señor la Vega on questions of general interest, and when I arose to go he grasped my hand, in true Mexican fashion, giving assurance that the call gave him great pleasure. The governor took me into a room and showed me what were real curiosities: the beautiful silk flag of Maximilian, and three of the rifles with which the emperor and Generals Miramon and Mejia were shot. It was painful in the presence of those relics to think of poor deluded Maximilian and the unfortunate Carlotta. These rifles are kept here as trophies, because three of the soldiers detailed to assist in the execution were from Nuevo Leon. The flag is a beautiful double silk banner, in which the colors are red, white, and green. The whole is richly bordered with gold lace. The center on both sides bears the old Mexican coat of arms, an eagle perched upon a cactus holding a serpent in its beak, and below are the words:
"Second Batallon de Linea."

The governor handed me the rifles one by one to examine. One is an Austrian gun, made at Liege. The other two are American, bearing the Harper's Ferry stamp. On the breeches of the three rifles are silver plates with inscriptions telling of the executions. The following is an inscription from one of them.

AL
EMPERADOR
FERNANDO MAXIMILIANO
1 BATALLON DE LEON
2D COMPANIA DE CAZADORES
SARGENTO 2D,
ANGELL PADILLO
JUNIO 19 DE
1867.

Angell Padillo was the soldier who used it in the execution. It will be remembered that Generals Miramon and Mejia had espoused the cause of the empire and were executed at the same time and place with Maximilian. ✗In speaking of this tragedy, the governor said he always felt sad himself over the fate of Maximilian, but as a lawyer he must say there was absolutely no other way. Maximilian must be shot. He also informed me that just before the order was given to fire, the emperor turned to Miramon and said, "General I am not worthy to stand in this place, I wish you to change positions with me." "No," said the brave Miramon, "I am content to stand next to the emperor." On the 19th of June, 1867, in the city of Queretaro, the commandant raised his sword and the crack of twelve rifles rang out, and emperor and generals weltered in their blood. ✓

Monterey was founded three hundred years ago, and like all other Mexican cities its history is blended with the annals of the Roman Catholic Church. The Spanish priests, who came over to convert the Indians, often laid the first foundations of civilized life in Mexico. In 1592 Fray Andres de Leon established a mission on the site of Monterey. The first building here was a mud hovel. The Aztecs were gathered together and the nucleus of a city was formed. That primitive hut still forms, it is said, a part of the Iglesia de San Francisco, now one of Monterey's fashionable churches. Every thing here is venerable. It would not be very difficult to write a book about Monterey, where the tourist can ascend the rugged heights, or roam about through the rich plains which engirt it, or climb the moldy towers of its numerous churches and look down upon the courts and plazas and narrow streets. But I must refrain.

Here, as every-where in Mexico, many legends are told in reference to the founding of churches. I must relate one in particular, connected with the Church La Capilla de la Purisima. It runs as follows:

"About a century and a half ago there came a great deluge, when for forty days and nights it rained without intermission. Great floods, pouring down from the Sierra Madre, came surging through Santa Catarina, carrying all before them, and Monterey was in imminent danger. An Indian woman, who made shoes for a living, possessed a wooden image of the Virgin, and when the floods were rising in the suburbs she took it to the water's edge and prayed to it, when, lo! the torrent immediately receded, and the city was saved! Then this poor woman and her humble neighbors erected a *jacal* (or hut) upon the spot, called *La Casa del Virgen*, in which the precious image was enshrined. Here the women for miles around were wont to come and pray; and by and by a rich lady, dying in Monterey, left a legacy with which to build a better house of worship. La Capilla de la Purisima is the result, a handsome little church upon the site of the old *jacal*.

"So many believing creatures desired to be buried where the great miracle had been performed, that a populous grave-yard once occupied the spot; but the growing city spread out all around it, and in 1858 the bones were removed. When those now living in the vicinity have occasion to dig in their door-yards, or the courts of their houses, it is no uncommon thing, to this day, to turn up skulls and bones."

Other stories are told which illustrate the current superstition of the Mexican people. There is here a church called El Roble—The Oak—which has been a great while in building. It derives its name from a legend connected with one of its small chapels. The traveler is shown there an image of the holy Virgin which is very dark, almost black. Many years ago a pious monk was in the habit of attending to his private devotions beneath the spreading branches of a live oak. One morning this image was found standing in the heart of the tree, and soon the tidings spread and great was the desire of the people to pay their devotions to her. So that it became necessary to erect a chapel and enshrine her therein. Nevertheless the Virgin preferred the oak, and no matter how securely the doors were bolted at night, in the morning she was always found standing in the tree. One day, during a violent storm, the lightning shivered the oak, and ever afterward she was content to remain in the chapel. But in time the new Iglesia Mayor, or great church, was completed, and the bishop desired to place this particular Virgin in a special niche prepared for her. With much ceremony the transfer was made, amid an adoring crowd.

The cathedrals and churches are always opened at break of day in Mexico, and on the very next morning after the transfer, when the cathedral was unlocked, lo! the Virgin was not there. Soon a messenger was dispatched to the Chapel of the Oak, and there she was in her chosen place, her sacred garments dusty and soiled from the night journey through the streets of Monterey from one sanctuary to another! All these mythical stories, of which I have many to record, are believed by Mexicans and related to the traveler, who offers an affront if he shows any signs of incredulity.

An old American gentleman, who went to Mexico with Taylor's army, and who so fell in love with the climate, and especially with a Mexican señorita at the same time, that he has resided there ever since, accompanied me one afternoon to the Virgin's Bridge, which spans a small stream running through an obscure portion of Monterey. The structure has upon it the undisputed marks of time. Standing there in the shade of a tree, he said that many years ago a number of Americans were in prison in the city, who had fallen into the hands of the Mexicans in some of the frontier raids which had been quite common. Like all other prisoners, they were forced to work in the road gangs.

A bridge was needed at this place, but great difficulties were in the way. The current was deep and strong. Adobe would not do, and rocks could only be had in the somewhat distant mountains. At length the American captives were offered their freedom by the authorities if they would bridge the stream with stone within a given date. The time allotted for the completion of the work was limited, and no facilities for such an undertaking were within their reach. But they were spurred to great exertions by the thought of freedom. They quarried the stone in the mountain under the eye of a military guard, and bore them on their bleeding backs to the spot. Day and night, with sore feet and blistered hands, they brought the work to completion within a few hours of the allotted time. The next day they were to go out free men. Morning came, and, at break of day, all stiff and exhausted, they were marched out of the filthy and gloomy prison in which they were locked at night, two by two, into the middle of the bridge they had built, when, without a word of explanation or time to offer a prayer to Heaven, a squad of soldiers fired upon them, and all fell dead upon the bridge which their own hands had built.

"Do you see that statue of the Virgin?" asked my venerable friend, pointing to the image which stands upon a pedestal. He continued, "These people never cross this bridge without crossing themselves and bowing to the Virgin."

CHAPTER VI.

LAND OF THE BEAUTIFUL VIEW.

Hacks and dust—Spiral railways in the Sierras—Old craters—Mexican houses—A street front in Saltillo—Outside and inside—Flowers and fountains—Battle-field of Buena Vista—An unequal contest—Thermopylæ of America—Nearly whipped and didn't know it—Wanderings over the plains—An incident—Unwritten history—"When she says she will, she will "—Joe Hooker outdone—Soothed by sweet songs—A remarkable señorita.

OUR train pulled away from the depot at Monterey on a clear, bright afternoon. The depots in Mexico are generally a mile or two from the towns, either because the right of way could not be secured, or because the Mexicans do not wish to be disturbed in their repose by the screeching of locomotive whistles and the rumbling of car-wheels, or because they expect their cities and towns to have such an enormous growth at some time in the great hereafter that they will extend out to them; or, more likely, it is the result of a conspiracy between the railroad authorities and street-car and omnibus companies, that they may be partners in subtracting as many shekels as possible from the innocent tourist.

As a rule, at all events, one must breathe the dusty air for half an hour, more or less, before he can sit down in the cool shade of the hotel veranda after a weary journey by rail. The distance from Monterey to Saltillo (pronounced Sälteyo) is about seventy miles, and is a very pleasant one. The roadway winds almost like a spiral around the spurs of the Sierra Madre.

sắl—tēl—yọ.

The valleys through which the road passes are narrow, and bounded by steep, rocky ridges and serrated outlines. Wherever vegetation can grow the almost universal mesquite and nopal cactus are seen. All along the way, especially on the right, are rocky formations which nearly resemble the Giant's Causeway, in Ireland. They are circular and semicircular openings in the mountain sides, from a hundred yards in diameter to several hundred. The sides of these openings are columnar, giving them quite an architectural aspect. I have not seen them described by any writer. They deepen the impression one gets of the age of fire, when there were mighty convulsions of nature throughout all this region. These circular openings were small craters, doubtless, through which the pent-up forces within found means of escape.

At Monterey the elevation above gulf level is a trifle below two thousand feet; at Saltillo it is a little more than five thousand feet, an ascent of about three thousand five hundred feet in seventy miles, or fifty feet to the mile on the average. But, taking out a few level plains over which the road passes, it will be seen that there are ascents which tax the energies even of the locomotive.

It was just getting dark when the train ran up to the station at Saltillo, and I was soon seated in a *coche*, ready to be driven, through dense clouds of dust thrown up by hack wheels, dogs, and donkeys, as we came from the station, up this street and down that to the Hotel de San Esteben, the Fifth Avenue of this Mexican city.

At first I felt quite vexed at the stolid driver, to think that he should be so forgetful of an opportunity to show off his city as to take a traveler who was there to see the very best they had through narrow and obscure streets, instead of conducting him through the principal avenues. But I learned afterward, by a personal inspection, that I had been driven through the most elegant thoroughfares of the metropolis of the State of Coahuila de Zaragoza. The streets in these old Mexican cities are very narrow and the buildings small, consequently the population is very compact.

Saltillo has a population of ten or eleven thousand; some say twice that number; yet when I went up on to the highest point of land near it which I could reach on foot, I should have estimated the population at not over a couple of thousand at most.

I wish now to give the reader a description of Mexican houses in the villages and cities of the interior. The remark has been made that when you have seen one Mexican city you have seen them all. That is not quite true. In some respects there is a sameness, but there is also a difference in the size as well as in the quality of the structures, both public and private. A street front in Saltillo, for example, resembles a mud wall twenty-five or thirty feet in height, but varying in places as the builders on their respective lots have determined. They are generally constructed of sun-dried brick, called adobe. In some places there are more two-storied buildings than in others. Monterey is a finer city than Saltillo, because the houses are larger and better. San Luis Potosi is finer than either of them, for its buildings are still larger, and of better construction. A row of houses fronting on a main street looked to me like a simple wall, say thirty-feet high, and extending along for half a mile, sometimes higher and sometimes lower.

Into this wall, corniced neatly at the top, are openings for windows and door-ways. The windows always have on the street side a sort of iron or wood cage, resting on a projecting stone base or set into it. These are securely fastened to the main wall by iron clasps, and are never removed. In hot weather, while the doors at night can be shut and securely bolted, the windows can remain open; and are proof against intruders of any kind. You walk along a street in the evening, and the children as well as grown people are perched upon the inside, looking at you through these iron, or in the case of less expensive residences wooden cages, for I don't know what else to call them—which gives the establishment a prison-like aspect not the most pleasant to behold. This street front is not uniform in its appearance, for in some places it is painted in bright colors, and ornamented with kaleidoscopic or geometrical figures, at others it is only tinted, and anon presents simply the natural appearance of the adobe brick or cement, according to the taste or purse of the owner or occupant. But let us enter one of these door-ways in this apparent wall. Here one is surprised. The interior of a Mexican house far exceeds the promise given by the outside, which is often very plain, though sometimes it is finely ornamented.

You enter generally through a high and somewhat pretentious door-way. Having passed this you are in an open court, or *patio*, as it is called, and which is usually paved. Into this *patio* open the rooms of the family. Then in the rear is another and inferior *patio*, devoted to the servants and the animals. When the building is a two-story one a stone stair-way leads to the upper apartments. These also open into a broad balcony. It often happens that all the light and air you get comes in through the windows and doors opening into the court; the other three sides of the room being simply solid walls, white and hard and smooth. The court is roofless, and is frequently decorated with vases

Spanish, and good English. The obese sleeper had left us. I could speak English after a fashion, and German after a poorer fashion. But here, in this group of travelers, were spoken Spanish, French, German, Welsh, and English.

These pistols they carry don't mean any thing. The story is told of a man in Texas who said to his wife: "Come, Kate, get me my pistol; I am going to prayer-meeting." The poorer class can't afford pistols, and hence carry knives. But, somehow, a Mexican likes to go armed, whether he uses his arms or not. Our passengers, with all their pistols and belts, were gentlemanly, and I would not be afraid to make the circuit of the globe with them.

Through the whole day we journeyed along the great plain, flanked on either side by the mountain ranges. Every-where the same almost unendurable dust and heat, the same poverty-stricken country, the same palm or Yucca trees, the same varieties of cactus, the same mud huts, and the same half-naked peons greeted us. Only one sight broke on my vision to relieve the monotony during the day, and that was but a momentary attraction. Over the plain, at a distance of a mile or two, I noticed a moving cloud of dust which seemed to hug the tops of the cactus bushes, and, wondering what caused it, I turned my glass in that direction, and saw, what is quite common here, a flock of antelopes, a species of gazelle, which swept round us within rifle shot, for they are exceedingly fleet of foot. They were about the size of sheep, but very trim and pretty. The little creatures wander over these interior regions in search of water, and, as they sped by us, I thought of what the Psalmist David had said of them long ago, "As the hart panteth after the water-brooks, so panteth my soul after thee, O God."

perfection of melody at once powerful and pathetic. The señorita sings as principal soprano in the parochial cathedral, a very fine old church on the main plaza.

She is under as good training as her city can furnish, and seems to be over fourteen, say about sixteen; but, then, girls reach maturity earlier in this latitude. If she were trained by a real master for a couple of years, and should then go to New York, or Boston, and sing some evening and be criticised right thoroughly by the reporters in the morning papers, on the second evening there would not be a hall in either city large enough to hold the audience.

The señorita turned from the piano, as if to say, "I have done my best to please the visitor," at which I arose to take my leave, in true Mexican style, giving her my hand with a cordial grasp, expressing myself with a "muchas gracias."

of flowers, playing fountains, and cages of birds. I have sometimes counted from six to twelve cages in a single court. The mocking-bird is a general favorite, especially so with Mexicans. He is very funny, but a little selfish, for he preserves a studied quiet during the day, so as to give himself full liberty to keep people awake at night with his ceaseless chatterings. Around the court border will be seen vases and earthen pots of growing shrubs and flowers, often in great numbers, and containing rare and beautiful varieties. Then comes a wide corridor, with rows of stone pillars supporting, in the case of two-storied dwellings, the upper balconies. All the rooms of the house open into this court, which is delightfully cool.

These apartments are often most elegantly furnished, and constitute homes which boast of every modern luxury. This is the old Moorish style of architecture, and is admirably adapted to a warm climate. The people generally live in much smaller apartments than in the United States, and hence a greater population is crowded together in the same space.

Saltillo is situated at a considerable height, but is very warm. It is jocularly said here, in reference to the remarkable healthfulness of the climate, that people never die in Saltillo. They just live on and on until they "dry up" and disappear, and nobody knows where they go.

The first thing I wanted to do, after getting well settled in my hotel, was to visit the famous battle-field of Buena Vista (pronounced Wana Veesta), which is about eight miles from Saltillo. A party was soon made up for the trip, and we were not long in reaching the historic place.

The name Buena Vista means beautiful, or good view, and really it is a *buena vista*. It lies between two spurs of the beautiful Sierras, the valley being, at its widest point, not over three miles, narrowing down to less than one mile.

After the fall of Monterey General Taylor's forces entered and occupied Saltillo without opposition. On the heights overlooking the city he threw up some earth-works, remains of which are yet faintly visible. Knowing that Santa Anna was approaching him with a large army, General Taylor pushed on a large force to a village twenty miles beyond Saltillo, called Agua Nueva, or New Water, on the San Luis Potosi road.

The American army had been greatly weakened by the withdrawal of a large portion of its best troops for the purpose of re-enforcing the army of General Scott in the campaign against Vera Cruz.

Agua Nueva was selected by General Taylor, not as a battle-field, but as a point well supplied with water, and which would be a suitable spot to drill the new recruits sent to replace those who had been withdrawn. But the stay there was short.

On February 21, 1847, scouting parties discovered that the Mexican army was coming down upon them in great numbers, and a battle was imminent. Taylor was always quick in making choice of a position, and never made a mistake. He at once decided to fall back to the pass of La Angostura—the Narrows on the Saltillo road, at the Hacienda of Buena Vista. The valley here has a V shape.

General Taylor occupied with his whole force the apex of the V, where the valley narrows down to a mere pass, which, on this account, proved a very Thermopylæ.

" Early on the morning of February 22, 1847," wrote an eye-witness, " great clouds of dust were seen rising in the air in the direction of Agua Nueva, which told of the advance of Santa Anna. It was an anxious hour for the brave Taylor, who, with four thousand five hundred men, must either retreat rapidly to Saltillo, within his defenses, or meet in battle at least twenty thousand of the very best troops of Mexico. At four o'clock that day the long roll of the drum signaled the onset of battle. Infantry, cavalry, and artillery took positions. Two miles away were seen the columns of the enemy advancing in perfect order. The sun gleamed from the bright lances and bayonets of the Mexicans. Their artillery carriages rattled over the hard road. Their horses were gayly caparisoned, as is their custom. Their bugle notes sounded and echoed among the rugged heights of Buena Vista. Never was an enemy more confident of victory. Why should not twenty thousand men overwhelm an enemy less than one fourth their number. General Taylor had the advantage of the best position on the battle-field, and was on the defensive."

On the left rises a mountain to an altitude of two thousand feet, some distance up which I clambered. It seemed marvelous that troops could ascend it, as did some of Taylor's men, making the declivity a sheet of flame.

The battle of Buena Vista was begun by an attempt on the part of Santa Anna to get possession of this eminence. It was good generalship on the part of the Mexican commander, but the flank movement was a failure. On the right of Taylor's position were precipitous ravines impassable to either cavalry or artillery.

Notwithstanding Santa Anna's army greatly outnumbered that of Taylor, he was slow to make the attack. Before advancing to battle he sent a flag of truce, bearing the following note to the American commander:

"You are surrounded by twenty thousand men, and cannot by any human probability avoid suffering a rout and being cut to pieces with your troops ; but as you deserve consideration and particular esteem, I wish to save you from such a catastrophe, and for that purpose give you this notice in order that you may surrender at discretion, under the assurance that you will be treated with the consideration belonging to the Mexican character; to which end you will be granted an hour's time to make up your mind, to commence from the moment when my flag of truce arrives in your camp."

Taylor responded laconically :

"In reply to your note of this date summoning me to surrender my forces at discretion, I beg leave to say that I decline acceding to your request."

Again he sent another messenger to ask General Taylor what he was waiting for. Taylor's cool reply was:

"I am waiting for General Santa Anna to surrender."

That battle, if not the greatest, was one of the fiercest ever fought on this continent. The Americans were at times overwhelmed with numbers, but so determined were they that at the close of the second day, February 23, 1847, the Mexicans retreated toward San Luis Potosi, and the Americans were masters of the field.

Less than five thousand Americans had met and defeated over four times their own number. Taylor's army numbered four thousand five hundred men, with less than five hundred regulars; while Santa Anna boasted that his numbered twenty thousand men. It would have been no disgrace to Taylor, confronted as he was by such a numerous foe, had his army been routed ; though it would have been a reproach upon the government, which had so greatly depleted his forces to strengthen the army of General Scott.*

Three times during the last day of that battle, all seemed lost but honor. The artillery was splendidly handled, and it was here that General Taylor is said to have given the characteristic order, "A little more grape, Captain Bragg," which was followed with terrible destructiveness. It is only just to the Mexicans to say that they fought heroically. But they were without spirit. Their commander says, in his report of the battle, that his army was composed of men "torn with violence from their homes," and were both "hungry and poorly clothed."

When one reads history and learns facts the great glory of victories is dimmed. There mingles with the shouts of gladness the pitiful moans of the helpless and injured. Alas!

I spent half a day wandering about this field of the "beautiful view," climbing some of the steep places, and going down into several of those ravines. It called up the feelings of my boyhood days, when I read in the papers the thrilling account of the great victory that General Taylor gained over the Mexicans at Buena Vista. An incident is said to have occurred at this battle, the relation of which, without vouching for its absolute truthfulness, may not be out of place here. General Taylor had been the commander of a military post in Iowa, at Prairie du Chien, and had under him a young lieutenant whose name was Davis, a graduate of West Point. Young Davis fell in love with a daughter of the then Colonel Taylor, and the colonel was bitterly opposed to the match. But the young folks had made up their minds to spend the rest of their lives together, notwithstanding the hostile attitude of *paterfamilias*.

* At this battle the American loss was 264 killed, 450 wounded, and 25 missing. Mexican loss, in killed and wounded, 2,000 men.

You see, "when she says she will, she will, and when she wont, she wont." This time the young lady willed. The couple eloped and were married. The young lieutenant resigned from the army, went to Mississippi, and took up a plantation. When the Mexican war broke out, among the men who first offered their services to the country was Jefferson Davis. Raising a regiment of Mississippians he was mustered into service, and assigned to duty under General Taylor, his own father-in-law, to whom he had not spoken since the day he had refused him the hand of his daughter. Now for the sequel: At this famous battle of Buena Vista, Taylor was well-nigh defeated. The Mexican general is said to have declared, in language not the most polished, that Taylor "did not know when he was whipped." General Taylor had even given orders for a retreat, at least to a stronger position, which Colonel Davis misunderstood, and advanced with his Mississippians to a new charge, and, lo! the Mexicans were panic stricken and fled. General Taylor was victor. Then he sent for Colonel Davis, gave him his hand warmly, and said that the past must now be forgotten, while he must confess that his daughter was a better judge of men than he was. Such is the story as it came into my mind on the battle-field of Buena Vista.

Not even a vestige of the earth-works remains. Much has been said about "Joe" Hooker's battle on Lookout Mountain, Tennessee, in the War of the Rebellion, spoken of as the "battle above the clouds." The battle of Buena Vista was fought at a greater altitude—nearly as high above the level of the sea as the summit of Mt. Washington in New Hampshire, a region of perpetual snow. Snow is seldom seen here.

On the Fourth of July, 1884, some Americans in Saltillo went out and celebrated our national independence by holding a picnic right where the men of 1847 fought and fell. That battle was the turning-point in the Mexican war, and "Jeff" Davis's mistake made his father-in-law, General Zachary Taylor, President of the United States. The Americans always vote for the man who wins, and Taylor won.

It was about eight o'clock in the evening when I reached my hotel, the San Esteben, in Saltillo, and sat down to write up my notes. The evening was one of the most beautiful ever seen. The dark Sierras lift their frowning summits to the east and to the west.

My door opens into a large court, paved with solid blocks of stone, and in the center a small fountain plays. A few vases, out of which grow some tropical plants, border the court. Some cages, containing mocking-birds, hang around the inner corridor. I was far from home and friends. The evening so beautiful, balmy, serene, invited me to a stroll in this old Aztec city. But were I to venture out without a guide, what might become of me? *Quien Sabe?* I sat down to write, and was fairly under way, when the sound of a human voice, unusually sweet, was wafted to me on the evening air. It was a very melodious voice and of unusual compass and power. I laid down my pen and listened while wave after wave of sound came floating on the air, as if vieing with the silvery moonlight to touch my soul into tenderness. "But this will not do," I said, and I picked up my pen, spurred by the recollection of the old saying, " Business before pleasure," "this writing must be attended to." Some coy expressions were floating through my brain, like fleecy clouds in the summer sky, and I tried to woo them. It was all in vain; the voice did not hush, the piano accompaniment was indistinct, the words of the song I could not catch, and if I had caught them should not have understood them, for they were in a foreign tongue. There was no use in trying to write in such a perfect paradise of song, so I folded my port-folio, walked out into the court, looked up through the deep foliage, but it did not come down; I followed in the direction whence I thought it came, and was led toward the street. Reaching the arched entrance-way, the *porte cochere*, I discovered that it issued from an opening in one of those low flat-roofed adobe houses, directly across from the hotel. I stood there until the singer ceased to sing, stood there until the dim light vanished, the curtains were dropped, and the "sweet singer" of Saltillo had gone to rest. I went back to my room and sat down to muse. "Is she a finer singer than one ordinarily hears? or is this strange spell which has come over me due to these mellow surroundings? Is it because I am tender from the recollections of the past? or is this a songster of wondrous sweetness, or what?" I could not write, but just resigned myself to night and dreams, made all the sweeter because of that music. In the morning I said to the clerk of the hotel, who spoke some English, "Who is the lady who sang so beautifully across the street last evening?" He gave me her name as Señorita ———. "Could I hear her sing this evening?" "O yes, I think so," replied the clerk. "I will see, and, if possible, make an engagement for you to hear her." He succeeded, and at eight o'clock we went over; the hotel clerk to be the interpreter and make the formal introduction to a little miss of Aztec blood, fourteen years old, born of respectable parents, in the middle walks of life.

The room was furnished in a simple way. It was clean and neat, and rather above the average of the common people in Mexico. There stood an old piano, of English make, and only second-class at that. "Can this plain little maiden sing as she seemed to sing last evening?" I said to myself, as she gave me her hand. The Mexicans are greatly given to handshaking. The clerk told her I was an "American traveler," and wished to hear her sing. Now, it was very remarkable, but true, that she never said a word about having a "severe cold," or being "out of practice," or "not having her music with her;" no, she never made a single excuse, but sat right down to the piano and sang and played several pieces, then modestly paused.

I told her, through the interpreter, that I was greatly delighted, that it was unusually fine, and that I wished her to continue the pleasure she gave me. Then she asked me if I ever played. Now I had to be honest and said I did, but my music was of a very simple character, and would not sound well after such music as she had given. The little rogue insisted and insisted that I should play something—any thing; but I assured her that I was "entirely out of practice." Then she wanted to know if I would sing. Imagine my embarrassment. I told her I was a basso in a choir long ago, but that now I made no pretensions in that line. I then flanked her movements by asking her if she would have the great kindness to play and sing the Mexican National Hymn for me, which she did; but when I called for the "Star Spangled Banner" she gave me a significant look, saying she did not like it as well as the Mexican. She evidently had a traditional hatred of the "Yankee." But turning on the piano-stool she played John Brown, as an instrumental, following it with

"Away down upon the Swanee River."

The words I did not understand, for they were in Spanish, the melody I did, and I really thought she sang it as I had never heard it sung before. It was the very

CHAPTER VIII.

HUT LIFE AMONG THE AZTECS.

Crosses by the way-side—Old Spanish claims—Adobe huts—Peonage—Prince and beggar—Building a house—Back to first principles—Tortilla making—A yard of beefsteak—Water carriers—A new discovery—Beautiful Salado—The school-master abroad—Hungry—Lulling music—Change in temperature.

OUR diligence had been rumbling along through the forenoon amid clouds of dust, with almost as little to interest the traveler as a journey through the Desert of Sahara. It was very apparent that I was in a land where the Roman Catholic Church had full sway, for crosses were to be seen every-where.

Often they stood by the way-side as *memento mori*, made of wood or stone, and were intended to designate places where persons had met death by violence of some kind, either by the hand of man or by accident. Then I observed, also, that stacks of straw or grain in the fields were frequently surmounted by this sacred symbol; whether to charm away the lightning, or to indicate the mortgage the Church has on the property of Mexico, I do not pretend to know, but there were the crosses. Any one who has not seen this region of the globe can form no accurate idea of the habits and condition of the common people of the interior of our sister republic. At each stoppage for exchange of mules the passengers are allowed half an hour to stretch their limbs and rest from the jolting of the coach. These stoppages, by day and night, gave me a fine opportunity to see the natives

CHAPTER VII.
AMID THE SIERRAS.

Historical romance—Needed courage—Mexican severity—Value of a white neck-tie—A mixed company—Slow, but sure—A Mexican freight-train—Pounding the mules—Stage-driving a profession—An early start—La Ventura—The ranch—Grease and the greasers—Fleeing the fleas—Babel of languages in a coach—Monotony broken.

FROM earliest boyhood I had cherished an ardent desire to see the land of the Montezumas. This feeling was doubtless stimulated by reading accounts of the Mexican war which filled the newspapers of the time. The names of Generals Taylor and Scott were familiar to all Americans, young and old. The victories of Palo Alto, Resaca de la Palma, and Buena Vista had thrilled all hearts. Then in later years Prescott's *Conquest of Mexico* was eagerly perused, a work which every body ought to read and which nobody should fully believe.

It is unsurpassed as a specimen of elegant writing, an almost matchless piece of word-painting, and at the same time equally unsurpassed as a historical romance. One can scarcely believe that the early Spanish chroniclers, who accompanied Cortez and followed in his tracks, and whose writings furnished Mr. Prescott the data for his history, did not, in a large degree, draw upon their imaginations for their facts.

It required no small degree of courage to start off alone on a five or six hundred mile diligence journey amid the Sierras. That trip was taken through a region which has had the reputation for many years of being infested with roving bands of banditti; though, to the credit of Mexico, let it be known that the supreme government has determined to rid the country of these outlaws and cut-throats. Whenever caught they are shot down without mercy, and sometimes it is said without even the form of trial.

I was strongly urged, by a few friends, not to undertake the stage route, for it has been considered quite hazardous; but others insisted that the real danger was largely imaginary. I never like to retreat from a position once deliberately taken, if it is at all tenable, and so I "screwed my courage to the sticking place," and set out from Saltillo for San Luis Potosi—distance well on toward four hundred miles. This was the first regular run.

I had met a lady at Hot Springs, Arkansas, who for many years had been a resident of Mexico, and who gave me some advice in reference to diligence travel. One thing was to go plainly dressed, and to keep out of sight as much as possible costly jewelry and other signs of wealth. This I at once determined to do, and so decided, as far as possible, to make myself look like any other ordinary citizen! I was dressed in a plain suit of traveling clothes, and had with me a light overcoat and shawl. This is a very warm climate in the daytime, but the nights are cool and one needs an extra wrap. Then I wore a regulation white neck-tie, which would indicate that I belonged to the clerical order, and if the bandits should attack the stage, the white cravat would indicate to them the utter barrenness of the soil, in a financial point of view. But what shall I do? I cannot converse in Spanish, and how shall I get through for six or seven consecutive days of diligence travel in the midst of Spanish Aztecs?

There was positively no way left but to take my

chances, and, like an "illustrious predecessor," the great Cortez, burn my ships behind me and go forward. *Nulla vestigia retrorsum.* At four of the clock in the morning, under a clear sky and a bright moon, the coach rolled out of the *patio* of the Hotel San Esteben, at Saltillo, toward San Luis Potosi. There were four of us in the diligence. One was a dapper little Spaniard, well-dressed, well-behaved, silent, and, as I subsequently learned, a perfect gentleman, though he could not speak English. I observed that under his coat was a leather belt stuck full of cartridges, while a heavy revolver rested on his hip.

A Mexican does not regard himself well-dressed without his ammunition box and revolver. Next to him sat a very large man, with shaggy eyebrows, black mustache, shod with heavy boots, the tops of which came up to his knees. On the rear seat of the diligence was another person of obese proportions, with a very foul breath, and who, like some people in church, slept most of the time. Next to the obese man sat a pilgrim, whose defensive armory was limited. The only revolver I carried was my cranium, where my thoughts revolved. I had a light silk umbrella, which could be used either to keep off the rain, or as a sun-shade, or a walking-stick. My grip-sack contained such articles as a tooth-brush, a comb, celluloid cuffs and collars—indispensable articles to a traveler in Mexico—two or three changes of linen, a little medicine provided for emergencies, some paper and envelopes, a stylographic pen, and a field-glass. Thus armed *cap-a-pie*, I sped forth on my journey over roads smooth and roads rough—smooth in spots, but very rough in more spots.

The modes of transportation in the Republic of Mexico are various. Now you are hurried along in a railway train at a rate of speed not exceeding twenty miles an hour. Owing to the fact that Mexico is a mountainous region, the grades are heavy and the curves very sharp, hence the average speed is less than in our own country. But the railway train in Mexico is swift compared with the stage or diligence. These diligences are made in Mexico after the old Concord pattern, and are drawn by a little drove of mules, on the principle that "three make a crowd."

Then if one tires of riding he can walk up the zig-zag roads over mountain steeps, or he can ride on the back of a burro, a species of donkey. This little animal one meets every-where in Mexico. It is said to have been imported from the East by the monks two centuries ago. The burro is a diminutive creature, but has great strength and powers of endurance. He eats but little, lies down to rest or sleep anywhere, is seldom sick, can carry a weight of two hundred pounds all day, and besides is docile and patient. For two hundred years the burro has been the freight-train of Mexico. He can climb up the rocky slopes of the mountains with almost as much agility as a goat, laden with wood, charcoal, silver ore, corn, crockery, poultry, men, women, and children. In short, he carries every thing that needs to be moved. I have seen a Mexican burro loaded down with adobe bricks or stone from the quarry, and with a good-sized man sitting on behind the load, trudging along through the sand and heat at a very remarkable rate of speed for a burro. There are ranches all over northern Mexico where they are raised by the thousand for home uses. Mexican industry in times past would have suffered without the burro. I always liked the little animals; if they throw you off you wont fall very far, and besides, one can either ride or walk without the trouble of dismounting. Stretch out your limbs and you are walking, draw them up and you are riding—figuratively speaking.

The railroads have now come into Mexico, and the burro has a little less to do than formerly. The passenger train is also supplanting the old-fashioned diligence. But for a great many years the diligence system has been spread over Mexico like a net-work, and travelers, whether for business or pleasure, have had to patronize them or stay at home. Great fortunes have been made by the general diligence companies. In all the principal cities and villages may be found the *Hotel Diligencias*. It used to be and is yet so arranged on some lines that the traveler could deposit his funds with the company at the beginning of a journey, and check out from day to day to meet his traveling expenses, and then at the end of the route draw out any balance that might remain to his credit. This was one method of putting a check on the bandits, who never cared to waste time on empty pockets. The Mexican coaches are exceedingly clumsy. They are made not to break down, yet they do sometimes, as one did in my case. A Mexican driver often whips his mule team into a gallop where the roads are very uneven and rocky, and then lets them walk where they are smooth. These mules are arranged in a particular order. When twelve of them are attached to the coach, there are two in the rear to act as wheel mules, and to guide the vehicle—two sets of fours in the middle, and two in front as leaders. The mules are exchanged for new relays every dozen miles or thereabout, and one can always tell the character of the road immediately ahead by the number of animals harnessed to the coach at the relay station.

Stage-driving in Mexico is a distinct profession, and he who acquires a knowledge of this business can seldom settle down to any thing else. On each diligence there is, first, the main driver, who sits in the *boot* and handles the reins. This position is one of considerable dignity.

He answers to the engineer of a railway train. Then he has an assistant who is called the "whipper," a position equal to a fireman on an engine. The main driver uses three different whips: first, a short and stubby lash, with which to harass the two wheel mules, which are almost directly under him; then he has another, just long enough to reach those in the middle, a whip with a lash and "cracker;" besides he carries a very long one, with which to reach the leaders away out in front.

I have watched the driver by the hour to see with what cruel skill he could strike any mule, or any part of any mule, with his stinging lash.

Now he "draws a bead" on a particular ear, and it seems as if the poor ear must fall to the ground and drag its owner with it! Anon he cuts into the "fetlock," and the laboring mule will hold up that foot for a rod or two, and hobble along on three legs. But this is not all. The assistant, the fireman of the train, carries a whip, also, and like a squirrel on a tree runs up and down the outside of the coach, and whips this mule or that one, either because the beast, in his judgment, needs it, or because he thinks somebody or something ought to be hurt. And then he gathers up a hatful of stones, and, from his lofty seat, pounds the poor things with them. He aims at the shoulder of one, the leg of another, the ear or the neck of a third, and does it with an accuracy that can only come of long practice. He hurls his bolts with almost the precision of the rifle's aim, if not with the penetration of the lightning's fire. One thing is certain, and I know what I say, having deliberated the matter thoroughly, I would not like to be a mule and be under the lash of a Mexican driver.

The passengers were always awakened at about three o'clock in the morning, in order to allow ample time to swallow our "bread and coffee," so as to start promptly at four o'clock. Our course, the first day, lay along the Sierras, in a country the most destitute and wretched I have yet seen. Look which way one will, nothing comes into view but barren rock and glaring sand. If a tree appears in sight, it is a species of palm, seemingly from ten to twenty feet high. Several varieties of cactus are seen, which will be described farther on. Once in a dozen miles we pass a few huts, in which the lowest class of Mexicans stay, for it cannot be called living. I found myself saying to myself, again and again, for I could not say it to those about me, " What is there here to live for?" The day's drive ends at about four to five o'clock in the afternoon, when the diligence reaches its appointed destination. Our first day brought us to La Ventura, on the hacienda of General Treviño, where we were five thousand eight hundred and fifty feet above the placid waters of the Rio Grande. General Treviño is reported to be very wealthy. This hacienda, or farm, is large. It is possibly thirty miles long, and fifteen to twenty wide, for it reaches across the valley between the ranges of the Sierras, and we traveled through it nearly half a day. It is not a farm, for very little of it is tilled, but rather a roving ground for stock, and in that lies the general's income. A fair Mexican horse can be bought here for four to five dollars, so that if a man raises three thousand horses a year, and they cost in the raising almost nothing, the income must be very large. Besides these there are cattle and sheep and burros by thousands all over some of these immense ranches. The Hotel Diligencias, on General Treviño's ranch, is any thing but a comfortable place to stay. My room was on the ground floor, which is made of cement. The springs on my bed seemed to be made of two-inch plank, judging from the utter absence of elasticity.

Our supper consisted of tortillas, which are a species

of cakes made of pounded corn and water. Butter is unheard of; the coffee was thick and black. The meat is always fried in grease of some kind, and flavored with extract of onions and garlic. General Treviño is a very popular man in Mexico, and is a standing and promising candidate for the presidency, but he can't keep a hotel, or else I am no judge. It is due to the general to state, however, that he does not wait in person upon the guests. His clerks and peons do all the work. But when he becomes president I can call upon him at the Mexican White House, and claim acquaintance on the score of having once been nearly devoured by the fleas which swarm in the Hotel de la Treviño, at La Ventura.

At four o'clock in the morning we fled from the fleas we knew to others that we knew not of, and continued our journey toward Cedral. Our course lay mostly along a wide valley, with the frowning mountains on either hand. I was greatly pleased with the appearance of things at certain points along this road, and especially with my stop at the Hacienda del Salado, which is said to be partly in four different States. These ranches often cover such great areas that they may, indeed, reach into several States. This is one of the largest and best in Mexico. Among its stock are eight or nine thousand head of horses, and five thousand head of cattle. By the time the stage had reached the Hacienda del Salado the members of our company had become tolerably well acquainted with each other. It had not changed very much since the start from Saltillo. The big man, with heavy boots, shaggy eyebrows, and revolver, was a Hungarian, and had resided for many years in Mexico. He spoke German, Spanish, and a little English. The silent little Spaniard spoke French as well as his native tongue. A Welsh gentleman, who had come in away back in the mountains, spoke his own language, some in their rude and simple habitations on the table-lands of the interior. It is a region of haciendas, or great landed estates, which date back to old Spanish times, when Mexico was ruled by the viceroys, and these estates were granted by royal charter to men who, in some office, served the kings of Spain. They are often very large, their boundaries being somewhat indefinite, and in the original grants were to extend, for instance, as far in a certain direction as a good horse could travel in a given number of hours, or to continue in a specified course to the most rapid portion of a particular stream of water. As a result of such indefiniteness there have been many litigations in modern Mexican courts over boundary questions. In some places along the route these boundaries have now been legally adjusted, and great, solid stone walls, two or three feet thick, and four or five feet high, have been constructed, sometimes extending from the valleys to the very crest of the mountains. At some point on a hacienda there is a cluster of adobe huts called *jacals* (pronounced hackles), where dwell the men and women who do the work on the ranche, or hacienda. I was in probably twoscore of these rude structures between Saltillo and Lagos.

These people are the peons of Mexico. They belong mostly to the aboriginal tribes, and are held in a kind of semi-slavery. A peon is not a legal serf. He is free to go when and where he pleases. But he is always, as a rule, in debt to the owner of the land, the haciendado, and so long as the debt remains uncanceled he is in bonds to his master. If he removes to some other part of the republic he can be followed by his creditor, who may garnishee one third of his wages until the debt is discharged. The highest price paid a peon laborer is thirty-seven and a half cents per day. He may have a wife and family to provide for, but his wages remain the same. Then there is always a store at the headquarters of the hacienda, where are kept the necessaries of life, such as cotton cloth, coffee, sugar, corn, etc. If the peon uses them, he is forced to make his purchases from his employer at one or two hundred per cent. above the original cost-price of the articles; so that debt is inevitable and the owner of the land virtually gets the labor necessary to the care of his stocks free, while he holds the laborer in bonds almost as severe as that which held the Negro on the plantations of the South in the old days of slavery. They are a hard-worked people, and it is not strange that they wander about, vainly hoping to better their condition. The owners of these immense ranches are generally wealthy and usually reside in the principal cities of Mexico, if not in New York, London, or Paris. No wonder they are rich when they have inherited the land they control, pay not a dollar of tax on it, and in addition get their labor virtually free. If Mexico could have one more revolution, which would break up these vast landed estates and place them where they could be divided into small farms for the common people, it would advance the civilization of the country. The ownership of real estate is always a stimulus to a people, and besides it would fill up the treasury of Mexico and place her on a better financial footing. There is very little emigration to Mexico, which must always be a drawback to her prosperity. The country is favored with a climate which admits of out-of-door work all the year through, and though many of the uplands are barren, other sections are fertile. The great North-west of the United States attracts people from Europe by tens of thousands, simply because land is cheap and abundant and the emigrant can own the soil he cultivates. The land in Mexico is owned in large tracts by a few people. I have seen the statement, that fifty thousand people, or six thousand families, own Mexico to-day, so that this monopoly of the soil is largely the cause of the backward state of the country. The Roman Catholic Church at one time owned almost two thirds of all Mexico, and church property could not be taxed. I suppose this to be the origin of their land system. On the other hand, every thing produced or grown for the market is subject to taxation. This is the way they " grind the faces of the poor " in Mexico.

But now, what about the mode of life among these peons? They are clad not only in the cheapest of fabrics, but the dress is scanty enough. Their houses are the merest huts. Sometimes they are built of adobe and are well roofed. But in thousands of instances along the course of the journey they are made by piling up a few stones in a square or semicircle; then driving into the ground a few stakes and covering them over with straw, or the broad leaves of the maguey plant, and the house is completed. A gentleman wished to hire a peon to do some work for him on the following day. The man said he could not come, for he had some work to do for himself.

"Can't you come in the afternoon?" he inquired.

"Yes," said the peon, "I can."

"Why not in the forenoon?"

"Because," said he, "I must build a house to live in during the forenoon."

Surely that was a sufficient plea. I saw many cases where men, with their wives and several children, lived in just such huts, where there were neither bed, chair, table, nor dish, at least none that any one could see, and surely there was no such thing as a cupboard in which to store the crockery. At night these people lie down on the ground, with at most only a piece of ma-

HUT LIFE AMONG THE AZTECS.

nilla cloth between them and the earth, their covering consisting of some greasy blankets. They sit on the ground, or on stones, or blocks of wood. The food, such as it is, is cooked on an earthen platter, called a *comal*, over a pot of charcoal, which is the universal fuel, and is carried to the mouth either with rudely made wooden forks and spoons, or with the fingers. It would tax the imagination to draw a picture of human degradation that would exceed the facts as they appear on the table-lands of Mexico, among the people who live in these rude *jacals*. Their food is cheap. Everywhere they seem to live almost entirely on the tortilla, a species of corn cake. Making tortillas is the hard work of these poor women. The corn is cracked with a stone rolling-pin on a slab of stone inclining at a certain angle. The housewife, on her knees, in the door of the hut, spends many hours of each day in pulverizing the corn and rolling it into the right consistency for tortillas, and then, after patting them into cakes, baking them on a *comal*. They are exceedingly difficult to masticate and have but little taste, but are not lacking in nourishing properties.

The tortilla is eaten with chile sauce. The latter is made from the pods of the piru-tree, a species of red pepper which grows in the tropics. When taken into the mouth this sauce is suggestive of fire and brimstone. If they have meat, in which they indulge occasionally, it is usually fried in fat, and seasoned with onions and garlic. Beefsteak in Mexico is not sold by the pound, but by the yard. They have a way of cutting it into ropes, which can be hung up in the sun and dried without spoiling, owing, I suppose, to the great amount of ozone in the atmosphere. It seems odd to see street peddlers carrying trays of fresh meat on their heads in the sun, with the thermometer up in the nineties; but one gets accustomed to almost any thing. When a Mexican slaughters an animal of any description, he obeys for once a certain scriptural injunction, ₍and "gathers up the fragments, that nothing be lost."

These hut-dwellers I am describing are most devout Catholics. The hut may be destitute of all furniture, dishless, bedless, chairless, and cheerless; but it will not be without its cross and candle, and image or picture of the Virgin. These table-lands are quite destitute of water. It had not rained there for eight months at the time of my visit. Hence it is a region of droughts. Pools of stagnant water are seen here and there, and great basins have been excavated out of the earth in some localities, which fill up in the rainy season and last through the dry, for the use of both man and beast.

Women are the universal water-carriers in the country. I have seen them all along this journey, in twos and threes, going to or coming in from some distant pool, spring, or well, bearing on their shoulders large water-pots, shaped precisely like those used in Bible lands and times, and borne on their shoulders or head in the very same way. Doubtless many a Jacob has met his Rachel at the well in Mexico. History repeats itself.

These days of travel were made all the more uncomfortable on account of the dust. To breathe at times was almost impossible. I was fortunate enough to find an old empty bottle at one of our stopping-places, which I filled with water, and saturating my handkerchief occasionally, held it to my mouth and thus strained out the dust. ⊦My fellow-passengers looked upon it as a very wonderful discovery. ⊦

A sudden change had come over the spirit of my dreams as our diligence came whirling into El Salado, out of a region quite void of vegetation save only a few clusters of huisachi, mesquite, and a species of palm, called the Spanish dagger. To my eyes the Hacienda del Salado was like an oasis in a desert. I gazed around in mute astonishment. Had I gotten suddenly out of Mexico? No! for yonder are the Sierras. It was a pleasant place to rest a day. Every thing was bright and pretty. The streets were clean and the houses neat. I looked about me and could not discover a cross on any building, and so I concluded that the owner of El Salado could not be in much sympathy with the predominant religion of Mexico. My surmises were true. This estate is one of the largest and finest in all Mexico, and the owner is one of the richest men in the republic. His straw and haystacks and buildings are not covered with crosses, but he has a fine school-house, and supports, at his own expense, a first-class teacher, who instructs the children and youth of his employees in the common branches of study. I found there such educational equipments as outline maps, terrestrial globes, blackboards, geometrical forms, etc. The school at the hour of my visit was orderly and quiet and the pupils were bright and interesting. This gentleman is well-known in Mexico. He denounces Romanism, and thinks that if that system of superstitious belief represents Christianity, the world can get along without it. But, like thousands of other thoughtful men in this country, he believes in the morals of the New Testament and in the liberal education of the masses. Such men are called infidels by the priests, and from the stand-point of Romanism they are such, but from a more liberal point of view they are subjects of pity rather than blame. They are too logical to live in their native land.

I turned away from El Salado with a feeling that, after all, there were some green spots in what was almost a desert. After about thirty miles of journeying we came to Cedral, all covered with dust and quite overcome with heat. I was thirsty, but was cautioned not to drink the blue limestone water, on grounds of health, and hence must wait for coffee. No matter how hungry and thirsty the traveler may be, he must endure it until about seven in the evening before he can procure any refreshments. These hotel keepers are not willing to change an old custom. The coach arrives at about five o'clock, and the cook and porter sit around waiting for night before any thing is done toward making the traveler comfortable. Thus our coach came rushing into Cedral, awakening boys and dogs. I was shown to a room in the Hotel Diligencias, which was a decidedly cheerless place. At seven o'clock I sat down, with my fellow-passengers, to devour another dish of frijoles, to masticate more tortillas, and to be made half ill with the same onions and garlic, and then in time to be roused from my slumbers at three o'clock in the morning to pursue the journey.

Soon after retiring to my quarters, and just as sleep was settling down on weary eyelids, I was aroused by the strains of a small band on the plaza, almost directly in front of the hotel. Though not so intended, I complacently assumed that the serenade was for me, and laid awake for an hour or two drinking it in. In an attempt to analyze the sounds, they seemed to come from a cornet, two or three flutes, a clarionet or two, and a harp or guitar. There were no clashing cymbals to deafen the ear, no huge base-drums to drown with sonorous thuds the delicate notes of flute and guitar. Such music as that on the plaza at Cedral, under the clear skies and in this soft tropical air, would not answer in a military camp the evening before a battle. It would make the soldiers homesick. But it was delightfully soothing to a tired traveler, and under the spell of harmony I fell asleep.

In this tropical latitude the days are very warm, the thermometer rising into the nineties at times. The evenings are balmy; but in the morning the air is uncomfortably cool.

The usual signal for starting was given at four o'clock, and we went forth under the blue heavens and the bright stars. The breakfast always consists of bread and coffee, which must suffice till noon. A good hearty meal after the American style would be a help to the traveler, but he is summoned to his *pan y café*—only a few minutes before starting, so that if one wishes to take a second cup and a little more bread, the tramp of the mules and the sound of the driver's horn prevent it. They only provide a single cup of coffee and one nodule of bread.

The bill you pay at one of these "hotels" includes a supper of frijoles, some tortillas, fried meat, onions, garlic, chile sauce, dead flies, bed as soft as a flagstone, coffee and bread in the morning—all for two dollars. Cheap as dirt—and dirt it is, generally.

CHAPTER IX.

VILLAGE LIFE ON THE TABLE-LANDS.

Almost left—Shaking out scorpions—A scare at day-break—Fourteen robbers—Stealing silver—Embodied ghosts—Strange noise—Escuela Parroquia—Religious duties relaxed—Liberalism—A scene in the sanctuary—Kissing the floor—Educated *versus* uneducated —Two millstones—Revolutions.

IF there is any one thing which tries the patience of a traveler in the interior of Mexico it is the village hotel. The one at Cedral, where sweet strains lulled me to sleep, compares favorably with those of its class generally; but that is not saying much for it. They are usually so wretched, that to remain in one over night is a matter of dread, especially if you are accustomed to English or American hotels. There are some places of ten thousand inhabitants in Mexico, I was informed, where no hotel of any kind, good, bad, or indifferent, exists, because such towns are off the main lines of travel. Those in villages are of two classes: first, such as are designed for tourists, which are always under the control of the general diligence companies; and others, called *mesones* and *posadas*, kept by any body who pleases, intended for live stock as well as persons. In this they are like Noah's ark, they take in animals as well as human beings—dogs, donkeys, pigs, cats, and fowl come in and go out of some of them at will.

I overslept myself at Cedral; at least the first sound that stirred me from my dreams was the rattling of the chains and other noises incident to harnessing up the mules in the patio adjacent to my sleeping apartment. There was barely time enough to get my bread and coffee before starting. The only thing I had to do in making my toilet was to put on my shoes and hat; for it must be borne in mind that while it is very warm during the day-time, the temperature rising to seventy-five or eighty degrees, at night it grows quite cold. The bed covering is scant and often not very clean. Certain vermin, too, infest the premises, and, at some seasons of the year, become so numerous that travelers inclose themselves in rubber sacks as a protection. Thus I justified myself in doing what might be considered a gross violation of the proprieties of life.

It is always well for a traveler in Mexico to shake out his shoes before inserting his feet, as it would not be a pleasant sensation to find one's self compressing under the sole of his foot a live scorpion or tarantula. I was told that scorpions abound on these uplands, though I saw none. They multiply with marvelous rapidity. A scorpion will become a grandparent in a day or two. They hide in the crevices of the wall and in the openings in the cement floor of your room. If a piece of manilla cloth graces the floor of your apartment, under its folds may lie concealed a nest of these poisonous vermin. Therefore it is well for the traveler to do with his garments as he does with a bottle of medicine, "shake well before taking." The scorpion does not cut into the flesh with his teeth, but stings with his tail, and when tortured, it is said, they will actually sting themselves to death. They are greatly feared in these parts by young and old. When one of these venomous creatures injects its poison into the flesh, especially that of a child, convulsions ensue, accompanied with foaming at the mouth and with other signs which indicate the near approach of death. A Mexican, when stung, resorts to the use of powerful stimulants to counteract the virus. Neither scorpion, tarantula, or centipede ever gave me any trouble.

From Cedral to Metahuala (Metawala) the distance is only a dozen or so miles. It was reached just a little after day-break. We were now in the neighborhood of Catorce, a place of over ten thousand inhabitants, and a region proverbial for two things : its extensive silver mines—some of which are the richest in the republic—and its name. Catorce means fourteen. The place was so named from a band of fourteen robbers, who for many years infested these mountain regions, making this their head-quarters. After leaving Cedral, and when we were fairly under way, at a distance of about two miles, and before it was light, there came dashing up after us a man on horseback shouting with a stentorian voice to the driver to halt. We were in the neighborhood of Catorce—that place of former robber renown. The situation was alarming. At length the driver halted and a parley ensued, which increased our anxiety. I feared the parley might be only a sort of ruse, designed to hold the diligence until the other members of the bandit crowd came up. Soon the coach made a circuit over the broad plain, and back we went to Cedral again, the driver having forgotten to call for a couple of passengers who had booked themselves for this particular coach. It was only a scare.

We soon reached Metahuala, a small city containing a number of *haciendas de beneficios*, as these silver smelting works are called. The roads in the early morning were lined with peons of every description, on foot and on donkeys, coming in from their huts in the outskirts to labor in the silver works. The peons handle the wealth, but do not own any of it. When they leave the premises in the evening they are all searched by an officer appointed for the purpose, that not a single grain of the precious metal may be surreptitiously carried away. One of these poor fellows, however, notwithstanding the vigilance of the officer, succeeded for a time in purloining it in a very adroit manner. He had constructed for himself a pair of sandals with double soles, between which he somehow managed to secret small fragments of silver each day, and, without exciting the suspicion of his employers, accumulated quite an amount. He was detected, however, and imprisoned for a period double the length of time it would have taken him to earn the amount stolen. Even in Mexico "the way of the transgressor is hard."

Thousands of these poor Mexicans of the lower order are driven to crime through the oppressions to which they have been so long subjected. The meager pay, the natural demands of life, the moral darkness which surrounds and envelops them, palliate but do not excuse theft and robbery. Their condition should excite the pity and help of mankind.

Evening brought us to Charcas, a typical Mexican village in the Sierras. As the drive during the day was an easy one, we came in quite early, so that ample time was given for seeing the sights—and a Mexican village has some sights worth seeing. The diligence was driven into Charcas amid a cloud of dust, and after a few turns, first to the right, then to the left, we passed through the arched entrance-way—the *porte Cochère*—under heavy stone vaulting into the court-yard, about which the meson was built.

Around the court ran an arcade, with flag-stone pavement. I was soon in my *cuarto*, or room, where, notwithstanding the heat without, it was delightfully cool. As these rooms receive their light mostly from the roofless court, it seemed almost like twilight, which was a pleasing change from the monotonous glare of the sun on the white sand during the day. To sit there for an hour would have been a delight, but time was too precious to be allowed to pass unimproved in this wild, romantic region, which I shall probably never see again. The furniture of my room were relics of a former generation. The human beings around me, in their dress, manners, and customs, resembled more the embodied ghosts of a long-gone past, than the people of this advanced age of the world. The tourist is not obliged to stop always at the Hotel Diligencia, though it is a little more convenient in the morning at starting time, besides you are not so liable to be left. There was another hotel in Charcas to which some of the passengers went. But generally in a Mexican village, no matter at which one you do stop, you always regret that you had not gone to the other. These villages on the table-lands are like the eddies in a river, where the waters go round and round ceaselessly, while the great mad current sweeps ever onward toward the sea.

The contact of these people with the outer world is so slight that they are not changed by it. Gazing at them one is carried back even beyond the times of the old Spanish kings and queens. We are pointed by some historians to the glorious past of Mexico, but now we see only degeneracy, lack of ambition, and want of education, other than that which is included in the dogmas of a despotic Church.

The first thing which attracted my attention at Charcas was a singular kind of noise I heard. I could not divine what caused it, but, prompted by curiosity, I at once set out to ascertain. A block or two brought me to an old stone building, which had a fortress-like appearance. These buildings are suggestive of their history. They seem in many places to have been built as much for defense against revolutionists as

for security against rain and sun. I noticed that the
doors of this edifice were of heavy plank, so that they
could be fastened with ponderous bolts. The windows
were guarded with heavy iron bars, through which a
violent mob would find it difficult to penetrate. This
particular building was a school-room, a place to im-
press the heart and train the mind of childhood.
It was as somber as a prison. Without ceremony I
walked into the street door-way, which was standing
wide open, and at once found myself in a long dismal corridor opening into a room whence came the
strange noises that had attracted my attention. As
I reached the end of the hall-way next to the room a
lady met me, evidently startled at my boldness, for which
I apologized as well as I could. Surmising my purpose,
she gave me to understand that it was the *Escuela Parroquia*, the parochial school. There were in that room,
which was comparatively small and very dingy, not less
than two hundred pupils, ranging in age from six to sixteen. They sat in rows, on high benches without backs
with their feet, in the case of the smaller ones, dangling
in the air. Each had a book, held with both hands directly before the face. It was study-hour, and every
child in the school conned the lesson aloud. Being in
Spanish, I could not tell what it was they were vociferat-
ing, whether grammar, geography, or the catechism; most
likely the latter. Some had voices peculiarly shrill,
others quite subdued. The noise was like the chatter-
ing of a great many blackbirds in a tree. Tenor, treble,
alto, and bass voices blended in the strange medley.
They all swayed back and forth in rhythmic measure to
the very unmusical sounds. Two male teachers, young
men preparing for the priesthood, I imagined from their
appearance, were in charge. They walked up and down
the room, with small sticks in their hands, keeping a

strict watch on every child, and when any one became weary or indolent and slackened up the voice, that child had a head to be hit. These poor little creatures were bright-looking in the main, and deserved a far better fate than to be driven through a book of some kind, like donkeys through a mesquite grove. Not a map, globe, blackboard, or flower was there to grace the room, such as I saw at Salado. Only the hideous pictures of some seedy old saints hung on the time-stained walls, to add, if possible, a deeper gloom to the exceedingly gloomy place. Poor children! thought I, as I bowed myself out with a *gracias* to the teachers. How strangely this contrasts with the graded schools of our own beloved land! No wonder the priest-ridden people of Mexico are ignorant and superstitious. In the interior villages, owing to their isolation, the priest has far more influence and power than in the larger cities. It would be a blessing to all Mexico if the power of the priesthood were entirely broken, as it will be finally; for nothing lives which God has ordained to die, and it must be this rank weed will ultimately perish, though, like all other weeds which infest the soil, it taxes the patience of the world, greatly hindering true progress wherever it takes root.

Mexico has been nearly crushed by this monster. In the villages and small towns the curates have been absolute tyrants, fleecing their flocks to the utmost extent without remorse of conscience. And so, when the government decreed that the payment of tithes should be voluntary, a majority of the people in some sections refused to respond to the demands of the Church. With those decrees came a decline in the influence of the clergy. Religious duties were relaxed on the part of many, mass was attended only on Sundays and fast days by the male population, and then more through habit and ostentation than from any real spirit of devotion, while the confessional was avoided almost entirely, except by the women.

The separation of Church and State, under republican rule, grew out of the power of the clergy over the bodies and souls of the people. In this revolution they lost their prestige in a large degree; but their wealth was great, and right well was it used in fomenting the different factions that for many decades had desolated the country. In time the liberal government felt itself strong enough to sequestrate the property of the Church for the uses of the State. The effect of this measure on the part of the government was to separate many of the clergy, either on scruples of conscience or love of money, and in just so far curtail the influence of the Romish hierarchy. The combination of the priests with the French invaders in 1863 had much to do with increasing the strength of liberalism.

To-day, beneath the surface of the best and most intelligent society in the larger cities, there is a marked indifference to the papal Church, but in the rural districts it holds on its ancient way.

After visiting the school at Charcas, and partaking of my evening repast, I went to the principal church. It was in the dusk of the evening. There was no special service, but about forty persons were there on their knees in various parts of the sacred building, many of whom were repeating audibly their devotions, making almost as much noise as did the pupils in the school. There were old women and young women, rich women in black silk mantillas, and poor women in plain blue and gray rebozos; there were a few men and boys mingling in the worshipful company; some had open books, out of which they seemed to read their Ave Marias; others were mumbling something as they counted their beads. All were on their knees upon the sandy floor. There are wooden floors in a few Mexican churches, though some one writes to the contrary. They are not so common as stone and cement. These women would kiss the floor with their bare lips again and again over which the crowd had walked with sandaled and unsandaled feet. No one could question their sincerity or help pitying their ignorance and degradation. The life these people live is doubtless fully up to their capacity of appreciation.

It must be remembered that the education of human tastes and the multiplication of human wants keep pace with the increase of popular intelligence. But we must make a distinction between a want and a necessity. The necessity measures the minimum of life's demands. The study of how to reach that minimum is the sure pathway of descent toward barbarism.

Mere necessity contracts the soul and dwarfs the powers of the mind. On the other hand, the wants of mankind measure the maximum of life's demand, so that if the study of the minimum tends to dwarf us, the study of the maximum tends to develop and enlarge us. It requires far more to clothe, feed, and shelter a people who are educated than it does one who are not; for cultivated people have wants which come with their development, spontaneously. These wants are never indigenous in a soil which has not been stirred by educational forces. Furthermore it is true that many of the wants in cultivated life are artificial. The mere utilitarian philosopher will argue against expensive pictures, elegant carpeting, richly bound books, fine pianos, costly bric-a-brac, etc. But nevertheless they come with civilization as the flowers come with summer sunshine, and he might as well argue against the flowers of summer as to argue against the flowers of society.

Education may be an expensive luxury, but without it

we should drift rapidly back to savage life, and, like our Anglo-Saxon ancestors, dwell in caves and clothe ourselves in the skins of wild animals. Education increases the wants of mankind, but, at the same time, it augments the ability of men to produce. There is no power on earth quite equal to brain power.

Here, in this interior region of the Republic of Mexico, the Church of Rome has held the people with hooks of steel to mere forms and ceremonies. Churches, convents, and monasteries have been numerous, schools few. The result is, the people have but few wants for themselves, while their earnings have gone to enrich the Church. Their necks for three centuries have been under this galling yoke. Between the civil exactions of Spanish rulers on the one hand, and the spiritual demands of the Church of Rome on the other—one representing the upper and the other the nether millstone —the poor Aztec people have been ground almost to powder.

Mexico was conquered by Spanish arms at a time when the authority of Rome was supreme in Spain; consequently that form of religious tyranny came to be supreme among the Aztecs. The fruits most congenial to Rome have every-where and always been ignorance, degradation, and slavish submission. Women were taught to be entirely satisfied with their own ignorance, and to be controlled by the priesthood. These ecclesiastics regarded themselves as the disposers of the people from the cradle to the grave, and even in the world to come. Still there are some who actually realize the condition of Mexican society. They are revolutionists, or reformers, a class in advance of the common horde. There will always be upheavals in Mexico until the people who live in intellectual and moral darkness are educated to an understanding of their civil and religious rights. Mexico has not advanced as far as old Spain itself in some things. But advance it must and will, though it be through revolutions and blood, until it takes its place in the procession of the nations.

> "For ever the right comes uppermost,
> And ever will justice win."

CHAPTER X.

THE EYE OF THE SIERRAS.

Hacienda life—Picturesqueness—From cellar to garret—Isolation—Source of wealth—A forest of cacti—Fantastic forms—Designs of nature—Vegetable reservoirs—San Luis Potosi—A cheering voice—Acres of flat roofs—The Sunday market—At the point of the bayonet—In a box—The rescue—The army—Ambitious generals—A bath amid blossoms.

THE region between Charcas and San Luis Potosi belongs to one of the great table-land systems of Mexico. The distance is a little less than one hundred miles, the road running almost directly southward. The elevation above sea-level is over six thousand feet. The days are hot; the nights, especially toward morning, cool. The great attenuation of the atmosphere affects the breathing, especially of those unaccustomed to it. The highway traversed by our coach was as smooth as one could expect in such a region. These table-lands are not like a western prairie, but are, in the main, rolling, with scattered patches of quite level country inclosed by lofty mountain spurs.

This is a land of haciendas. A hacienda seemed to me to be the lonesomest place conceivable. They are very much alike in general characteristics, though variable in size, ranging from a few hundreds to many thousands of acres. On every one we passed there was a central point, where stood at least one stone or adobe fortress-like building, with bastioned outer walls, corner towers, and barricaded windows, strong enough to withstand the attack of a revolutionary army.

One of these vast estates is usually under the management of a principal agent. The owner, who may reside far away, seldom sees his property, though he receives any profit which may remain after the agents, clerks, and peon laborers have pocketed their share. A hacienda is a little world by itself. The community is regulated by its own social laws and customs; has its own church and priest; gets up its own amusements, and pursues its own way undisturbed by any contact with the great outside world. The main building, occupied by the administrator of the estate and his subordinate officers, is generally rudely furnished with wood benches, iron bedsteads—put up when needed—pine chairs, and deal tables. The walls of the buildings are white within and without, and seen from a distance, from some eminence, surrounded as they are by a number of smaller houses occupied by the peons, present a picturesque and very beautiful appearance—the white walls contrasting markedly with the deep green of the tropical foliage, especially in well-watered places. This little "city" has its store, shop, church, and indispensable plaza. Leather checks are given to the peon laborers, which represent money, and are exchanged at the store for the necessaries of life. His isolation compels the peon to make all purchases there at whatever price may be demanded. On some of these estates, like that of Salado, the proprietor resides and superintends the work in person. In some such instances great magnificence is displayed. The family mansion is the scene of culture and gayety. The children are educated abroad, especially in Madrid or Paris. Flowers, birds, music, and riding lend their charms to this grade of hacienda life.

In all these vast ranches, however, there is a feeling of solitude realized, more possibly by the tourist than by the resident. There is a vastness of desolation which is inexpressible. One feels as though he had traveled quite beyond the bounds of civilization, or had wandered into some other world. To leap out of our own country into this table-land region of Mexico is like going out of an elegant parlor into a garret, where the dust of generations has accumulated, and every object is festooned with cobwebs. The monotony of this interior life is seldom disturbed by any event of sufficient importance to stir the pulse to quicker beat. The coach passes by with rumble of wheel, rattle of hoof, and crack of whip. A few passengers possibly alight, stretch their limbs, and hand a few centavos to the beggars, young and old, who throng around, and then are off again. Ere the dust raised by the diligence has settled down the former stillness reigns. I quote from a recent writer:

"Most of the lonesome hacendados have few books, no daily mails or newspapers, and no amusements, except such as they can create for themselves. Hence a visitor is hailed as a boon from heaven, and kept as long as he or she can be prevailed upon to remain. In former times — in fact, in days not altogether passed away in some portions of the country—there were no inns, and persons traveling from place to place with their retinue of armed attendants—as was necessary for personal safety — were fain to depend upon the hospitality of the haciendas for nightly stopping places. And so generally was this expected that the proprietors, quite as a matter of course, set apart a generous sum in the provision for annual expenditures for their *administradors* to use in the entertainment of chance guests—rich or poor, friends or strangers, and whether or not they came with letters of recommendation. But when a troop of friends invade some lonely hacienda for a visitation—then great is the rejoicing! Not only is the fatted calf figuratively slaughtered, but the finest bull the estate affords is sacrificed upon the altar of hospitality, in the form of a bull-fight, for the amusement of any who may care to witness. The great court-yard, in the center of the square of buildings, is transformed into a temporary *plaza de toros*, professional matadors and picadores are sent for, and word goes to all the outlying ranches that a free show is about to transpire. At the appointed hour a crowd is certain to appear, even in the most isolated sections, where one had supposed no human being dwelt outside of the hacienda; and with the graceful hospitality which is the heritage of this easy-going race from their Moorish progenitors, all are welcome to come in and make merry with the lords of the land."

But little farming is done, in the American sense, on these vast ranches. They are not suited to the growth of cereals save in a few places here and there. The chief business is stock-raising. Cattle are grazing over the plains, flocks of sheep are clinging to the hill slopes, and droves of mules and burros are congregated about the ponds of stagnant water. These constitute the wealth of the lordly hacendado.

I could not help thinking as we rode along of the diminutive specimens of cactus one sees in the dooryards and green-houses in the United States. They were called up by the laws of association, just as a very large man reminds you of a small one. The cactus plant in Mexico is not cultivated for ornamental purposes; it is very useful. The mullein is treated by us in this country as a weed, neither useful nor ornamental, but rather indicative of a poor soil, while in England they cultivate it in their gardens, and call it "The American Velvet Plant," esteeming it a "thing of beauty."

Cacti grow here to perfection. Look in which direction you may, you see some variety of this species of vegetation. There are several hundred varieties known to the botanist. This is their native climate. They seem to thrive in a dry and arid region. In one place they stand before you great thick fleshy-stemmed shrubs, single-branched in one instance, and double in another. Notwithstanding the dryness of the earth on the table-lands and the apparent absence of moisture from the atmosphere, these plants are soft and juicy, insomuch that the roving herds of cattle break them down with their horns and chew them as a means of quenching thirst. This is certainly a provision of nature to meet a want of animal life. They live through long droughts and are natural reservoirs.

The great variation in their form exceeds the imagination. The most majestic and beautiful of all the species is the so-called organ cactus, a purely tropical growth. It rises to a height of twenty-five or more feet, resembling not a little the seven branched candle-sticks of Moses, or the pipes of a great organ, whence its common name. Another kind resembles cannon balls lying loose on the earth. They are globular and are called the melon cactus. Here they stretch along the ground in a snake-like appearance, and there spread out into a fan-like shape, resembling a magnified rabbit's ear. This is the form of the universal nopal, which grows from a few inches to several feet in height, in leaf-like articulations covered with sharp spines. The later variety, sometimes called the prickly-pear, produces the *tuna*, or Indian fig, which, if not "beautiful to the eye" is "good for food;" besides, it is used by the natives in preparing a species of strong drink, and in furnishing from its parasitic insect the *coccus cacte*, a bright dye for their fabrics. Certain species take on the tree form, attaining often a height of fifty feet. These wonderful vegetable productions are of all forms, flat, ribbed, and cylindrical. The cactus is of use to the people, but not of so much importance as some other things. The maguey is the most useful of all the species, and is cultivated by the Mexicans systematically. It holds about the same relation to the Mexicans that wheat does to us, or the family of palms to the Hindus. But of this more hereafter. These peculiar plants put forth vigorous life through a portion of the year and then rest. Nature has constructed them to live not only in a dry and sandy region, but to resist, by their tough and impervious skin, the heat of the tropical sun. I have seen them growing out of what seemed to be naked lava rocks in the volcanic districts, their roots penetrating the crevices of the lava-bed and disintegrating it. In this case they are the forerunners of other and more useful productions. It is difficult to see how the people could live on these uplands without the cactus. Their flowers are very rich in color, and those of some of the better species are very fragrant, but all are very short-lived. Some burst out in the night-time, and when morning comes are gone. It seems marvelous that such pulpy, thorny, ill-shaped plants should produce flowers so lovely in color and fruit so delicate to the taste as the tuna. But such is the provision of the Author of nature. I could not help thinking, in passing through the land of the Aztecs, where palms shoot up great white blossoms which rise above their tops in tall and graceful plumes, and cactus flowers present the brightest of colors to the eye of man, that in like manner God can cause to grow out of this barren human soil a people who shall be his delight and who may reflect his glory in the land of their ancestors.

Nearly one hundred miles over hills and through valleys, amid heat and dust, not a little weary with the long jaunt, brought me to San Luis Potosi, the "Eye of the Sierras," possibly never so-called before.

I was very glad when we came in sight of the city. It was a very tedious journey from Charcas to San Luis, but one which afforded considerable variety to the eye, if not to the palate.

Such a trip is one not soon to be forgotten. We came into San Luis, as they call it for short, with a rush. These drivers always leave the stations in a whirl, urging their teams forward at full speed, and keeping it up until they are well out of town. I noticed that usually, as we drew near our stopping place, Jehu would slow up, in order that the mules might have a breathing spell, then he would come through the village or dash into the city on a gallop, so as to make the innocent people think we had been thundering along at that rate of speed all day. When our diligence landed us in San Luis Potosi it was in the dusk of the evening, and in front of the Hotel Diligencia. As I stepped out upon the sidewalk, amid a group of hotel runners, I heard one voice which, in true American fashion, said, in plain English, "The San Fernando is the best hotel." That was just what I was anxious to hear—that is, the language—for all the rest spoke Spanish. Of course the San Fernando was selected, not because it was the best hotel, though it was very good, but for the reason that the colored runner, formally a slave in old Virginia, could be of service to me by his ability to converse in both languages. A single night's rest and a good bath completely rejuvenated me. I was as fresh as when I started from home.

I shall not soon forget San Luis Potosi and the impression made upon the mind as I gazed over the acres of flat roofs—Azoteas—and beheld before me the Spanish

Renaissance cathedral, whose matin bells had roused me from my slumbers. I was looking out of a window in the upper story of the hotel upon antique houses built along exceedingly narrow streets, which were well paved and tolerably clean. It was Sabbath morning, and the thoroughfares and plazas were bustling with excitement. The day was beautiful, and in these Southern lands there is a gayety about life which is peculiarly fascinating. Under my window marched a band of musicians arrayed in flashy uniforms, followed by a crowd of youth who danced along the pavements to the strains of the music, while mahogany colored duennas and senoritas, from the door-steps and windows across the way, gossiped and flirted with the opposite sex.

San Luis was an improvement upon the Mexican cities which I had seen. It has a population of about thirty-five thousand souls, and lies at an elevation of over six thousand feet above the level of the sea. The city is regularly laid out. It is the capital of a State of the same name. There is here a larger proportion of two-story buildings than in either Monterey or Saltillo. The city extends over a considerable area, and boasts of a number of plazas. In our approach to it, during the last two-hours' drive, we passed through a very rich section of country. All it needs to convert it into a garden-spot is Yankee enterprise and more water.

A gentleman of high standing informed me that the thermometer never reaches the freezing-point in San Luis Potosi, nor is it ever excessively warm. In all these cities the places of most interest are the cathedrals, the principal parochial churches, and the plazas; and they are numerous. On Saturday, as we drew near San Luis, say within thirty miles, I noticed great numbers of poor peons wending their way toward the city to spend the Sabbath. Burros by the score, driven by their masters, were bearing their burdens toward the markets of San Luis. They were freighted with jugs and skins filled with pulque, bundles of wood, hay, straw, pottery, onions, and many other things I cannot describe. Sunday is the great day, in Mexico, for marketing, praying, and bull and cock fighting. I went and looked upon the motley crowd of men, women, and children squatting in the market-places on pieces of old oil-cloth or skins of animals, having before them little piles of potatoes, onions, tomatoes, meat, etc., for sale. A man and his wife will travel from five to thirty miles through heat and dust with produce not worth over two dollars, sell it if possible, remain over the Sabbath, sleep on the ground in any corner, go to mass in one of the churches, attend the cock or bull fight in the afternoon, if there be one, then go home, and, I suppose, think they have had a good time!

San Luis now contains a number of ruins; that is, old churches and convents sequestered by the government, and now used for State purposes and for various mechanical industries. The city is poorly lighted with candles and petroleum. It has good water. Some of the buildings are of lofty proportions. Many of them are painted on the outside in bright colors, after the Mexican style. It is a *costombre de la pais*, as they say—the custom of the country. These colors are quite durable and pretty. The main plaza is ornamented with a bronze statue of the patriot Hidalgo, one of Mexico's illustrious sons. Street-car lines are in operation as a result of American enterprise. Telephones are in use, though the electric light had not yet been introduced. Several regiments of Mexican troops were stationed here. One morning, as I was prowling around sight-seeing, I heard the sound of a bugle, and thought correctly that I might have an opportunity to witness a military parade, and, accordingly, followed in the direction whence the notes of the bugle came, until I found myself directly in front of the soldiers' barracks, and very innocently walked into the archway, and was rapidly pushing on toward the *Plaza de Armas*, when a couple of soldiers raised their muskets and called out sharply, "Alto!" I altoed. Just then the officer of the day, who had gone aside from his post to converse with some one, perceived the dilemma I was in and came to my aid. I told him, in a mixture of English and Spanish, compounded of three parts of the former to one of the latter, that I was an American tourist and was out sight-seeing, that I wished, if permission could be allowed, to witness some military evolutions. He was very polite, gave me his hand cordially, and, in a commanding voice, said to the guard, "Paseo!" I paseoed, and remained there half an hour, entirely satisfied with the exceedingly ill-looking fellows and the horrid stench of the place. I don't know but these soldiers, according to the Mexican *code militaire*, might have shot me on the spot, not for "hauling down the American flag," but for running up the American impertinence.

Government troops are met at all prominent points in the republic. As a people, they are fond of soldiering. Indeed, ever since the day of her independence Mexico has cultivated a military spirit, which has consumed her very vitals. She needs the plow and the loom far more than the sword. The resources of the country have largely been squandered on the army, and the army, through its ambitious generals, has been the real government. The blessings of peace have been despised, while the citizens, instead of contending for the common weal, have been divided into factions led on to blood and disturbing revolutions by rival chieftains. Revolution has succeded revolution rapidly, one aspiring chieftain supplanting another, so that in fifty-six years they have had fifty-five presidents, one regency, and one emperor. Civilians have rarely been placed at the head of affairs, which shows plainly that the people have but little voice in politics. The reins of government have almost invariably been committed to hands that wield the sword.

The history of the country is a record of military insurrections and usurpations, in not one of which an oppressed people, as a whole, have struck for their

> "Altars and their fires,
> God and their native land,"

but in which some ambitious general has tried to rise by crushing some one else. Even when invaded by a foreign foe, military factions and rival generals have paralyzed the power of the nation and rendered her an easy prey. A Mexican gentleman told me that at the battle of Buena Vista the real cause of their defeat was this sort of rivalry. They hindered rather than helped each other on the field of battle. Through all the past, records bear witness to the fact that popular military leaders have been the chief disturbers of Mexican republicanism.

When General Santa Anna returned from exile, at the beginning of the war between this country and Mexico, in 1846, and again took the leadership over all his rivals in military and civil affairs, the city of San Luis Potosi was the point where he concentrated his great army, with which he expected to overwhelm the forces of General Taylor, and when defeated he marched back upon it again with the remnant of that army. This city is very pretty, and has many fine buildings, private as well as public. Its public baths are equal to those of any country. It is a healthful region, and when the railway reaches this point from Tampico, on the Gulf, it will become a resort for pleasure seekers, as well as a sanitarium for invalids. Who has not heard of the famous bands of music of which this old Aztec country boasts? I thought the accounts had been exaggerated, but, after hearing one of their very best, I concluded otherwise. I sat for two hours one evening on the main plaza listening to one of these military bands. It was formed in a circle in front of one of the state buildings, and numbered thirty-six pieces, including various horns, flutes, clarionets, etc. The horns were burnished silver. I failed to understand how there could be a finer band of music. If every thing one sees here were as good as the music, then Mexico would be a paradise indeed.

CHAPTER XI.

THE HAUNTS OF THE BANDITTI.

Distance in the mountains—Roadways toward the skies—The age of ice—Primeval ocean—A good acquaintance—A hard customer—High places of Baal—City of seven hills—Beggars—Conscience and cash—Children the hope of Mexico—A pen portrait—Robberies—Dress that is cheap—An Aztec bath-house—Crockery and cooking—Fire-water—The husband and weaver—The christening.

MY rest in San Luis Potosi was one of much delight. It lingers in the recollection—even now, like a beautiful dream. The fine old churches, the plazas, the music, the clear skies, and the salubrious air of the table-lands have left only pleasant memories.

It was at six o'clock instead of four o'clock in the morning when I took my seat in the diligence, along with a number of passengers, all of whom were strangers to me, and began to climb the Sierras. We cross them now, on our way toward the capital, in a zigzag course, bearing a little to the south-west. The road in some places is exceedingly rough, and in others as fine as a roadway can be. This is an old highway, which has been cut out of the mountain side throughout most of its extent. In some of the steeper portions, as we near the summit, where we are eight or nine thousand feet above the level of the sea, the lower side of the road is walled up by solid masonry from fifty to a hundred or more feet.

One must guess at distances here with the possibility of being greatly mistaken, underrating rather than overrating always. The road-bed is forty feet wide, and in many places is as smooth almost as a Nicholson pavement. The Sierras are a continuation of the Cordillera of South America, taking the name of Sierra Madre in Mexico. Their trend is north-westerly from the isthmus of Tehuantepec. In the southern part of Mexico their elevation is moderate, but as they extend northward begin to rise up grandly, until they attain a mean altitude of about nine thousand feet, while Popocatepetl, Iztaccihuatl, and Orizaba push their summits skyward nearly twenty thousand feet, according to recent estimates. The former is the culminating point of North America. I had crossed the eastern range, which includes in its valleys the cities of Monterey, Saltillo, and San Luis Potosi. It must have required no small degree of engineering skill to construct this highway. Up, up we go, around this curve and around that, still on and up, until we exclaim, "Will the end never come?" We look back, and mountains which seemed high as we crossed them, or moved around them in spirals, now resemble mere hillocks below us. Far in the distance and far below us, set like an emerald in its mountain fastness, lies quietly and beautifully San Luis Potosi, the "Eye of the Sierras," which seems at this distance about the size of a Mexican village. Not a tree is visible on these heights, for nothing grows on the rocks save a few dwarfed specimens of the universal nopal cactus. This is a region interesting to the geologist. The rocks show us that old mythical Pluto once held sway here. They are metamorphic in character. Here are granite, gneiss, clay-slate, basalt, trachyte, and porphyritic feldspar. The region is volcanic, though no volcanoes exist at present. I was impressed, also, with the fact that, subsequent to the great upheavel of the Sierra Madre chain, the waters covered this part of the globe. When we were at the greatest elevation, I saw acres and acres of water-washed bowlders covering the slopes near the summits. They lie in vast masses, and also single bowlders, ranging in weight from a few pounds, as round as cannon-balls, and looking not unlike them, up to those weighing several tons. The lower summits are far more angular and castellated than the upper. The latter are rounded off, and made more dome-like in their contour. They were "sand-papered" off some by the ice-floes. All this seems to show that this was once the bottom of a sea. The higher elevations were near the surface of that sea, and may have projected even above it. The signs are that they were washed by the waters and worn by the chafing ice of that epoch. Over the lofty summits the tides of a primeval ocean ebbed and flowed, and vast sea-monsters sported in the waters that once concealed these precipitous heights. But, then, to use a common Mexican expression—*quien sabe?* Having reached the summit, we did not descend on the other side, for the reason that here begins the central tableland, which has a mean altitude of between seven thousand and eight thousand feet. We have climbed to a greater height now than before reaching San Luis Potosi. Our first stop for the night was at Ojuelos (Owhalos), a lofty but lonely place to stay. Two armed guards went with the diligence, for the route has always been famous for its brigands. They each carried breech-loading rifles and revolvers. The passengers were six in all. The men wore the usual belt of cartridges and hip pistol. The two ladies and I were unarmed. We had one gentleman in our company, a native Mexican from the city of Leon. He was a civil engineer by profession, and could speak English tolerably well, which with my trifle of Spanish enabled us to get along very comfortably. As soon as he spoke to me in my own tongue in the diligence I felt quite at home. I recognized him at once as a cultured gentleman, and such he proved to be. At the hotel at Ojuelos, the landlord assigned me to a room along with one of the guards who had accompanied the diligence, an exceedingly rough-looking fellow, against which proceeding I protested stoutly, assuring the keeper of the house that I would not occupy the same apartment with an armed stranger, even if he were a guard. At once the gentleman from Leon was quartered with me. Hotel rooms here are generally furnished with two and sometimes four single beds. No sooner had the diligence driven through the arched gate-way than half a dozen beggars beset us. Here in the mountains Romanism has been supreme and unmolested for ages, so that crosses and beggars are very numerous. Mountainous regions are well adapted to the religion of Rome.

Romanism thrives well on the high table-lands and amid the mountains. Count Gallitzin retired from Maryland lowlands to a rocky portion of the Alleghany Mountains, in Pennsylvania, to found his Catholic colony. The early settlers of St. Mary's chose a lofty and almost inaccessible spot, passing by the rich bottom lands east and west of them.

Among the rugged Alps, near Modana, stands a chapel on the top of a rock, which is not only visited by the common people, but occasionally by those of noble and even royal birth On the top of Mount Cenis, the highest of the Alps that can well be reached, is a chapel in which religious worship is conducted every August, even at the risk of life on account of tempests. It might be deemed unjust by some to trace a connection between the customs of the Roman hierarchy and paganism, but on seeing the hill chapels in Mexico, they bring to mind the high places of Baal in the far East. The heathen believe that their gods love to dwell in high places. That same opinion prevails to-day in both the Greek and Latin Churches. No one can visit Cholula and Guadalupe, in Mexico, without seeing, in more ways than one, the connection between Romanism and paganism. The population through this part of the territory are Romanists of the rudest and most bigoted type. Papal Rome boasts of her civilization, and seeks to dominate over the whole world. Even some Protestants are beguiled into the belief that Catholic schools are superior to those of the Protestant faith. Rome has been master of Italy for centuries, but look at that fair and sunny land to-day, and behold the effects of the Catholic religion upon the people!

Catholic writers are in the habit of lauding the beneficent influence of popery in the city of Rome. It is very true that great sums have been lavished on that city in an artistic way. Magnificent churches and grand museums have been reared and stored with paintings and sculptures of unsurpassed excellence. Some travelers go to Rome and see only its art; others see its people, and conclude that any government which does not educate its children and elevate them fails intellectually and morally—fails in its mission. Judged by this last standard, the Church and government of Rome are every-where a stupendous fraud and failure. One goes to Italy and visits the gorgeous palaces, the great church of St. Peter and the stately Vatican, the marvelous frescoes of Raphael, and cries out, " Wonderful! " This kind of visiting makes Catholics. On the other hand, a journey through the suburbs of the Eternal City, or through some of the papal States, tends to unmake them. One traveler says: " We often observed in our journeyings plenty of farm hands, mostly women, but saw no houses, and were told that the people lived only in the cities and villages as a means of protection from robbers. This is, however, untrue. I have since seen the fact fully confirmed that there exist no predatory bands in this country, for the good reason that there is not enough on the farms to support them. Should they take it all they would have no booty. The robbers have long since quit, because there is nothing to steal outside of the churches. The land, so beautiful and productive to all appearance, is a barren waste. Not from want of natural gift, but from want of cultivation. We saw rolling tracts of land containing many thousands of acres utterly abandoned to the wolves and foxes of the distant Apennines. The people living in the villages and towns were unfortunate enough, but those that lived outside were almost reduced to the level of the brute creation. The condition of the people, especially the women, who are too poor to have homes near the fortress, is fearful. We went ourselves into the fields and inquired of them about their condition and wages. We were informed, by the more intelligent of them, that their pay did not average five cents a day, and they board themselves."

If it is the mission of the Church to keep men in ignorance, superstition, and poverty, then the Church of Rome has been a success in Italy and Mexico. The latter has been the paradise of priests for centuries, and at the same time a land of beggars. No matter where the stage stops, in the country village or city, at once the beggars appear on the scene. Lieutenant Baker says that, when hunting in the upper Nile regions, when an animal of any kind was killed, though at the moment not a vulture was in sight, in an hour afterward the air would swarm with them. They seemed to come down out of the skies or up out of the ground, attracted by the sight or smell of the dead beast. So Mexican beggars light down on the traveler at every stoppage of train or stage. Among them are old wrinkled men and women, filthy and cadaverous, mere lads and lasses, and at times even little children, who hold out their hands and plead for *cuartillso* and *centavos*, the smallest of Mexican coins. These poor creatures are the filthiest and raggedest human beings I have ever seen anywhere. At first they moved my compassion, causing me to deal out small change to them, but I soon learned that to continue it would exhaust the capital of a national bank, and, not having one with me, I desisted.

I had to study the question in order to justify myself in what, at times, seemed hard-heartedness. I reasoned in this way: The Catholic Church has had the exclusive and absolute training of these people for over three hundred years, and to-day they are the most degraded and abject people in the civilized world. They are wretched, almost beyond endurance. Life to them means nothing; it is the merest vegetation. The present generation of Mexican Romanists is beyond redemption. To help them is but to prolong a miserable existence and foster a bad custom. Better death than the life which tens of thousands of them are living. They are as good now as they ever can or will be. They can hope for nothing better in this life or the next by praying to the Virgin and doing penance. Much as they move me to pity, and gladly as I would give to them, where is the real benefit? The hope of poor down-trodden Mexico is in the continuance in power of the Liberal party and in the children. The Liberal party befriends Protestant Christianity, and the latter will do something for the children; and thus, in future generations, a new life will come to this land. The most forbidding people I had seen since I came into Mexico were at Ojuelos. They were far removed from the centers of business and of modern civilization. There is a class of the population called *leperos*, who are a mixture of the worst Spanish with the worst Aztec blood. These people, far from being to blame for their bad origin, are rather to be commiserated for their ignorance and moral degradation. A description of the lepero, at once graphic and true, has been given by Brantz Mayer:

"Blacken a man in the sun, let his hair grow long and tangled, and become filled with vermin; let him plod about the streets in all kinds of dirt for years, and never know the use of brush or towel, or water even, except in storms; let him put on a pair of leather breeches at twenty, and wear them until forty without change or ablution; and over all place a torn and blackened hat, and tattered blanket begrimed with abominations; let him have wild eyes and shining teeth, features pinched by famine into sharpness, and breasts bared and browned; combine all these in your imagination, and you have a recipe for a Mexican lepero."

To lie down at night in the midst of such a people to sleep was, doubtless, quite a safe thing to do in view of the strong hand which the government has laid upon these marauding bands, that have been for ages the dread of tourists in the Sierra regions. Formerly along this route robberies were of frequent occurrence, and many a diligence company has been forced to surrender at the point of the pistol or dagger, and every dollar and every article of value, whether jewelry or clothing, taken from the passengers, without regard to sex, who have been left in a state of at least semi-nudity, to go on their way as best they could. It is said that the danger is now past; if so, it is only because the government keeps along these mountain highways a strong force of mounted police, known as the *Guardia Rurales*, who are fully armed.

The seven States and one Territory which constitute more than one half of the national domain do not contain over one and a half millions of people, and they are the least thrifty of any in the republic. Great thoroughfares extend over this section of the north and north-east, along which travel is quite considerable. Besides, these mountains have been mined for silver and gold, which have had to be carried through their passes to market, and hence they became the natural hiding-places of banditti, who have impressed their band names upon several localities.

One of the things which is very noticeable here is the dress of the natives. If the mode of their life is simple, as they lie down on their mats to sleep, or sit on the ground to eat their food, not less so is the style of their wearing apparel. The Aztec Indian wears short, wide trousers, made of coarse cotton cloth or the skin of the deer, and which seldom extend more than half-way between the knee and foot. Over these are a sort of loose frock, made of the same material, but colored. A girdle often encircles the waist. Both men and women wear cheap sombreros, woven of straw or sea-grass, which cost only a few reals. A pair of leather sandals protect the feet from the hot sands. As a rule, they are exceedingly untidy in person, though it is due to the Aztec Indian to state that he does take his bath once in a great while. He uses the ancient *temascale*, a steam bath at that, administered in an adobe oven built just high enough to enable one to preserve an upright sitting posture. Stones are heated and water is poured on them in sufficient quantity to generate steam—a process less complex than the modern Turkish bath and fully as efficient. I heard of these baths, but saw none, and, judging from the appearance of the inhabitants, concluded the story of the *temascale* must be mythical.

The dress of the women is equally simple. They wrap around their persons a piece of coarse cotton or woolen cloth, passing it about the body twice, and holding it in position by a broad band. Over the shoulders is worn a wide and very loose garment, with openings for the arms. The hair hangs down the back in two plaits, and when the toilet is made for some special occasion, as a bull-fight or a christening, is fastened with high colored ribbons. They take great delight in earrings and other flashy ornaments. The races of northern Mexico distinguish their tribes by the color and fashion of their costume. The huts along the way are the very cheapest of structures. In the wooded districts, which are not numerous in this part, they build with a little more permanency than on the plains, using timber and thatch. At other points the houses are built of adobe.

Simplicity reigns in these mountain huts. The crockery consists of a few unglazed pots and pitchers, some cups and dippers made of gourd shell, an earthen yessel in which to burn the charcoal, answering the purpose of a cooking-stove, with the omnipresent comal, or earthen frying-pan, on which to cook the meat and tortillas. These constitute the rude outfit for housekeeping through all this land of robber celebrity.

In such huts life is passed, if it can be called living, children are born and reared, and men and women sicken and die. Their wants are few, for they are children of nature, with whom a little goes a great way. Like the dwellers on the table-lands of the eastern range, described elsewhere, a mat of rushes or palm-leaves answers for chair, table, or bed, and for winding-sheet at death.

THE HAUNTS OF THE BANDITTI.

This rough mountaineer distills and brews his own liquors. Almost every hut by the road-side has an opening of some kind, often a mere hole, in the rude wall, in which is placed a mug of pulque, or some other strong drink, to draw a few centavos from the pocket of the traveler, and add to the wealth of the inhabitant. The maguey plant furnishes him pulque, which produces a stupid sort of intoxication, or he utilizes the universal nopal cactus by expressing the juice of its fruit, the tuna, and fermenting it. He lives mostly on fruits, and when he attempts to cultivate the soil he does it with a rude mattock and hoe. The wife does her part in the home economy. A good wife gives emphasis to the meaning of the word which signifies *weaver*. It is her divine mission, in all lands, to gather up the tangled threads of life and weave them into garments of peace and beauty. Here she is a weaver in more than a figurative sense. With a few sticks she constructs a loom, and out of the coarse fibers of the maguey leaf weaves fabrics with which to clothe herself and her children, using as a needle the long, sharp point of the leaf, and its fibers for thread with which to do the sewing.

Ojuelos has its rough plaza and its old stone church. I had eaten an average Mexican supper, and was just about sitting down to write up the notes of the day, when the bell in the church tower began to clatter. The church bells in Mexico are rung as we ring our fire-bells when the ringers "ring with a will." One would almost think they must melt from the pounding they receive for something nearly every hour of the day. I laid down my pen and walked out toward the church, where a large company of people were gathering. On this occasion the people in the town were celebrating the twenty-fifth anniversary of the priest's assignment to this parish. A very indifferent sort of a band was endeavoring to discourse music to a very indifferent crowd in the plaza. Boys were playing at some sort of game which filled the air with dust. On the roof of the church, surmounted with a blackened old rococo dome and steeple, some colored lights were gleaming out of the gathering darkness. The church was illuminated with a great many candles. It was an hour when babies should have been in bed, but on this occasion one was to be christened in honor of this event. A large number of people were assembled—women in black shawls, and other women in coarse gray rebozos; peons in broad-brimmed sombreros, hiding their faces in the folds of their zarapes, and beggars in rags and dirt. Some were on their knees before the high altar, others crowded around the main entrance awaiting the child with its parents and god-parents. It is customary, as Señor ———, the civil engineer, informed me, for people in good circumstances to open their purses, if not their hearts, and scatter some silver coin among the poor on such occasions. There was a considerable pushing and scrabbling as the expected party arrived upon the scene, but, so far as I could discover, not a penny went into a beggar's hand. The organ and choir chanted something soft,

"Sweet and low"

as the company entered the nave of the church and approached the *pila bautismal*—the font. It was ceremonious, but almost as devoid of reverence as an auction. The little procession was preceded by several small boys carrying lighted candles a foot or two long. At a certain stage in the proceedings these tapers were handed over to a couple of red-faced, plump-looking men in surplices, who placed them in tall candle-sticks within the altar. In doing this they had to pass by one of those gaudily dressed little images of the Virgin, before which they invariably made a courtesy in a very mechanical sort of way.

Following these boys, and surpliced somethings, came the reverend " father," a smooth-faced, well-kept man, who evidently intended that this christening service should be conducted with all due ceremony. The parties stood before the font in perfect order, and the god-mother, I suppose it was, took the child in her arms as soon as its blankets could be removed.

The priest read the prayers in Latin, with a rich mellow voice, while the boys and surpliced men responded the amens almost like genuine Methodists. The lights about this time had grown quite dim, for the movement was rather slow, so that I could not see; but my friend, who was reared a Catholic and is now a liberal, explained to me the custom. First salt was placed on the child's tongue, oil was rubbed on the chest, forehead, back, and cheeks. Next its head was douched with cold water, at which the feeble little thing issued a vigorous protest, raising an audible squall. This over, it was rubbed with a towel, refolded in its blankets, and passed over to the arms of its mother or some relative. The priest pronounced what I understood to be a benediction, every body bowed to the Virgin except the two travelers, and the scene was ended. The custom on christening occasions is for the priest, the parents of the child, and relatives to repair to the child's home, and for the parents to bestow various presents on the different members of the family which are understood to be precursors and symbols of the child's future abundance in the things of this world. As I trudged back to my hotel through the dust and crowd of people, including every size, shape, color, and grade of life, I said to my liberal friend and companion, "If these people are so rough *with* their

9

religion, what would they be without any?" His reply was to the point, "If Mexico had not been Catholic, lying, as it does, so near the great United States of the North, it would long ago have been Protestant and progressive." To all of which I assented. I was soon at rest in my room, and in the early morning we started on our way through El Passo de Cuarenta, once the home of forty robbers.

CHAPTER XII.

THE HOME OF FORTY ROBBERS.

Rough, rougher, roughest—Scarcity of timber—Burning wooden saints—Too much pulque—Breakdown—Forced march—Huts and pistols—Under the rock—The true gentleman—Confessions of a Liberal—Revolution—Too big a story—Jaunt in a cart—Home of forty robbers—Valley sights—A garden of sweets—Dogs and donkeys—Dead flies—Music hath charms—Onward by torch-light—Rest and rails.

THE first time I took my seat in a Mexican *diligencia*, I thought, whatever else might happen, one thing was certain, the cumbersome vehicle would not break down. The roads across the mountains are as smooth as the physical condition of the country along with its financial state will warrant. They test the strength of any carriage, no matter how strongly built.

We started on our way from Ojuelos in the morning at the usual hour of four o'clock. The coach was drawn by a full team of mules. When the passenger looks out of the coach window and sees twelve of these animals attached to it, he knows what kind of roads are ahead of him. All through the forenoon our course wound about among the mountains. Now we went up and now down. Once in a while we came to a small level spot, over which we glided quite smoothly, hoping the mountains were past. But the first thing we knew our mules were drawing us up some long rocky winding slope again. We occasionally crossed river-beds that were waterless, channels which only fill up in the rainy season, and then soon run dry. This region is quite timberless, the mountains are rocky and lofty, and the soil hard, so that when the rain does fall the waters rush down the valleys in great, and often overwhelming, floods. Nothing strikes the traveler more than the great absence of timber. Forests are few. Is it any wonder, when for centuries the people have been burning it into charcoal and cutting it off for other domestic purposes, and never planting a tree! The Emperor Maximilian, it is true, did introduce into Mexico the eucalyptus, a species of Australian gum-tree, which is of rapid growth, attaining a height of fifty or sixty feet in a few years, and, besides, is quite ornamental.

The railroads are using the mesquite for fuel, a shrub-tree which abounds over all the land. It is a small, but very compact, species of timber. About twenty-five per cent. of the cost of Mexican railway management is the fuel bill. In one instance I heard of a wood-purchasing agent for one of the railway companies buying three hundred wooden saints for fuel, which he bargained for at forty cents a head! They were furnished by the natives, and on delivering them no questions were asked. A good coal mine in Mexico would be a greater bonanza to its owner than the best silver mine they have. We had passed high noon, had eaten our lunch in as wretched a tavern as ever sheltered a mountain tourist, and were descending a long slope, which was exceedingly rocky, at a rate of speed that threw us at times out of our seats, making what the printers call "pi" of the passengers, when all of a sudden "crash went the crockery!"

The driver on this run was not as good as some others we had had. His flushed face and stolid appearance plainly indicated that he was entirely too full of pulque to handle the reins properly in such a region as that through which we were passing. The way he would rush down the steep places, and around the curves, was almost frightful. The lives of the passengers were in peril. It was when descending one of these roughest spots, and just as we reached a small stream of water in a valley, that the right rear wheel directly under me was wrecked and the coach brought suddenly to a halt. We were in a place called the *Puerta de Cuarenta*, the pass of the forty, nine miles from the next relay station, and thirty miles from Lagos, the terminus of the diligence line. The accident was no small one if it was but the breaking of a coach wheel. There were no telegraph or telephone lines that could be called into use by which to order a new coach to replace this wrecked one.

The assistant driver had to take the harness off one of our mules and ride to Lagos, a distance of thirty miles over a rough mountain road. The new coach must return over the same thirty miles to our rescue, and then carry us on to Lagos. Ninety miles of mountain roads must be traversed, and every body detained and put to great inconvenience and personal discomfort, because a drunken driver whipped his mules into a stiff gallop where they should have been allowed to walk. These coaches, though so stoutly built, soon wear out, owing to the hard usage to which they are subjected.

We were nine miles from Cuarenta, the only place where we could obtain food, or lie down to rest. We were in a dilemma surely. Some of the passengers could not walk that distance and hence had to remain with the disabled coach. To be compelled to stay until midnight or after in the heart of the mountains would be quite a tax upon one's patience, as well as trying to his nerves, for it was a dismal, lonesome place. There was no time to be lost, and accordingly Señor ——, the civil engineer, his relative, and I concluded to take passage on *walker's line* for Cuarenta. It was quite an undertaking for me to walk nine or ten miles at that great elevation owing to the rare atmosphere, to say nothing of the heat of the sun. Kossuth said, " Nothing is too hard for him that wills." We "plod our weary way" as rapidly as Gray's plowman. The road we traveled had the advantage of being uneven. It is far less tiresome to walk where you ascend and descend alternately, than to trudge one's way over a level monotonous plain. At some points the ascent was quite steep, however, and consequently a little taxing to the muscles. At the distance of about five miles, which we were two full hours in making, I found myself quite exhausted, not because I was weak, but owing to the region we were in. To proceed farther seemed impossible, to return to the broken coach equally so. Here and there stood rude cabins near the road, to enter one of which might have been at the peril of life. Indeed, I noticed that my fellow-travelers, both of whom were native Mexicans, always drew their pistols out of the sheaths and held them in readiness for use, as we were passing these huts, or going through any deep ravine which might shelter a brigand. Señor —— said it was a dangerous road to travel. Once he politely offered his pistol to me, which I respectfully declined. At one point the road made a great bend, and I saw how we could save time and strength by a shorter cut, but which would take us near a hut and over a part of the ground adjacent to it. This movement required a little diplomacy. In the door of the hut sat a man with bronzed skin, and dark and shaggy beard, very roughly clad, holding between his teeth a pipe.

The gentlemen with me walked up to a stone wall in front of him, with pistols in hand, but cleverly concealed, and in Spanish pleasantly and politely asked permission to cross the ground, and the privilege was as pleasantly and politely granted. "Muchas gracias," they said, with a bow, and we went on our way.

About this time I was very much overcome with the heat, and began to look for a good place to sit down and rest my tired limbs. Near by I saw a great porphyritic rock protruding from the side of the mountain, the sight of which recalled the words of the Hebrew prophet: "And there shall be a tabernacle for a shadow in the day time from the heat, and for a place of refuge, and for a covert from storm and from rain." I thought, too, of another Rock, and also of the "shadow of a great Rock in a weary land." As we crept under it into the deep shade, I realized that I was there in a land once noted for its banditti, and near a town known formerly as the rendezvous of forty robbers. I was there unarmed with two men, men whom I had never seen until within a day or two. I was lying under a great rock, which may have secreted many a daring bandit waiting for his victim, and yet I was almost as unconcerned about my own personal safety as I would have been in my own home. The men in whose company I was journeying bore the unmistakable stamp of honorable manhood. There is a royalty outside of king's palaces. It is often found in the humble and quiet walks of life. Our conversation during the day had been on various subjects, but now it happened to turn on questions relating to the Church and government of Mexico. It came easily, naturally. Perhaps my own thoughts were started in that direction by the associations of the great rock in whose cooling shadow we were reclining for a little rest preparatory to a further prosecution of our journey. Señor —— was the younger of the two Mexicans, and was the spokesman. The other gentleman was the silent man of the party. I cannot now recall the precise words of my own, which sent the conversation along the particular line it took, but as I was studying the interior life of the people of Mexico, every utterance impressed me, and while I could not retain in my memory the exact wording, I could the substance, which was all I cared for. The spirit is more than the body—the meaning more than the mere words. It was easy to be seen, from several expressions he dropped, that the civil engineer was not much of a churchman, and so I felt all the more ready to call him out. He possessed several qualities that rendered him just the kind of man I desired to meet. He was intelligent and very gentlemanly, and was well-educated, having, as he told me, spent several years in Europe, as a student, after passing the curriculum of the best college in his own land. I believed what he said about it, for his general conversation and references to places abroad were to me convincing proofs of his truthfulness. Besides he was a *liberal*, which, in Mexico, signifies that a man is no longer willing to give all his earnings to the Church, and to be led by the priest, as if he had no right as a man to think for himself.

I said something about the numerous political revolutions in Mexico, as indicating a restless spirit. "Foreigners," said he, "who are not acquainted with our country, have an idea that we are wholly given up to anarchy and misrule, and charge us with loving revolutions as a sort of pastime for excitement. They think we delight in war. Never was there a greater mistake. We love revolutions," he said, with a significant look, "when our rights are usurped by a foe who resides under the sunny skies of Italy, and then we believe in the logic of the sword."

He went on to say that there was a party in Mexico, who were regarded by Romish priests as atheists, because they did not patronize the Church by the payment of tithes and attendance upon the confessional. "Pay tithes," said he, "and attend mass and confessional, and then go and do what you please. The worst brigands who infest the mountains are devout Romanists, and in the huts and caves where they hide will always be seen the crucifix and image of the Virgin."

As this last sentence fell from his lips, the señor's eyes fairly flashed and a glow came over his dark cheeks, which indicated that he felt deeply what he said. I asked him if he had ever been in the United States. He replied he had been in Washington and Baltimore, and longed to see his native land as prosperous as ours.

"You have Romanism in your country," he continued, "but it is not governed, as Mexico has been for ages, by a proud and avaricious clergy. The Church in Mexico has been the real government, imposing constant limits upon our rights as citizens, forbidding us to think, write, teach, or gain instruction. That is the reason why we are bankrupt in our national treasury and equally so in our morals. Ever since Spanish priests invaded Mexico, the rich mineral as well as all other resources have been seized upon by bishop and king, while the people have been held down under the most blinding superstitions. The Church gained possession of the mind, the heart, and the purse of the people, not by love, but by fear, and kept on adding to its wealth until it owned more than one half of the real estate of the country. This gave the ecclesiastics tremendous power over the masses. If they had but used it for the uplifting of the poor people, it would have been well, but you see for yourself what kind of a population we have."

As he said this his face wore, as I thought, an expression of sadness.

"But you have no longer the inquisition in your country," I remarked.

"Had it not been for the spirit of revolution," he answered, "we would to-day not only be governed by a foreign king, but we should be exposed to inquisitorial prisons and fires. The Mexican people," he affirmed, "really have no natural fondness for war above other nationalities. When large armies are needed, as when the Americans invaded Mexico, the soldiers are raised by conscription. The men who met the American armies in that war had to be driven from their homes at the point of the bayonet; that is a well-known fact in our history."

"That may all be very true," I said, "but you have had some revolutions arising from the desire for place and power on the part of ambitious generals, have you not?"

"Yes; the fact is Mexicans are human, and there was an opportunity afforded to gain power and glory by men who cared more for themselves than for their country. Some revolutions have come about in that way. There has been a feeling that things could not be much worse than they were in any event, while somebody might become a Washington. The experiment, it was thought, was worth trying. Indeed, we Liberals desire to be on a level, in point of free government and progress, with the United States. We desire to emerge from a shameful tutelage, under which we learned nothing more than to found monasteries of recluses and misanthropes, under which we had no better public spectacle offered us than that of the *auto-dä-fe*. In short, we desired a life of our own—constitutional law and liberty of conscience."

Turn the subject over in whatever light I chose, my friend the señor, would take up the points and trace them directly to the Church of Rome, as the main source of all the revolutions in Mexican history, as well as of the moral degradation and poverty of the people. Thinking to ascertain his religious sentiments, if he had any, I asked him if he ever attended the church. He replied that he did not, but that he believed in a God, and thought that no man was needed to come between him and that God. He believed that "Jesus Christ lived and died, and was a great teacher—possibly the greatest the world had ever seen, but that all the teachings of the only Church which he knew any thing about ignored, in fact, both God and Christ, and elevated to the throne of the universe an uneducated and simple-minded Hebrew woman, who lived and died about two thousand years ago. That," said he, "is too much of a story to ask a man who thinks to believe."

As he uttered the last sentence a smile of scorn passed over his face I shall not soon forget. Having taken a good rest, we arose and pursued our walk toward Cuarenta.

Soon after we had reached the highway again there came out of a by-road a peon, with a cart laden with straw and drawn by a mule. The wagon was a curiosity. As I remember it now there was not an ounce of iron about it. In Mexico wagons are frequently made entirely of wood. The harness was constructed of leather straps and some strings twisted from the fibers of the maguey plant. We made up a purse and bought his straw for *un peso*, one dollar, and had it dumped off by the side of the road, where he could get it again if he wished, and then for another dollar he entered into articles of agreement to carry us to Cuarenta. We composed ourselves as well as we could in the bed of the one horse or mule wagon, minus springs or seats, save such as we extemporized out of the straw. Then we set out at such speed as one might expect from a half-starved mule on a rough highway amid the Sierra. All went on gayly, for by this time we were rested and had become well acquainted, and it was a little easier riding, even in such a cart, than footing it. Presently we came to a place in the road where there was an old wash-out, when his muleship, despite the efforts of the driver, assisted by all the passengers, determined to go to the side of the road instead of walking in the wash-out in the middle. The right wheel, the one on my side, ran into the gutter, and over went the wagon, throwing us all out. I fell directly under and was completely, covered with the dust of the road, which at this point consisted of pulverized limestone. I was as white as a miller, but came out from under the nondescript vehicle unhurt. One of my "companions in distress," the silent man, did not escape so well. In the overthrow he suffered a severe wrench of the left arm, which quite disabled him. It would be a great calamity for a man to break a leg, or an arm, or to meet any other severe accident in such a place; for it is not likely that the aid of a physician or surgeon could be secured within less than thirty or forty miles, and then he might not be very skillful.

By and by Cuarenta appeared in sight at a seeming distance of a mile or even less. Such is the peculiar clearness of the atmosphere that distance deceives one. The town was about three miles away, judged by the time consumed in reaching the place after first sighting it. It was late in the afternoon when we drove up to the *Hotel Diligencias.* Did the reader ever before hear of the place? Cuarenta means forty, and, like Catorce, mentioned in a previous chapter, took its name from a band of brigands. I put up at this adobe hotel to await the coming of the stage. The region through which I had walked was one far remote from the busy marts. The stillness was marked. The silence, almost oppressive, is disturbed by nothing save the rumble of a passing coach-wheel or the occasional footstep of a wandering peon—the debased descendant of that mysterious people who came no one knows whence, and whose posterity, though numbered by the million in Mexico, now fallen from their former greatness, are mere "hewers of wood and drawers of water." But any sort of a stopping place was better than a stay of ten or twelve hours in a lone mountainous pass, or walking through the mountain defiles, under a burning sun, panting for breath.

I was in a town once celebrated as the head-quarters of a band of forty robbers! Cuarenta is an adobe village, with a population of about one or two thousand souls, more or less. Shall I describe it? Can I? The hotel is of one story, the rooms are three in number, a kitchen, a bar-room, and a "parlor." The walls are two feet thick, while the cement floor is a couple of feet below the street grade, hence in the hottest hour of the day the place is cool. In the rear of it is a very large garden, through which I wandered at will. Here grow a number of orange and lemon trees. The trees had on them flowers, as well as green and ripe fruit. Several thrifty fig-trees, also, were laden with fruit. Oleanders, covered with rich blossoms, grew there as large as apple-trees. Half a dozen varieties of roses, and as many of geraniums, all in bloom. There were many other flower-bearing shrubs whose names I did not know. It is filled with a great variety of flowers of many hues, blue, purple, red, golden. The cactus is here, as it is every-where. The place might be a paradise, but it is not. It is a poultry-yard as well as a garden—chickens and turkeys rove about among these flowers. Several dogs chase each other in their play under the foliage. It is a wood-yard where several donkey loads of the mesquite are piled, and where all the *débris* of the establishment finds lodgment. Mexicans are fond of bright and beautiful colors.

But let us look at an average street in an interior Mexican village. This street, on which stands the "hotel," is about a third to half a mile in length, and thirty feet broad. In front of the huts on each side is a narrow stone sidewalk, say three feet wide, and very irregular in its grade. In the dusk of the evening the sights are various and interesting to a stranger. The peons have quit work, and are squatting in groups about their humble door-ways. The streets are alive with half-clothed children of all ages. Such a scene! Dogs are nearly as numerous as the children, and are playing in the streets with them. Hogs go rooting about in the sand, and squealing around the door-ways. Donkeys wander up and down. Here and there sheep and goats appear on the scene. And then the Mexicans ring their church bells precisely as we do our fire bells, only with more vigor. So we have the clatter of several church bells mingling with the braying of asses, the barking of dogs, the squealing of hungry pigs, the shouting of boys and girls, and what not. It is difficult to characterize the spectacle. Shall I tell you what happened at our *table d'hote?* But I must say that the before-mentioned "parlor" is also dining-room, bedroom, and general sitting-room, dog kennel, and chicken coop, at the same time. At night, if the house is full, some of the guests can lie right down on the cement floor, which is dry and cool. At one end of this nondescript sort of place is a table, on which, over a white cotton spread, is a crucifix and some candles, with a picture of the Virgin, so that it is a church as well. Eleven willow cages are hanging on the walls, containing birds of rare and beautiful plumage. These denizens of the hill country are fond of birds. It is in this place I dine—on what? First, fried rice and tortillas, then some meat seasoned with the usual onions and garlic. Now it happened that on my "steak" were two dead flies, or insects of some kind, and I signaled to the head-waiter, a fifteen-year-old Aztec boy about the color of smoked ham, that I didn't like fried flies. He looked at me with a vacant stare, as much as to say, "They are as good as the meat, señor." The hostess saw my trouble, and, pushing the boy into the corner, relieved my embarrassment by deliberately picking off the insects with her fingers and throwing them on the floor. But I was not hungry for meat just then, and so did not partake. All she charged for this dinner, flies included, was half a dollar. Later in the evening I walked down the main street in this town of robber celebrity, and was not a little surprised to hear two young ladies singing, with a piano accompaniment. I could not help noticing the strange mixture of elements in this civilization. What reason had any one to expect a piano in such a place? These people, with all their degradation, are fond of music, flowers, and birds. It is a hopeful sign.

At two o'clock in the morning we were called up to take a new start, as our coach had arrived from the place of the breakdown. So, wrapping myself in my traveling shawl, I resumed my seat and my journey. Two guards rode ahead of us on horseback through the dark, carrying in their hands torches made of tarred rope, which not only lighted the way, but threw off sparks right and left, making one think of a wood-burning locomotive. At six o'clock the same morning, we were in Lagos, a city of ten thousand inhabitants, on the line of the Mexican Central Railroad, and, after a few hours' rest and a good breakfast, I was ready to resume my way. The days had sped away, and the long and wearisome journey by stage was at an end. It was one which I would not like to repeat, yet the experience gained in the trip is invaluable.

It seemed strange to travel where armed guards must protect person and property in a land of churches and priests, where the crucifix, which tells of the Saviour, is seen in every hut, stands by the roadside in many places, is cut in the rocks or carved in the clay banks that at times border the road, and crowns innumerable buildings; a land where the image of the Virgin Mary is continually before you, and yet a land that has been noted for its robbery and its crime.

From Harper's Magazine.

SAN ANTONIO RIVER.

CHAPTER XIII.

THE VALES OF ANAHUAC.

Ranges and peaks—Old safety-valves — Robbed—Scared — Out of the woods—Rich valley—An investment—Guanajuato and silver —Guadalajara and its plazas—Three rivals—Old Queretaro—Rich corporation—Scant garments—State rights—Oppressions—Grinding the poor—Custom-house exactions—Poetry and prose.

THIS title smacks a trifle of the romantic.
Writers on Mexican history and geography speak of the great mountain ranges which extend through the whole length of the territory from south to north. I suppose they do run in certain general directions called ranges, but really it seemed to me to be little less than a land dotted all over with mountains, here in clusters, there in single peaks, which seem to jut right up out of the plains. Go where you will in Mexico, especially in the central and southern portion, and a mountain or chain of mountains confronts you. The Mexican Sierras are regarded as a continuation of the South American Cordillera, which subside in Central America, and then rise again in Mexico. This is a volcanic chain throughout, according to Lyell, and in Mexico sends off a branch on the parallel of the city of that name, which is prolonged in a great platform between the eighteenth and twenty-second degrees of north latitude. Five once active volcanoes traverse Mexico from east to west, Tuxtla, Orizaba, Popocatepetl, Jorullo, and Colima— nature's safety-valves. There was a tradition among the ancient people of Mexico that their country extended

from the shores of the Caribbean Sea to Greenland, the *Ultima Thule* of the Aztecs. But Anahuac could not have included the whole of this vast extent. The word means *near the waters*, and hence the territory of the aborigines must have been confined to the region lying between the Atlantic and Pacific Oceans, with somewhat indefinite southern and northern boundaries. San Luis Potosi lies on the northern border of Anahuac proper. I had hoped to get through the haunts of the banditti and the home of forty robbers with safety to person and property, but failed to realize my expectations. I was robbed! robbed, too, right in *El Paso de Cuarenta*, at that. The story of the broken coach wheel has been related.

After arriving at Lagos, having come out into the region of railroads, I of course proceeded to make myself a little more presentable by a bath and change of linen. But on opening my satchel what did I discover! That it had been plundered by some one back in the mountains. The thief did not take the soiled or unsoiled linen, nor the celluloid collars and cuffs, nor tooth brush, nor comb. No; the denizens of the mountains have but little use for such articles. But a field-glass which had served me so faithfully, bringing remote objects into clearer view and making the magnificent scenery of mountain and valley to appear more distinct, alas! it was gone, hopelessly gone. At one point on the way over the mountain plateaus we were quite alarmed, however, at what seemed like being a genuine affair. As we were crossing the plains, at about two o'clock one afternoon, we beheld four men approaching us on horseback at their utmost speed. They drew nearer and nearer, and then swept into the road in our rear, and galloped after us until they came up to us, when one of the horsemen rode right by the side of the

coach, which was going very rapidly, and called upon
the driver to halt, which, after some moments he did,
when the rider handed him a package to be delivered
somewhere, and, wheeling his horse, rode off in the direction from which he came. As in a former case it
was only a slight scare. Imagine my feelings as the
coach rumbled into Lagos and I was once more, after
many days of staging, in sight of a railroad! What a
transition! No locomotive ever before looked so grand
to me as that one did that day in Lagos. It was a
three-wheeler, made in Philadelphia. I walked around
it, actually touched it, patted its iron ribs, almost
kissed it. Then there was the baggage and express
cars. What splendid structures! Then followed the
passenger coaches. In front, next to the express car
were those of the third-class, to accommodate the peons,
the lowest grade of Mexican people; next in order
came the second-class, for those of moderate means or
for any who chose to save their cash at the expense of
their dignity; and, lastly, the first-class, for rich hacendados—men who own vast ranches and mines—governors, generals of the army, merchant princes, bankers,
and tourists provided with free passes! That railroad
coach in which I took my seat seemed almost like the
czar's palace on wheels to me that morning. If six
hundred miles of travel in Mexican *diligencias* over
Mexican roads will not make a railway coach seem pa-
latial, I don't know what will. I actually felt so kingly
that at almost the first station at which the train stopped
I paid two *reals*, twenty-five cents, to an old Mexican
woman for a box of ripe strawberries, picked fresh from
the vines. They were exceedingly luscious, the large
berries on top, the small ones in the bottom of the basket.

I do not regret having taken this long interior
ride, for the day of the diligence will soon be over.

The railway here, as every-where else, is proving the death of the slow-going stage coaches.

I had now fairly entered the valley of the ancient Anahuac, a region of country which contains a thrifty population where many objects of interest attract the tourist. There is in this part of the Mexican Republic some exceedingly productive soil. Irrigation is necessary at almost every point, however. Water is drawn from wells by animal or human power, or is diverted by channels, *acequias*, from natural water-courses, and made to do the work of the clouds. Without this artificial method it would be difficult to raise any thing in many parts of the republic.

There are many cities of note in this famous valley. Among them Guanajuato, a place of over sixty thousand inhabitants, the capital of the State bearing the same name, and situated nearly three hundred miles north-west of the city of Mexico. Its foundation dates as far back as the middle of the sixteenth century. This has been for ages a region of silver mines, and one of the richest in the republic. Not less than three hundred millions of dollars' worth of silver and gold have been taken out of these mines to the present date. They have been worked ever since 1558. The ore must now be brought up from a depth of fifteen hundred feet by powerful machinery. Then there is Guadalajara, situated on the west bank of the Rio de Santiago, which in its magnitude is second only to the Rio Grande. The houses are substantially built. The streets cut each other at right angles, and are well-paved and unusually wide for this latitude. Both Puebla and Leon must yield the palm to Guadalajara. There are fewer foreigners in this city than in most others, owing to its remoteness from the railways. The churches are numerous and costly. The cathedral is one of the oldest and finest in all Mexico. It presents in its architecture a combination of the Arabian and Moorish style, with its pointed arches, clustered pillars, lofty towers, and flying buttresses.

Guadalajara has a population of about seventy-five thousand. Fourteen plazas adorn the city, the Plaza de Armas being the chief. It has an academy of fine arts and a university, besides, on the industrial side, several woolen and cotton manufactories. Like Leon, it lies in a section whose fertility produces a great variety of fruits and cereals. Lake Chapala, the largest in Mexico, having an area of four hundred and fifteen square miles, lies at a distance of forty miles from this city. Several islands are embosomed in its waters, which contain, it is said, some very ancient ruins. I might speak of Zacatécas, San Miguel de Allende, and distant Chihuahua, but as I did not see them they must be passed by in this account. The city of Leon does not lie directly in a silver mining region, but in an agricultural section, and is one of the most enterprising places in the republic. The inhabitants take great pride in their city, claiming a population of over one hundred thousand and holding it to be, next to the capital, the finest in Mexico. Leon, Puebla, and Guadalajara are like Chicago, Cincinnati, and Saint Louis in the United States. Each vies with the others for the palm of greatness. Leon lies on the northern border of one of the richest cereal belts in Mexico. I thought as our train swept over it that it could hardly be surpassed in richness of production in any land. It was here that I parted company with Señor ——, for whom I had come to feel a brother's regard. The time from this to the capital is about fourteen hours of continuous journey. The scenery along the line of the road is beautiful. The eye takes in an ever-changing panorama of mountain and valley as the train sweeps on around the great curves and over the plains of Anahuac. From north to south for nearly one hundred miles, and with a breadth varying from twenty to thirty miles from east to west, the country is almost equal to an Illinois prairie.

Queretaro interested me because it has such a history. It was founded by the Aztecs before Columbus discovered America, and at the time of the Spanish invasion it is said to have been a flourishing city. Lying in the heart of one of the richest valleys in the republic, with a temperate and salubrious climate, every kind of fruit, flower, and grain can be found in this market. A stone aqueduct, which calls up memories of ancient Rome, supplies wholesome water from a neighboring hill. One of the greatest manufacturing establishments in the country is located in the vicinity of Queretaro. The buildings and grounds are reported to have cost $4,000,000. It gives employment to over a thousand operatives, engaged in the manufacture of a coarse kind of cotton goods, worn mostly by the peons. The machinery of this immense factory is propelled by both steam and water power. The largest overshot wheel in the world is said to be in use at this mill. A corps of about forty soldiers, well armed with rifles and cannon, are in the service of the owners for defense against any possible insurrection or revolution. An attacking party, in order to effect an entrance, would have to scale the high solid stone wall, which incloses the property, in the face of musketry and cannon.

All along my journey the poorly clad peons, whether male or female, excited my pity. In the first place, the warmth of the climate might seem to be a reason why these people wear such poor, cheap, thin clothing. Men and women protect their shoulders in the evening with an extra wrap. The man will wind over his shoulders and face his woolen zarape—the woman covers hers with the universal rebozo. The transition in point of temperature is very marked, and the natives know by experience how to protect themselves against these changes. A foreigner who ventures out in the evening—and one can scarcely resist the temptation to remain out late in this climate—unprotected about the face is sure to take cold. The scarcity of water in the interior accounts in part for the filthy condition of their very scant garments. I have seen a great many instances where a dollar or two would purchase the wardrobe of a whole family, especially if goods were sold at New York prices. Take into consideration the climate, along with the ingrained habits of the people, the low wages paid for labor, and the prices demanded by the merchants for their dry goods, most of which are imported notwithstanding home manufacture, and it is no wonder one sees in Mexico so many half-naked people. The revenue laws are the most oppressive of any in the world. For example, all incorporated cities and towns exact tolls at their gates on all produce brought to their markets. The poor peon, who carries his crate of crockery or charcoal thirty miles on his back, must pay a duty before he can dispose of it. And if he has no ready money, must leave his zarape or some other article of sufficient value with the tax collector until he can redeem it with cash after he has sold his produce.

State rights are recognized in this our sister republic with a vengeance. The State is very independent. While by the Constitution all the States composing the federal union are required to pay out of their general treasury a pro rata equal to twenty-five per cent. of the total taxation for federal purposes, the general government is quite powerless to enforce the collection if the State authorities refuse to pay over the amount. This is often the cause of internal contentions. Mexico not being much of a commercial nation the import revenues are not large. The only custom-house which yields any considerable amount is at Vera Cruz. To support the general government by paying the salaries of the officials, keep up the army, meet the interest on the national debt, and provide for the various subsidies voted by Congress to public works, every industry is taxed. Besides, each State has its own system of internal revenue. The governor and other State officers must be paid, and their salaries are large. The Governor of San Luis Potosi has a salary of $8,000 a year, and $14,000 per year for office expenses. Whence comes the money? From the heavy taxation on all industrial pursuits, and the stamp duties on all sales. Every thing sold in the market must be stamped or assessed in some way. Every railroad ticket must have on it a government stamp. The soil alone is free from taxation. For instance, some dry goods, machinery, or any thing else, are ordered from New York, New Orleans, London, or Paris, to be sold at San Luis Potosi. These articles arrive at Laredo, Matamoras, or some other point on the Rio Grande. These dry goods, for example, must be taken to the custom-house at Monterey. The officers will not accept an invoice sworn to, but the boxes must all be opened, every article examined, and the duties levied for the State of Nuevo Leon. Having been examined and assessed, they are re-boxed, taken back to the railway station, at great cost of time and labor to the owner, who must furnish his own clerks to see to the account, and then are sent on to Saltillo, the capital of the State of Coahuila, where they are again taken to the custom-house, re-opened and examined and compared with the original invoice, and assessed for the State of Coahuila. Then again they are reboxed and forwarded to San Luis Potosi, where, for the third time, they are taken to the custom-house, opened, examined, item by item, and assessed for the State of San Luis Potosi. Now at last they are ready for the retail trade. Is it any wonder I paid nearly five dollars in Saltillo for a linen duster, which would have cost me one third of that amount anywhere on our side of the line. A box of snuff which costs $9 at wholesale in New Orleans must bring $50 here, because of the enormous duties assessed upon it as it passes through different States. An intelligent American gentleman, doing business in Mexico, informed me that he shipped some machinery from New York to Mexico, the cost of which, in New York, was $5,000. The freight charges on it to the Rio Grande were $785. The duties on it at the first custom-house in Mexico amounted to $2,300, with two and one half per cent. additional for handling. A carriage of any kind is taxed $100 a wheel when it crosses the line. A piano, costing in New York $350, when it reaches San Luis Potosi has cost nearly $1,200. This is ruinous to trade and proves a fearful drawback, especially to all the importing business. The authorities of a State may change the tariff even after the shipment of goods has been made, which must prevent any safe business calculations. But it is their way, and it will likely remain so until some new and great revolution, some time or other, brings a change. If the lands were taxed in Mexico the revenue would be ample, and then the poor would fare better. The owner of real estate would endeavor to make the land pay its way, which would lead to more and better agriculture, while the merchant would be relieved of the enormous duties on his importations. When a yard of calico, which is sold in New York for five or six cents, costs the buyer here from eighteen to twenty-five cents, the half-naked condition of the poor peons is easily explained.

Agriculture and grazing employ a large portion—perhaps seven eighths—of the inhabitants. The soil is noted for its richness and fertility, although portions are unfit for cultivation. The value of agricultural products is estimated at nearly $200,000,000 annually. The well-known mineral wealth of the republic constitutes the main basis of its foreign commerce. At the present time, however, the annual amount exported is as large as it is generally stated in statistics—probably not over $25,000,000 in silver, and in gold between two and three millions. There are also valuable mines of quicksilver, iron, and copper in operation.

Curious stories are related of the custom-house officials which show how business is carried on in the country. The custom-houses have on their lists nearly four hundred specified articles on which duties are assessed with regularity. Then when any thing is presented that is new to the officials, it is charged for after the manner of some article which it most nearly resembles. When celluloid was first introduced, the revenue officials did not know whether to assess it as bone or ivory, but decided to adopt the latter, to which it bears a likeness. As bone, it would have been assessed twenty-nine cents a kilogram; but as ivory, $2 20. A large difference. Hooks and eyes made of a metal somewhat resembling silver, though very cheap, when first introduced were assessed as silver, and instead of nineteen cents a kilogram, they were charged $1 15 a kilogram. An Englishman, after consulting with the Mexican consul at Liverpool, shipped a small lot of fancy goods to Mexico. The whole cost him in England $1,200. When he got through the custom-house at Vera Cruz the total charge on his stock amounted to $2,850. He sold the whole for $2,000, borrowed money to pay the remaining indebtedness, and returned home.*

* *Old Mexico and her Lost Provinces*, by Wm. Henry Bishop.

An American gentleman, doing some business in the city of Mexico, was in New York, and, thinking he might need some plaster of paris, purchased a barrel of it and shipped it to Vera Cruz. There it was opened and declared to be a valuable chemical of some kind, and was assessed at $80. This, added to the original cost of the article, with the freight bill, made it rather expensive. So he quietly thought to himself, the authorities might keep the plaster and do what they pleased with it. But notice was sent him that he must redeem the barrel or he would get into trouble. "A word to the wise" in that case was "sufficient." But $90 was surely a good price to pay for a barrel of plaster of paris.

The government, to exist at all, must have money. It gets it—but under such a system of State and national revenue no people can be highly prosperous, nor is it strange that the lower and poorer classes are so illy clad. In passing through the vale of Anahuac, one meets a good deal of poetry—in passing a Mexican custom-house he finds the prose.

CHAPTER XIV.

THE ADVENTURER OF MIRAMAR.

A notable spot—Causes of unrest—Strong language—Hidalgo the martyr—The two parties in Mexico—Banishment of the ecclesiastics—Maximilian a tool—The trailing banner—Napoleon's Latin race—Aztec prophecy—Relation of the United States—William II. Seward—Sympathy with Mexico—Sherman on the Rio Grande—The withdrawal—Escape possible—Courage of the emperor—The capture—Court-martial—Execution on the *Cerro de las Campanas*—" Poor Carlotta."—Last letter.

QUERETARO is a very old city, and contains about the usual number of narrow streets, flat-roofed houses, somber stone churches, and ragged peons, all mixed up with some good-looking people and fine edifices, both public and private. But that which will ever make the place memorable is the fact that here Maximilian, the adventurer of Miramar, with two of his generals, Miramon and Mejia, were executed on the 19th of June, 1867. The history of Mexico, ever since the days of Cortez, constitutes the pathetic chapter in the world's annals. I cannot do better than to quote from a distinguished Mexican writer, Señor Rivera y Rio:

" With the overthrow of Montezuma's empire, in 1520, began the rule of the Spaniard, which lasted just three hundred years. During this time Rome and Spain, priest and king, held this land and people as a joint possession. The greedy hand was ever reached out to seize alike the products of the mine and the soil. The people were enslaved for the aggrandizement and power of a foreign Church and State. It was then that the Church of Rome fostered such a vast army of friars, priests, and nuns, acquired those vast landed estates, and erected such an incredible number of stone churches, great convents, inquisitorial buildings, Jesuit colleges, and gathered such vast stores of gold and silver. All this time the poor people were being reduced to the utmost poverty, and every right and opportunity for personal and civil advancement was taken from them. They were left to grope on in intellectual darkness. They could have no commerce with foreign nations. If they made any advance in national wealth, it was drained away for royal and ecclesiastical tribute. Superstition reigned under the false teachings of a corrupt priesthood, while the frightful Inquisition, by its cruel machinery, coerced the people to an abjectness that has scarcely had a parallel in human history. Under such a dispensation of evil rule Mexico became of less and less importance among the family of nations."

Lampriere, another writer of these times, says:
"The Mexican Church, as a Church, fills no mission of virtue, no mission of morality, no mission of mercy, no mission of charity. Virtue cannot exist in its pestiferous atmosphere. The cause of morality does not come within its practice. It knows no mercy, and no emotion of charity ever nerves the stony heart of the priesthood, which, with an avarice that knows no limit, filches the last penny from the diseased and dying beggar, plunders the widows and orphans of their substance as well as their virtue, and casts such a horoscope of horrors around the death-bed of the dying millionaire, that the poor, superstitious wretch is glad to purchase a chance for the safety of his soul in making the Church the heir of his treasures."

In 1810 the tocsin of liberty was sounded. The instrument of the uprising was Hidalgo, a priest. It was, indeed, strange that a priest should sound the keynote of national reform, and raise the standard of rebellion against even those of his own faith and order. He was faithful among the faithless. Death by violence put an end to his efforts, but Hidalgo did not die in vain.

Nearly a dozen years of bloodshed followed the martyrdom of Hidalgo, but all the while the party of reform grew in numbers and in power. In 1821 Mexico was able to throw off the yoke of Spain. This was accomplished by a union of the Liberal party, the party of Hidalgo, with that of the Conservative or Church party. It was a strange coalition. Two avowed enemies unite in a common defense. This union was due to the act of the mother country. The Spanish Cortes, under a revolutionary impulse, had decreed a partial sequestration of the property of the Mexican priesthood. This touched them in a tender spot—the pocket. Out of this came the revolution and Mexican independence, but the yoke of the priesthood remained fastened upon the necks of the people, and two parties divided the country upon great issues of liberty. On the one hand the Romish priesthood openly avowed itself as the political party, using the confessional and Inquisition as its instruments, united with the aristocratic and monarchical element, comparatively few in number, but rich and powerful, in an unscrupulous opposition to every measure designed to elevate the down-trodden multitude, to educate the youth, and to establish liberty as the birthright of all, and as the fundamental basis of government. On the other side stood the party of liberty, originating in a natural reaction against despotism, becoming gradually more and more enlightened, and increasing in power under influences growing out from this our own country and from the Bible, which had found its way into a few hands and hearts. The struggle, at first for merely civil liberty and progress, was carried on with many vicissitudes and sore losses in life and property, yet with steady advance in the strength of the Liberal party. At length, as light spread by the introduction of the Scriptures, by intercourse with foreigners and the outer world, the press, and actual experience in governmental polity, they persistently proclaimed higher and juster ideas of the rights of man, until, by the remorseless persecution and crimes of the priesthood, they were led to espouse the cause of religious liberty, and embody it as a fundamental principle in their creed. The writer last quoted continues:

"The final issue of the struggle for constitutional liberty, just laws, equal rights, and freedom of worship, took place in 1857, when the priestly party was vanquished. The Constitution and the laws of reform then adopted, and still in force, emptied all the convents and scattered their inmates, separated Church and State, gave entire liberty of worship, forbade religious processions, the wearing in the streets of ecclesiastical robes, and the carrying about of the 'so-called host;' declared ecclesiastics ineligible to hold offices in the government, established civil marriages, nationalized the church property, guaranteed freedom of speech and the press; and in many other ways broke down the political power of Rome in Mexico. In vain did the Roman Church excommunicate those who accepted the Constitution of 1857 and the 'laws of reform.' In vain they inaugurated a civil war, and furnished treasure to military chieftains. In 1860 their cruel banner trailed in the dust—Miramon and his chieftains fled the country—and Juarez, the lawful president, fully inaugurated the new constitutional government."

The Church party was cast down, but not wholly discouraged. The bishops and their political leaders, banished as enemies of progress, fled to Europe, and sought foreign sympathy as well as foreign bayonets to quench the fires of liberty which had been kindled in their native land, to banish the Bible and the right of free worship, and to reinstate the old inquisitorial despotism by overthrowing republican institutions.

Through the influence of Labistida, the Archbishop of Mexico, a "Council of Notables" was created, composed of nobles, friars, priests, sacristans, and military men in the service of the Church. The pope, in the meantime, had selected Maximilian, Archduke of Austria, and brother of the reigning sovereign, who, with his wife, Carlotta, were most devout Catholics, to accept the crown of Mexico, with the titles of emperor and empress.* Napoleon III. and Eugenie, being also ardent as Catholics, were made partners in the scheme of holding Mexico in the bonds of Romanism. All this was done under the guise of collecting some money claimed to be due to France from Mexico.

The "Council of Notables," of course, voted for Maximilian, who accepted the position, was crowned Emperor, came to Mexico, and undertook the task of subjugating the people to his scepter, relying for support upon a French army. He began in the very start in the school-room, which would have been wise had he begun rightly. That Maximilian was sent to Mexico to be the willing tool of the pope in propping up a rotten and tottering structure is evident from one of his first official

---

*Maximilian was born July 6, 1832. He was married July 27, 1857, to Princess Carlotta, daughter of Leopold I., King of Belgium. He accepted the crown of Mexico April 10, 1864. Having no child, he adopted Augustus Iturbide, son of the Emperor Iturbide, a native Mexican, as his heir.

acts, the issuance of a notice to his Minister of Public Instruction. That tells the whole story.

In that document he says: "Religion is a matter of conscience for each individual, and the less the state meddles with religious questions, the more faithful is it to its mission. We have emancipated the Church and conscience, and I desire to secure to the former the full employment of her legitimate rights, and at the same time entire liberty in the education of her priests, according to her own rules, without any state interference; but she has likewise duties which she must perform, such as religious instruction, a duty in which the clergy of the country unfortunately have taken little or no part hitherto—consequently in your projects and proposals you will adhere to the principle that religious instruction in the primary and secondary schools shall be given by the priests of the parish using the books selected by the government."

Thus a government foisted on the Mexican people by the power of a foreign prince, purely monarchial and Catholic, must decide what books shall be used in all primary and secondary schools, and the teachers must be priests of the parish. Alas for Mexico under such a rule!

That the emperor inaugurated some works and reformed some abuses, and in several ways improved the condition of the country, is not to be disputed. But all that could not atone for the attempt made to overthrow the Liberal party, the party of freedom and civil progress, which for half a century had been gaining in power, and gave promise finally of the uplifting from ages of degradation the whole Mexican people. At the end of four years the flag of that pretended monarchy was trailed in the dust, its armies vanquished, and its leader slain.

11

The withdrawal of the French from Mexico was a grievous disappointment to the Jesuits and the Roman pontiff, as well as a most bitter day for the papal Church in Mexico. They had fondly dreamed that through the intervention of Catholic France the edict of the Juarez government, which expelled the bishops and other ecclesiastics, and sequestrated to the government the property of the Church, would be rescinded, and Mexico would once more come under absolute papal sway. It was quite logical, too, that the Church party should expect this from an emperor who had been raised to the throne and confirmed in its occupancy by the head of the Roman hierarchy.

Napoleon III. attempted to secure the predominance of the Latin race in Europe and America. To carry out his pet idea he had steadfastly opposed the accession of a Hohenzollern to the throne of Spain, which involved him in a disastrous war. The invasion of Mexico for similar purpose was a most ignominious failure. The Latin race holds to popery, and the world is rapidly outliving that effete form of religion. On the other hand, the Teutonic race holds to Protestantism, and Protestantism means progress along all lines. Germany, Sweden, the United States, Norway, England, are Teutonic. The Teutonic races believe in free thought in politics, science, religion, all things—the Latin race believes in the pope!

Queretaro, the place of the final collapse, has always been a Catholic stronghold. During the empire it was fortified with earthworks, and garrisoned with troops held in readiness for emergencies. The hill on which the emperor and the two generals were shot is called the *Cerro de las Campanas*, the scene of the last campaign of Napoleon's luckless *protégé*, and the tragic termination of the French invasion. The fatal spot is marked by three piles of stones, each surmounted by a rude wooden cross.

The Mexicans erect monuments of some kind to all their chieftains, whether liberal or conservative. Cities, hotels, plazas, and States are named after them. Thus the *Plaza de Zaragoza*, at Monterey; the Hotel Iturbide, in Mexico city; and other places. Vera Cruz is *Vera Cruz de Llave*, so called after a general and governor of that name. Puebla, also, is honored with the addition to its name of Zaragoza, the general who commanded the Mexican army at that place and won a great victory over the French on the 5th of May, 1867. Oaxaca (Wahacca) of Juarez is named after the Napoleon of Mexico, general and president, whose tomb is in San Augustine Cemetery, the Père la Chaise of the metropolis. That tomb is the most elegant mausoleum in the republic.

Guadalupe has the addition of Hidalgo. The latter is the most sacred Catholic shrine in all Mexico, and yet bears the name of a priest who first raised the standard of revolt in 1810 against Spain, and paved the way for the incoming of liberalism and the Protestant faith. He was the John Brown of his age and country, and, like him, was put to death for treason against the State. The Plaza Mayor, at San Luis Potosi, contains a statue to his memory, and the State of Hidalgo was named in his honor.

It is quite probable the time will come when Maximilian will be put into bronze, or marble; or some plaza or State will add to its name *de Maximiliano*, especially if the Aztec Indians gain the ascendency in the government. They are on the way up. Juarez was an Indian. President Porfirio Diaz is almost a pure-blooded Indian. There has been a tradition among these people for ages that a deliverer would come to them some time from the East. He would have a florid complexion and a red beard. So when Maximilian ascended the throne he answered the description, and hence was looked upon by the Aztecs with great favor. The emperor had a fine face and a long flowing sandy beard. It is said that at the execution he requested the soldiers not to shoot him in the face or beard. They acceded to his request, and aimed their rifles so low that the vitals were not touched, and consequently his death was a slow and agonizing one.

Some accounts state that the Liberal government was willing he should make his escape; others contradict the statement. The defenders of the republic argued that Maximilian was created emperor with legitimate succession by the solemn act of the Roman pontiff, and as the pope claims to be infallible, the dynasty of Maximilian must forever rule Mexico. This the Liberals understood, so they settled the question of the empire with the rifle, which they regarded as the only way out of the difficulty. It was heroic and very effectual practice.

No doubt there was power enough in France to maintain the empire in Mexico, had there not been another element to be considered. The pope and Napoleon moved upon Mexico at a time when they believed and hoped that the American government was powerless to interpose a substantial objection. But the war was over and federal authority was supreme over all the States. The United States government was willing that Mexico should have its own choice, whether that should be monarchial or republican rule, but it did not believe that the people of that land had been allowed by Napoleon the free exercise of that right. The Latin-race theory of the French emperor was very distasteful to the American people generally, and he was so informed by William H. Seward, our Secretary of State. Simultaneously sixty thousand troops of the Union were put in position near the Rio Grande, and Napoleon III. was given to understand that while we courted peaceful relations, yet this government felt called upon to guarantee to a sister nation the right to say whether their own people or a foreign potentate should bear rule.

For a time all the successes in arms seemed to be in favor of the empire, while the government of Juarez was reduced to a roving band, without any fixed capital. But they asserted that they could continue the contest until the troops of Maximilian were destroyed by casualties and sickness.

The United States government sympathized with the republican interests in Mexico, but had to move with caution, so as not to provoke hostilities with our old friends, the French. In proof of our sympathy with the Republic of Mexico as against the empire, our Secretary of State wrote to the French Minister of Foreign Affairs, stating that the "government of the United States had long recognized, and does still continue to recognize, the constitutional government of the United States of Mexico as the sovereign authority in that country, and Benito Juarez as its chief. The government, at the same time, equally recognizes the condition of war existing in Mexico between that country and France. We maintain absolute neutrality between the belligerents."

He also wrote to our Minister, Mr. Bigelow, at the French court: "The presence and operations of the French army in Mexico, and the maintenance of an authority there resting upon force and not upon the free-will of the people, is a cause of serious concern to the United States."

The utterance of these sentiments on the part of our government caused Napoleon and the pope to waver in their plans, whereupon the French Minister of Foreign Affairs wrote to our government, saying: "The French government wished the day to speedily come when the last French soldier should leave Mexico —that what was asked of the United States was that it should not impede the consolidation of the new order of things in Mexico, and the best guarantee would be the recognition of the Emperor Maximilian by the federal government." The correspondence continued, and Mr. Seward replied to the French Minister:

"The real cause of our national discontent is that the French army, which is now in Mexico, is invading a domestic republican government there which was established by her people, and with whom the United States sympathized most profoundly, for the avowed purpose of suppressing it and founding upon its ruins a foreign monarchial government, whose presence there, so long as it should endure, could not but be regarded by the people of the United States as injurious and menacing to their own chosen and endeared republican institutions. We have constantly maintained, and still feel bound to maintain, that the people of every state on the American continent have a right to secure for themselves a republican government if they choose, and that the interference of foreign states to prevent the enjoyment of such institutions deliberately established is wrongful and in its effects antagonistical to the free and popular government of the United States. Therefore the government of the United States hopes that France may find it compatible with its best interests and its high honor to withdraw from its aggressive attitude in Mexico within some convenient and reasonable time, and leave the people of that country to the free enjoyment of the system of republican government which they have established for themselves."

Members of the French Legislature thought it strange

that the French flag, which was once cordially greeted in America, should be less so now, declaring at the same time that " France was only in the habit of moving when she found it to her own best interests to do so." Napoleon, in his address to the legislative bodies, affirmed that " In Mexico the government, founded by the will of the people, was being consolidated, the non-contents were being vanquished, and that his troops were about to embark for home without compromising French interests." This he uttered at a time when he knew that the whole scheme of destroying the republic in Mexico was on the eve of disastrous failure. Napoleon took the hint from Mr. Seward's communications, and ordered a retreat, leaving Maximilian to his fate. The French soldiers

"Folded their tents like the Arabs,
And silently stole away."

I was informed by one who claimed to know, that after the French troops had been withdrawn, and the cause was utterly hopeless, an opportunity was quietly given to the adventurer to flee the country, and that he did descend the mountains to a villa on the way toward Vera Cruz with that intention, the railway having kept an engine fired up and a train in readiness for some hours to convey him to the coast, thus making his escape entirely feasible ; but he chose to return to the capital, still hoping, it is said, that the experiment of the empire might prove a success.

Before leaving Europe Maximilian had renounced all title to the throne of his brother, Francis Joseph, of Austria. Under such conditions a brave man would struggle hard. Whatever else has been said of him, he was not cowardly. He fled from the capital to Queretaro, where his small army was well fortified on the hill commanding the city. He was at once besieged by the

Liberal army, under General Escobedo, and sooner or later must fall. The final culmination was hastened by the treachery of a colonel in the army of the emperor. Maximilian was taken prisoner, and his forces surrendered to the Liberals.

A trial by court-martial followed, with conviction and sentence of death. Every effort was made by his friends to save his life. The seat of the republican government was then temporarily at San Luis Potosi, one hundred and sixty miles distant, and President Juarez was appealed to for pardon, but in vain. The government of the United States was also appealed to by Maximilian's friends, but it would not interfere. Napoleon had deserted the cause. Francis Joseph, of Austria, his own brother, could not come to his rescue. Carlotta was a devout Catholic, and, from the beginning, was the real instigator of the movement, in order to bolster up the Romish Church of Mexico. At this trying time she was in Europe, whither it was rumored she had gone with fresh appeals to Napoleon and the pope for continued aid, without which all would be lost. In that mission she failed, and, with reason wrecked, was taken home to her father, the King of Belgium, in one of whose castles she has been ever since. The hopeless maniac spends her time playing the queen, talking with imaginary courtiers, and arranging her toilet for state dinners. The last thing Maximilian penned, on the eve of his execution, was a letter to his absent wife:

"To my Beloved Carlotta: If God ever permits you to recover and read this, you will learn the cruelty of the fate which has not ceased to pursue me since your departure for Europe. You carried with you my soul and my happiness. Why did I not listen to you? So many events, alas! so many unexpected and unmerited catastrophies have overwhelmed me, that I have no more hope in my heart, and I wait death as a delivering angel. I die without agony. I shall fall with glory, like a conquered king. If you have not the power to bear so much suffering, if God soon reunites us, I shall bless the divine and paternal hand which has so rudely stricken us.

"Adieu! Adieu! Thy poor　　　　　Max."

Thus ended the career of Maximilian, the adventurer of Miramar, and with it Napoleon's Latin-race empire in America.

CHAPTER XV.

THE PARIS OF THE WESTERN WORLD.

The parallel—Struggles with speech—A dilemma—Settling the question—Politeness—Strange extremes—Ice from the mountains—*Portales de Commercios*—Street names—Church lotteries—Streetcars—Lilliputians—The washer-women—Burden-bearers—Fleet of foot—Street venders—Meal-time—Butter and bottom facts—Burial customs—Under the flags—Sleeping police—Days of knighthood—Force of law—Beauty shut in—Spangles and spurs—Shopping—Under electric lights—Pulquerias—Stupid and funny—"Floating gardens" that don't float.

THE Paris of the Eastern World is in the valley of the Seine; the Paris of the Western is in the valley of the lakes. The population of the former is nearly two millions; that of the latter about three hundred thousand. The Paris of the Old World is only two hundred feet above the level of the sea; the Paris of the New is nearly eight thousand feet above the sea. The Paris of France is surrounded by low hills; the Paris of Mexico crouches amid mountains, and in sight of peaks which shoot up ten thousand feet above her domes and spires. The Paris of the East was a collection of mud huts in the days of the Cæsars known as Lutetia; the Paris of the West was built much in the same way, and was called Tenochtitlan, the capital of Anahuac. The Paris on that side of the Atlantic was inhabited by a tribe of rude Gauls, called the Parisii; the Paris on this side by a roving band of half-savage Aztecs. The Paris of the Gauls suffered severely from frequent invasions by

North-men; the Paris of the Aztecs from the fierce warriors of Spain. The French capital has been the scene of many sanguinary revolutions, when its streets were crimsoned with blood; the Aztec capital has not only witnessed many revolutions, but has several times yielded to the might of invading armies. Paris the first, like Paris the second, has long since passed out of the era of mud huts into that of solid brick and stone; but their resemblance lies mostly in the gay and easy-go life which is characteristic of both. If Paris is France on one side of the Atlantic, Mexico is Mexico on the other.

When I reached this old capital it was late in the evening, and, as best I could, found my way to a hotel with a very high-sounding name. By this time I was beginning to grow discouraged, for I concluded that either the people did not understand Spanish or I did not.

It seemed to grow more difficult the more I tried to speak it, I thought, or else the native stupidity was increasing every day. "*Tres jolie pour le voyageur*" is true so far as the country itself is concerned; but to be among people you can't converse with without an interpreter is not so pleasant. Of course, I committed some blunders, I suppose, endeavoring to make myself understood. That much, in justice to the Mexicans, must be frankly admitted. At a hotel, on one occasion, I wanted to make my toilet for dinner, and asked the maid who showed me to my quarters for some *sopa*. She looked at me in the veriest wonderment, and said something in her own language, pointing to another room just across the court, which I did not understand. Again I looked at my hands and said, with much emphasis, "*Sopa! sopa!*" I was actually teazing the poor little Aztec for some *soup* with which to wash my hands. It was not to be wondered at that she pointed to the dining-room across the way, and most likely said I would get the soup over there. I should have called for some *jabon* instead. She was a better linguist than I, and brought me the *jabon*, and I ate my *sopa* in the form of a dish of frijoles afterward. On arriving at a hotel in the city of Mexico I was duly shown to a room and desired to change my linen, but the luggage was not sent up from the office. I waited quite a while, and at last rang for the *valet de chambre*, a young man about twenty-five years old, and told him to bring up my luggage. The Spanish word for luggage had entirely escaped my recollection. He stood as still as a post, and said something back to me, which, of course, I did not understand. Again I said, in a serious way: "Go and bring up my luggage from the office. I want to change my linen." But there he stood staring at me. " Luggage ! Baggage!" I shouted, pointing to the head of the stair-way. He only gazed at me, opening his eyes a trifle wider each time. Next I made signs, going through the motions of opening an umbrella, which constituted a portion of my traveling outfit. Then I said " zarape," the word for shawl, thinking he would take the hint; but no, he only stared at me in the most perfectly dazed manner. I was becoming desperate by this time, and, seeing that he could not take in the situation, I went through the motions of opening a valise and taking out some clean linen, pointing to my soiled shirt bosom, and again directing my index finger toward the head of the stair-way. But there he stood, muttering something about *señor*. These fellows will say " *Si, señor*," " Yes, sir," when they don't know what else to say. It was no use. Business had come to a stand-still, and there was no way left but to go down stairs myself for the satchel, shawl, and umbrella. But while I was rehabilitating myself for the descent I took occasion to say to him some things in language he never would forget, providing he understood it.

"Do you know that you are a very stupid Aztec?"

"*Si, señor*," was his courteous reply.

"Why, you couldn't extract the cube root from a pile of loose sand, nor pull up a yucca-tree by the roots from a Montezuma swamp, if you should try."

And again he said, "*Si, señor*."

"You ought to be sent to a lunatic asylum until your brain grows."

"*Si, señor*," was all I could get out of him in response to the most eloquent speech I could possibly deliver.

And so, having by this time suitably arrayed myself, I went down and brought up the luggage and showed it to him. Then he actually smiled, for he saw the point, and once more said, "*Si, señor*." These peons of the "male persuasion" are more stupid than those of the opposite sex. But, then, it only proves that women are brighter than men the world over. There is one admirable trait in the character of nearly all the people you meet here —low as well as high—they are exceedingly suave. They may rob you on the highway or pilfer your field-glass, or do any thing else, but they are exceedingly polite. If a Mexican bandit were to cut your throat he, no doubt, would do it politely, saying, I suppose, "*Gracias, señor*," or "*Muchas gracias, señor*," words one hears continually. A Mexican gentleman or lady is the embodiment of real politeness. The same is true of the children; they are taught to be courteous always and to every body. It is most admirable. An English poet has said,

"What strange extremes are centered in our make."

What strange extremes are centered in the make up of Mexican daily life! 1 have not seen it equaled anywhere. The cities of Europe in many instances look fresh and new compared with those of Mexico. It is one of the oldest-appearing countries in the world. To travel here transports one, seemingly, to the far East, and into the long ago. The architecture is Moorish, and was brought here from Spain, the Moors having copied the Romans. Hence the houses are built in the old Roman style, with courts and flat roofs, azoteas. The water pitchers, even, on the shoulders of the women, are constructed after the old Oriental pattern. The skin-bottle, the dress of the peon, also point to a remote past. The very soil itself presents the signs of age. Take the social life, as one sees it every day and every-where in Mexico, especially in the cities, and it presents the most marked extremes. There are millionaires who "live like princes," and anon myriads of the most abject poverty-stricken people, who live on tortillas and chile at a cost not exceeding six cents a day. One sees ladies most elegantly dressed riding in their carriages on the paseos, and then walking beside them, on those same streets, bare-footed and ragged women, bearing on their shoulders great bundles of produce toward the markets. A great many women are seen here in what fashionable society at home calls "full dress;" that is, in a state of partial nudity.

In Mexico every body smokes. They smoke in the street-cars, in the shops, and at the dinner table. I have seen a man upon his knees in a chapel, before an image of the Virgin, muttering his prayers with a lighted cigarette in his hand. Even old Popocatepetl himself, though no longer a volcano, emits his gaseous and sulphurous fumes from a crater that once poured out burning lava, and with the fire in his mouth lighted the ships at sea in their course. But Iztaccihualt, the "white woman," as the word means, and whose summit is perhaps two or three score miles from that of Popocatepetl, does not smoke. If ever she did, it was a long time ago, and she has reformed in her old age. Mexican ladies do not follow her example, but his, for they nearly all smoke. I have seen a beggar woman hold out her hand and plead for a few centavos with a cigarette between her teeth. And many a señorita may be seen sitting behind her barred window wreathed in the smoke of the cigarette. Mexican hotels never have parlors or smoking-rooms. The guest can indulge his habit in the dining-room, or the court, or the corridor, or anywhere else. If the traveler goes into a restaurant he will find some persons eating, and others, having finished their meals, leaning back in their chairs smoking. "No matter about the ladies," a Mexican will say; "light your cigar whenever and wherever you please." About the only offense you can offer them when you smoke, if you do so, is not to pass around your cigars or cigarettes. If you are sitting near a gentleman when he takes out his cigar-case to light a fire, he will most likely turn and offer you one, whether he knows you or not, and if you do not accept his courtesy he will regard it as almost an affront. If, however, in a very pleasant way, and with a polite bow, you say, "*Muchas gracias, señor,*" he will be satisfied.

The city of Mexico is the Washington of the *Estados Unidos del Sur*—the United States of the South—and must not be taken as a representative Mexican city, for it is built more after the fashion of the cities of Europe than any other in the republic. There are some portions of it which remind one of Paris. The Alameda, though not so large, is not unlike the Bois de Bologne of the French capital. At least it is about as easy to lose yourself in the one as the other.

In all Mexican cities one meets some things which are alike, for instance, the great number of one-storied buildings with flat roofs. There are some adjustments which come quite naturally. In a region of earthquakes people, by the instinct of self-preservation, would guard against lofty buildings, because of the danger of their toppling over in time of terrestrial oscillations. Seven stories and earthquakes would not go well together. Then, again, the very thick walls would prove to be a further protection against such calamities. I have seen walls built of adobe, stone, or brick, nearly a yard in thickness, especially in the mountainous districts. And besides, in a hot, dry climate there must be protection against heat, and this is secured by the very thick walls.

The city of Mexico, once the famous capital of the Montezumas, lies in the valley of Anahuac, surrounded by elliptical plains, inclosed by ridges of basaltic and porphyritic rocks, and at a remote distance engirt with magnificent mountains, two of which, some sixty or seventy miles distant, were once active volcanoes, and stood guard over ancient Anahuac, though it is a good while since they emitted their fires. The city covers a number of square miles, and is perfectly level. Go in what direction you may from the banks of Texcuco to the frowning bastions of Chapultepec, and the great "Snow Mountains" are ever before you. All the main thoroughfares of the capital center in the Plaza Mayor. Two great stone aqueducts bring water from remote springs into the city, where from central basins the *aguadores*, or water-carriers, convey it to the dwellings in earthen vessels for a fixed sum per day or load, according to the amount used or bargain made, very much as dairymen's carts deliver milk to the inhabitants of American cities. The water supply in the city of Mexico is sufficient to allow on the average forty gallons per day to each individual. Water is plenty, but cold water scarce, while ice-water is hardly used at all.

It is not much wonder, when all the ice is brought from Popocatepetl, sixty or more miles away, transported down the mountain on the backs of peons. It costs the consumer when delivered about ten cents a pound.

One grows very thirsty at this high altitude, and drinking does not seem to satisfy. The lips often become parched and cracked from atmospheric causes. The stranger must guard against this by the use of local remedies. A recent French traveler writes, rather exaggeratingly, of this city :

"Mexico is a grand city, in the Spanish style, with an air more inspiring, more majestic, more metropolitan than any city of Spain, except Madrid, crowned by numerous towers, and surrounded by a vast plain bounded by mountains. Mexico reminds one somewhat of Rome. Its long streets, broad, straight, and regular, give it an appearance like Berlin. It has some resemblance to Naples and Turin, yet with a character of its own. It makes one think of various cities of Europe, while it differs from all of them. It recalls all, repeats none."

"The second day," says Mr. Ward, England's former Minister to Mexico, "made converts of us all; in the course of it we visited most of the central parts of the town, and, after seeing the great plaza, the cathedral, the palace, and the noble streets which communicate with them, we were forced to confess, not only that Humboldt's praises did not exceed the truth, but that among the various capitals of Europe there were few that could support with any advantage a comparison with Mexico."

The climate does not vary much. It is like a constant recurrence of May and June days—never intensely hot, and never severely cold. In the United States the weather is a very convenient theme for conversation when people have nothing else to talk about. But in Mexico it is never discussed. I once said to a fellow-traveler:

" This is a pleasant day, sir."

" O yes," he replied, " all days are pleasant here.'

I saw the point.

This quaint old city has many objects of interest: its hundred and one venerable churches, used and not used; its great metropolitan cathedral; its public drives, thronged with the elite of the city in carriage and saddle; its Alameda, with winding paths, broad, smooth, clean, under the shade of the beautiful eucalyptus-trees. One can never forget the hours spent amid such surroundings. But these are not all. Yonder is Chapultepec not very far away, looking out on you from the tops of trees that were old when Cortez slaughtered the innocents. There is, indeed, much to interest the tourist in this Paris of the Western World. One never tires of strolling about through *los portales de commercios*, which consist of a succession of arcades around three or four sides of a large block of buildings where everybody walks and talks, and buys and sells cigars, canes, pulque, jewelry, dolls, notions, dry goods, etc. These *portales* are to the city of Mexico what the Palais Royal is to Paris.

In a city containing so much to see it was a question where to begin, so I started out on my journey to hunt up the curious part first. I was at once struck with the fact that each block along a given street had a different name, so that I soon became bewildered and had to call to my aid a policeman to extricate me. Some streets will have the same appellation for several squares. Take the principal street for example, the *Calle de Plateros*, which begins on the Grand Plaza where the palace stands, running to the statue of Charles IV. of Spain. Each block along that street has a name of its own, or there may be several blocks of the same name with numerals after them, as 1a, 2da, 3ra, etc., which greatly confuses a stranger in trying to find any body, for you must not only know the street but the name or the number of the particular block where he resides.

Here is a list of some of the principal names of streets. For instance, think of walking along "Crown of Thorns Street," or "Blood of Christ Street," or "Street of the Holy Ghost," or crossing a stream on "Holy Ghost Bridge." The Catholic Church has also stamped itself in such names as "Mother of Sorrows Street," and "Street of the Sacred Heart." At every turn you are importuned to buy a lottery ticket. Men, women, and children are employed to sell them. The principle lottery is that of "Divina Providencia." Along the streets are seen very attractive signs. Over a ladies' fancy store I noticed one which read "La Tentacion"—the temptation—a slight hint at woman's love of beautiful things. Over the door-way of one saloon I saw "El Abysmo," hell; over another, "El Delirio"—translated into English—the delirium. Both were appropriately labeled. Other places are more poetically named, such as, "The Ancient Glories of Mexico," "The Terrestrial Paradise," etc. Firm names are not often seen over store fronts. Fancy again comes into play, as in English, "The Surprise," "The City of Paris," "The Spring Time," "The Pearl," or "The Emerald." Over the door of a shoe store I saw "The Foot of Venus." Their boats on the canal bear such names as "La Ninfa Encantadora," the enchanting nymph; "La Flor," the flower, etc. The same is true of names of men, as "St. John of God Gonzales," or "La Santissima Trinidad Smith"—Most Holy Trinity Smith, if there are any Smiths in Mexico.

The street-car system is first-class. The cars do not go singly, but in trains of three, and are classified, as on other railways, into first and second grades. They run half a block apart, and each one is drawn by its own mule. Instead of the self-registering bell-punch, every car has, besides the driver, two men, one to sell the tickets and another to take them up, thus showing the need of putting a check on dishonesty. First-class fares are sometimes as high as twenty-five cents, especially when the distances are long; but the average is a *medio*, or six and a quarter cents. Second-class fares are always one half the amount of the first-class. The drivers carry horns and blow them when they approach street-crossings. Conductors, like nearly every body else, carry revolvers in plain sight.

It seemed very odd to see little girls five to seven years old trotting along the streets wearing full-length dresses, causing them to appear like a race of Lilliputians. Men were going about the streets bearing on their shoulders invalids and cripples to give them an airing in the plaza or Alameda. Never before did I see human beings on all-fours wandering around like dogs. I witnessed two such poor deformed creatures perambulating about one day, and a most sickening spectacle it was.

These people have no arrangement worthy the name for extinguishing fires. In cities built of stone and brick so universally, fires are of very rare occurrence. It is next to impossible to burn a building whose floors, stair-ways, casings, and roof are of stone or brick. A drug store burned during the time I was in the city, the fire department being entirely powerless to extinguish the flames. When the fire signal is given nothing is ever in readiness.

Never in my life before was I so embarrassed on account of my soiled linen. Washing is done here in a manner as trying to one's patience as to the articles cleansed. The washer-woman who undertakes the job of renovating your garments carries them away to some stream, pond, or canal, and with cold water, minus soap, rubs them between two stones awhile, and hangs them up to dry. Yet I must say that they looked very well, all things considered. My washing was kept for three full weeks on one occasion, though I repeatedly sent for it, and a portion of it has not been returned yet.

The price of wood ranges from $16 to $25 per cord, while imported coal costs $25 a ton; hence, if the weather is cool, you must stay in-doors and protect yourself by additional clothing, for there are no methods in use for warming apartments. It is commonly remarked that there is not a stove, grate, or furnace in all Mexico. The cooking in the cities is done over earthen or brick ovens heated with charcoal. The smoke and gas escape through openings above them. But in huts in the interior, the universal "cooking stove" is the *comal*, a mere earthen pot, simple and unexpensive, as well as portable. The natives have a belief that warming the atmosphere renders it unwholesome. It certainly must increase its rareness. In looking from some cathedral tower or lofty azotea the absence of chimneys is a noticeable feature.

The burden-bearers are before you at every turn. They carry on their backs almost every thing. For generations much of the labor of Mexico has been performed by these human machines, comparatively few carts or horses being employed. . Men carry wardrobes on their heads, pianos on their backs; stone, barrels of water, or pulque, and other heavy articles, are borne thus for long distances through the heat and over the sands with seemingly but little weariness. I saw one of these peons carrying twenty-four chairs tied together as one load on his back one evening, and another carrying two bureaus or chests of drawers bound together back to back. He was crossing the *Plaza de Armas* at a jog-trot under his heavy burden, but it evidently tested his powers of endurance. These people are trained porters, and will often go eighty or a hundred miles to market bearing their heavy loads of produce, which will bring them only a dollar or two at most. They keep up this gait hour after hour and day after day. If the Mexican is an expert rider, he is equally an expert footman. Indian couriers, through their knowledge of paths and by-ways, sometimes make better time between distant cities than the regular mail coaches. The Aztec Indian is contented with the little he gets, for, in his simple mode of life, his wants are few, the principal of which is his favorite pulque. Although the Indians live in villages in the interior, in the capital they dwell in suburbs distinct from the whites, though they mingle with them freely in the streets—a people within a people, interfering in none of the affairs of the upper and governing class. Their conversation and their deportment are humble and obedient. Their self-abasement is so marked, that they accept and apply to themselves the reproaches of the whites. A white man is to one of these Indians a *gente de razon*, a man of intelligence; while the Indian is called a *gente sin razon*, a man without intelligence. And he accepts the situation.

The Mexican Indians, who transport goods from the interior, are so trained that they will tire the strongest horse in equal time and distance, carrying on their shoulders at the same time from one hundred to one hundred and fifty pounds weight; and it is an actual fact, amply vouched for, that after making long trips thus heavily loaded, on their return they will fill their baskets with stones, their strained and distorted muscles seeming to require the burden to which they had been accustomed.

Women in great numbers sit around in the scorching sun, on the sides of the streets, using often the curb-stones for seats, sometimes with nothing to protect them from the sun's rays, selling fruits, meats, drinks, *dulces* (sweets), of which they have many varieties, etc., or they squat around in their humble door-ways, with the heads of their children in their laps, searching after the —secrets of nature!

As before stated, they are a nation of smokers, but their filthy habit of chewing is almost unknown to them. The Mexican is not always the most polished sort of an individual, but one thing may be spoken to his credit, he does not befoul the floor of his *jacal* with tobacco juice.

Their hotels are not like our own of the higher grade, which generally have ample bathing accommodations. If you want to take a bath here you must go to a public bath-house. You will find them every-where in the large cities, and their appointments are first-class. In the best hotels in the cities travelers are waited upon by men servants, but in the villages by women. There are no reading-rooms, with files of newspapers, to accommodate the traveling public. They are kept on the European plan, and sometimes you must walk a block or two to find a good *fonda*, or restaurant. You take your *pan y café*, bread and coffee, in the morning at seven or eight, eat your breakfast at eleven to twelve, and dine at four to five o'clock. Some of these *fonditas* in the city of Mexico are very fine indeed; others are very wretched, as I found out by experience. One of the scarcest and most expensive articles, as well as one of the poorest, is that great American luxury—butter, and costs about one dollar a pound here. It is churned in the skin of an animal of some kind, a sheep, hog, or goat, out of which the beast has been extracted by some process. The skin is made milk-tight, and is filled with cream, and then dumped up and down by a spring pole, or rolled about over the ground by the children until the "butter comes."

One who is fond of getting at bottom facts can always have the satisfaction of knowing the color of the creature whose skin formed the churn by the color of the hairs in the butter, for in the process of construction the outside of the animal becomes the inside of the churn.

Funerals are conducted in a way curious enough to an American. In one instance the street-car answers the place of hearse for the corpse, and carriages for the pall-bearers and mourners. If the family is very poor, the dead is carried through the streets to the place of interment on the shoulders of men. Those who can afford it bury their dead in coffins; but poor people cannot do this, for, owing to the great scarcity of timber, coffins are very expensive. There are persons who keep them to hire, and, in such cases, when the cemetery is reached the body is transferred to a cheap, rough box, or wrapped in manilla cloth or a blanket, and thus buried. The coffin is then returned to the owner, to go again upon a similar errand. The tombs of the wealthy, however, in the fine cemeteries, are both elaborate and beautiful.

The hack accommodations are good. The hackmen are all under the most careful police surveillance, the rates being fixed by law and regulated according to the condition of the vehicle and the horses. Each hack carries a small tin flag. If the flag be green, the price is $1 50 an hour, as only he whose carriage is new and horses good and harness genteel is permitted by the authorities to sport a green flag. If the flag be blue, the price is $1 an hour, with a corresponding diminution of style. If you cannot afford so high a price as $1 an hour, you can select a carriage with a white flag, and pay seventy-five cents an hour. But you can go even below this, and ride under a red flag at fifty cents an hour, where you have reached bottom price, and if you escape going to the bottom before the ride is over you may consider yourself a lucky fellow.

The capital, as well as all other principal cities, is under good police regulations. The police force comprises three grades: first, the roundsmen, who patrol the streets on horseback, armed with carbines and sabers, closely resembling cavalrymen. There are also patrolmen who, on foot, have their regular beats. Besides these there is another grade still, who take their positions through the night at the street crossings. They carry lanterns, placing them in the intersections of the thoroughfares, and then find a place near by where they can sit down and go to sleep! In this there is an advantage, however; a policeman can always be found quickly, for, whether awake or asleep, he is near his lantern. He carries a club and revolver, and, clad in scanty linen and sombrero, with his zarape thrown over his shoulders, and his rusty old-fashioned cavalry saber dangling at his side, is quite a formidable-looking figure. I have perambulated the streets of Mexican cities far into the night, and must say that they are very well governed. A recent writer in a popular magazine says:

" Here are no drunken riots, no saloon brawls, little thieving, and less murder within corporate limits. The least disorderly action, even loud talking in the streets, causes prompt arrest, and to be suspected of being a disturber of the public peace is almost as dangerous to personal liberty as actual commission of crime. It is so little while since revolutions were the order of the hour that Mexico has not yet become accustomed to the situation, and modified her laws to suit a time of peace. An American finds himself environed here, on every hand, by laws which he cannot comprehend. For instance, any one carrying a package upon the streets after eight P. M. is liable to arrest. A person either walking or driving after eleven o'clock at night is accosted by the watchman with the query: *Quien es?* or *Donde vive?*—' Who are you?' or ' Where do you live?' Receiving no reply, the vigilant guardian of the peace may shoot if he pleases. This is rather severe on those luckless Americans who do not even understand the language, and whose replies are generally more forcible than elegant. I never heard of the law being carried into full effect, but, nevertheless, it stands upon the statutes, and is liable to be enforced. In Mexico prisoners are never pampered, as sometimes by over-zealous philanthropists in our *Estados Unidos del Norte*. Here the penitentiaries are bare of all but the merest necessaries—tortillas for food, a stone bench for a bed, unremitting toil, and most rigorous discipline." *

The police are not only vigilant, they are equally polite. A policeman will stop a street-car and assist a lady to enter it with a gallantry that reminds one of the days of knighthood. If a man commits a crime in any principal city in the republic, he must either flee the country or pay the penalty. An instance came to my notice illustrating this. In February, 1869, a prominent lawyer in the city of Mexico was killed by one who entertained toward him some enmity. The murderer was arrested, tried, convicted, and sentenced to be shot, but escaped and fled to France. He remained away ten years, and then, thinking that his crime had been forgotten or would be condoned, returned. But he was soon in the

* Mrs. F. B. Ward.

clutches of the law, and, after ten years of voluntary exile, was executed by shooting—the mode of capital punishment adopted by the Mexicans.

On pleasant afternoons, and, excepting in the rainy season—there are but few unpleasant ones—carriage driving and horseback riding are the order of the day. The great boulevard, which was laid out under the reign of Maximilian, the *Paseo de la Reforma*, or "Empress Drive," so-called in honor of Carlotta, and which extends from the Alameda to the castle of Chapultepec, a distance of three miles, is the great driveway of the capital. It is said that the carriages usually contain the culture and beauty of the metropolis. As they are generally closed, it would be hard to disprove the statement. I never saw a light carriage—a phaeton, for instance—in Mexico. Ladies do not ride on horseback to any extent, and if they do in individual instances, social etiquette requires them to be accompanied by a near relative. But with men horseback riding is a national amusement. In the cooler hours of the evening or morning, the streets are full of horsemen in some sections. The gentlemen are very fastidious about their riding attire. A broad-brimmed sombrero costs all the way from three dollars to two hundred and fifty dollars, and is the main feature of the equestrian outfit. In that the *caballero* is lavish of expense. If he earns fifteen dollars a month he will spend three months' wages on a hat! With his silver-trimmed sombrero, his tight leather trousers, with rows of silver spangles up and down the outer seam, his gayly embroidered jacket, scarlet sash, sword, revolvers, and silver spurs, he presents a very striking appearance. Nor must his saddle suffer in the comparison with these other gay trappings. His silver-mounted bridle must match the silver-trimmed sombrero. All must be in harmony regardless of expense. Such an outfit costs at the highest, including the horse, about a thousand dollars. They are expert horsemen. I saw one in Monterey lose his hat in the wind, and putting the spurs into the sides of his fractious steed, swept round in a circle to where it was lying in the street, and swinging over the saddle, while the horse was in active motion, picked it up and placed it on his head with the utmost ease.

The shopping is always done by ladies of the upper class in carriages. They do not enter the stores; but have the goods brought out to them for inspection or purchase. In some of the larger and more fashionable establishments parlors are fitted up, where a lady can sit at ease in seclusion and have the goods brought to her, if she chooses.

Etiquette is carried so far that a gentleman will not be seen on the street with any sort of a package in his hand. He can carry a book, however, provided it is not wrapped in paper. Only foreigners and common people stand at counters to make purchases or carry parcels to their homes or hotels. Goods are not delivered at the residences of purchasers by the merchants, as is customary in American cities. If a package is too bulky to take with you in your hand or carriage, a licensed carrier will deliver it at your expense.

Each carrier wears on his breast a brass badge, like that of a policeman, which contains his registered number and is the sign of his office. If he does not deliver the goods, promptly, and in good condition, he is liable to be reported at the police head-quarters, where he is heavily fined. But if he fails to find your residence, or if any mistake has occurred in the directions given him, it is his duty to take the goods to the police head-quarters, where the purchaser can recover them, as well as learn the reason why they were not delivered.

In the less pretentious places of business there is but little system in the classification of goods—silks, cottons, and woolens are mixed together somewhat indiscriminately. Shopping, therefore, requires great patience. A lady informed me that she went one day to buy a pair of gloves. The clerk pulled open a drawer in which were shoes, corsets, ribbons, and gloves. There being none to fit, he kept on searching until he found some in another part of the store.

The Plaza Mayor is the great rendezvous in the evening. Here the crowds gather, the old and the young, the rich and the poor, a promiscuous mass. A military band discourses music several evenings in the week, under the brilliant electric lights, and finer music is seldom heard. The scenes are not so rich and gay as those of the Paris of France; but a larger variety of face, form, color, and picturesqueness appears in the Paris of Mexico. You do not see crowds sitting around under the street awnings sipping wine and gossiping with each other, as in the French capital; but go to the *pulquerias*, where the national beverage is sold, and the crowds will be seen, gay and hilarious, in true Mexican style.

There is a great amount of drunkenness in this old city, but not much rowdyism, owing to the vigilance of the police and the nature of the intoxicant. People who indulge in too much pulque—and a very little is too much for one's good—are rendered too stupid to quarrel and fight. Pulque is the daily beverage of the rank and file of the people. It is said that if a peon earns a dollar and a half, he gives one dollar to the priest, spends forty-five cents for pulque, and provides for his family with the remaining five cents! Even that is not so bad as when some Americans spend all their earnings for vile whisky, and leave their families to shift for themselves.

Of course I had read of the floating gardens, the *Chinampas* of the historians of the olden times, and was eager to see them. So I went up the Santa Anita canal adjoining the *Paseo de la Viga* on a feast day, and edged my way amid a motley throng of all ages, grades, conditions, and complexions. The banks of the canal were lined with people, and the waters were covered with boats of every description—long boats, short boats, flat boats, clean and dirty boats. The jolly crowd sang songs, played on rude instruments, laughed, danced, smoked, flirted, and drank pulque. Mothers sat about, crooning something to their mahogany colored babies, boys played with the dogs, and tried to push each other into the water. There was no quarreling and fighting, but all was hilariousness and rude gayety. But where were the far-famed "floating gardens," these wildernesses of sweets and blossoms, far surpassing the Alcinas and Morganas of the sunny land of Italy, which are said to have dotted the lakes of Anahuac, three hundred years ago? Alas! like Rachel's children, "they are not." But, doubtless, they did once exist, and were formed of reeds and rushes and the branches of young trees woven firmly together, and covered over with alluvial earth sufficiently deep to allow of the growth of vegetation, flowers, and very small trees. They were even capable of sustaining small huts for the residence of the gardener. Remains of them still exist. I walked over one of them, but it did not float, though I could feel it tremble, under my weight. The poetry of the "floating gardens" of Montezuma remains, but the gardens have ceased to float.

CHAPTER XVI.

WANDERINGS ALONG OLD PATHS.

An old tradition—Brave barbarians—Sacrificial stone—A royal seat—Sculptures and paintings—A vandal act—Various institutions—An old canal—Entering a pawn-shop—" Raising the Wind "—First train to the United States—Solemn smiles—A new conquest—Enterprise that failed—Egyptian plows, bottles, and brooms—Preferring the smoke—In no haste—Extremes—Too many houses.

TO walk about the streets of the city of Mexico is to wander along old paths. Ages before Columbus discovered America the valley of Anahuac thronged with a great population, and Mexico, derived from the word Mexitli, the name of the Aztec war-god, was a city of rude grandeur, if we may credit the chroniclers of the olden times. The ancient city was founded by the Aztecs, who marched into this valley from the north after suffering defeat in a battle with the Colhuans, a rival tribe. An oracle had foretold them, as tradition relates, that they should found a city when they came to a spot where an eagle would be seen standing upon a rock. It was on the shores of Lake Texcuco—now spelled T-e-x-co-co—that the long-sought eagle was seen perched upon a branch of the nopal cactus growing out of the crevice of a rock, and holding in its beak a serpent. This is the origin of the Mexican national coat of arms, which is stamped on its coin and inscribed on its banners. Into this ancient capital Cortez entered in 1519, and from which he was compelled to retreat in seven months. Desperate and daring, he re-collected and reorganized his forces, and again attacked and captured the Aztec stronghold. The brave barbarians, who could only defend themselves with rudest implements of warfare, held out against his horse and cannon for seventy-five days, fighting with the courage of despair, but at last were vanquished, and the Spaniard was left master.

To write all that might be said about this old capital would require the space of a volume. Much, therefore, must be passed over in silence. The sights are various. There is the Academy of San Carlos and School of Fine Arts, with numerous sculptures and paintings. As one enters the court, or patio, he sees a large collection of images—hideous, monstrous-looking things, which could only have been produced by a people possessed of the very crudest idea. That which attracted my attention first was the *piedra de los sacrificios*, the "sacrificial stone," a basaltic rock, circular in form, and of enormous weight. It measures about nine feet in diameter, and is three feet thick. Cut all over its rim are hieroglyphical representations of the subjugation of an inferior by a superior people. At the time of the conquest its destruction was practically impossible, hence it was buried in the main plaza, where it was found in 1791, since which time it has been preserved as a curious relic of the past. In its center is a deep cavity with an outlet seemingly begrimed with stains through which flowed the blood of the thousands of victims said to have been offered upon it to the Aztec idol, *Teoyaomiqui*. Whether the idol or the name was most hideous, the reader must judge. A few paces off is the stone yoke used in securing the victims while their hearts were being torn from the quivering flesh, the priests making the incisions between the ribs of the doomed victims with obsidian knives. To be appreciated it must be seen. In a room off the patio, under lock and key, is preserved, as a curious object, the state coach of the Emperor Maximilian, the grandest vehicle in America. I opened the door and took my seat on the crimson plush where royalty once sat. When I dismounted the attendant assured me that it was against the rules to do as I had done, but he did not refuse to accept the small piece of money I gave him, not as a bribe, but as an expected fee. After wandering about among the curious old images of beings with hideous forms and faces, such as feathered serpents, and certain nondescript animals in stone, dug out of the earth all over Mexico, relics of a rude and barbarous age, and brought here for the inspection of the curious, I entered the academy proper.

It was with no small degree of interest that I had sought the large building near the great *Plaza de Armas*, where may be seen the fruits of native as well as of foreign artistic genius. When I thought of the numerous revolutions which had diverted the Mexican mind from themes of peace to those of war, and the many revolutions which had drained her treasury, it was something of a surprise to find any thing worthy the name of a picture. The first place entered was the gallery of sculpture, where, as usual, may be seen a great collection of Greek and Roman figures, or rather copies of them. The usual hideous and impossible things one sees in such places, and which, by common consent, are called "beautiful," are displayed here in plaster. They are awaiting transfer to marble when the expense can be afforded. But passing to the upper part of the building, I was pleased to find nearly a dozen rooms whose walls were overhung with paintings, many of which were worthy of any art gallery. Some of them represent events in the history of Mexico, from the invasion of Cortez until the present time, while others were evidently intended to preserve certain legendary scenes in ancient Aztec land. One painting particularly interested me—the dead Aztec; or, "Friar Las Casas protecting the Aztecs." I suppose it was intended to show the horrors of the conquest. Most of these paintings are the work of Spanish artists, and were, doubtless, the property of the Church at one time. At the seizure of the convents by the government these pictures fell into the hands of the lovers of art, and now go to constitute the National Gallery. Among those which are most striking is the "Dead Monk." It is a wonderful conception, and a most impressive Catholic painting. Several "Hagar and Ishmaels," by different artists, are there. Another, a "Dante and Virgil gazing down into Hades," is so real that, as one said, it seems as if their cheeks would scorch from the fires. Many of the pictures are a little too dark, owing to the too free use of bitumen. "Columbus Contemplating the Sea" and the landscapes of the Sierra valleys are among the most attractive. The Mexicans, with all their failings, have an eye to the beautiful, as the flowers and the picturesque costumes of the people and the colored geometrical forms on the outside of their buildings give ample evidence, though I did not admire the latter. This School of Fine Arts —the Academy of San Carlos—has been in existence for over a hundred years, and yet these people are far from being patrons of high art. The average Mexican house is satisfied with the cheapest sort of pictures, providing they represent some old saints or the Virgin Mary. The brightest paintings one sees generally are those on the walls of the pulque shops—the native "gin-mills." Here the Holy Virgin is brought out arrayed in the most gorgeously colored robes. The earliest Mexican paintings are the best, for they were nearest to what is called the Renaissance period. Mexico ought to be a land of artists, for the time was when the Aztecs had no other way of communicating their unspoken ideas than by picture-writing. But, alas! when the Spanish invaders came, bringing with them their religion, the first bishop, Zumarraga, thought it would aid him in overthrowing the whole religious system of the inhabitants if their pictures and images were all demolished, and, accordingly, he ordered a universal destruction of all manuscripts and Aztec hieroglyphs. Only a few specimens escaped this vandal act, but for which some definite information of the origin and history of the peoples who had dwelt amid the mountains of Mexico since the earliest times might now be in possession of the world. That act was a very zealous one, but it was a " zeal without knowledge." Segrade and Obregon excelled in portrait painting. Some of their works are on the walls of the Hall of Embassadors in the National Palace. One of the first of native artists was Cabrera, in whose veins flowed pure Indian blood. The original Mexican pictures, like the pronunciamentos of her various revolutionary generals, are too grandiose. They magnify their subjects far too much. Several works of the old masters are pointed out here; but whether they are genuine or not the ordinary tourist has really no means of knowing. " That is a Murillo," " This is a Ribera," " Yonder is a Rembrandt," the guide will say. Yes, but I am a little like the man who always goes to sleep during the sermon, knowing that his minister is strictly orthodox. I know that if these pictures were painted by the old masters, as represented to me, they must be all right, whether I can see it or not. It was Mexico that I was studying, and so I wanted to see what Mexican artists could do. Of the natives there have been a number who excelled, but none were equal to Louis and José Juarez, whose works, it seems, would do credit to any nation or to any age. Among these I particularly noted the "Good Samaritan," the "Hebrews by the Waters of Babylon," and "Noah Receiving the Olive-Branch." Valesco's sienna colored "Valley of Mexico" is a painting of which one never tires.

The city boasts of a Mining School of high grade, a Museum, a College of Medicine, a Military College, a School of Agriculture, a Conservatory of Music and Oratory, Geographical and Historical Societies, Society of Architecture, Government Mint, and Custom-house. Also a House of Correction, a general prison, and hospitals for infants, insane, and blind.

The old Aztec capital was situated in the midst of the highest salt-water lake in the world—Texcoco, which received the overflow of five other lakes that were above it, and hence the city was exposed to occasional submergence until a suitable outlet was made through the mountains which border the valley on the north. I passed through this *desague*, the cut or "Tajo of Nochistongo," on my first entrance into the city, when the thought came into my mind with a good deal of force that Mexico is much older than my own country. All things considered, that was one of the most remarkable hydraulic operations ever undertaken by man, and was begun thirteen years before the pilgrims landed on Plymouth rock. It is over twelve miles in length, three or four hundred feet deep and wide, and the excavations were all carried away on the backs of peons.

Walking along one of the main thoroughfares, I noticed a sign which attracted my attention, and so unhesitatingly walked in to see what I could. I found myself in a pawn-shop. It was not that I had any thing to pawn that took me there, but rather curiosity to gratify. No one visiting the city of Mexico can afford to miss seeing this curiosity shop, for such it is. This great national institution is called the *Monte de Piedad,* and has branches in different cities through Central Mexico. It was founded for a beneficent purpose. I was shown the first entry upon its books, which bears the date of 1775, in which a loan of forty dollars was made by a gentleman on a set of diamonds. The intention of the founder was a good one, that of keeping the people who by circumstances might at times be forced to pawn personal articles to obtain temporary relief, out of the hands of swindlers, whose ulterior object would be to get entire possession of the property pawned at a fraction of its value. This institution loans its money at the rate of twelve per cent. per annum, and carries the property pawned for eight months. Every article entered is appraised carefully by an officer of the institution, and if at the final sale it does not bring the amount of the original debt and interest, the appraiser is held personally responsible for the difference. There is not much danger of his appraising goods at too high a figure. Money in some amount can be loaned on any article of personal property from a pocket knife to a piano or coach. People pawn their clothing, which is common, silver-ware, furniture, pistols, or any thing else to obtain money, and often to enable them to attend the opera or a bull-fight.

I was in the city of Mexico when the first through train started on its way for Chicago and New York. It consisted of a locomotive, tender, baggage car, dining-room car, and three parlor coaches. About five thousand people, more or less, gathered at the depot of the Mexican Central Railroad to witness the departure of that train. The fare, including every thing, was $150. The event signaled a new era in Mexican history. The capital of the *Estados Unidos del Norte* connected by rail with that of the *Estados Unidos del Sur* shows that the world moves. It was an occasion which might well call out a crowd, and suggest the firing of cannon and other popular demonstrations. But such was not the case. A few handkerchiefs were waved and a few *adios* spoken, and that was all. The Americans in the city were generally present, and hailed the event with joy. The faces of the Mexicans wore rather solemn smiles. I was told that the Mexican people are not very demonstrative, they certainly were not at this time. If it had been in New York or Chicago, such an event would have been celebrated with sound of cornet and thunder of artillery. The Mexicans feel a trifle uneasy and suspicious, as they view the inroads made upon them by American capital as well as genius. They say we conquered them once by our arms, now we are subjugating them by our inventions and our machinery. The priesthood are particularly bitter against the innovations caused by our people, which disturb the ancient quiet and loosen the hold the Church has had for so long a time on the popular mind. These dozy old Spaniards and stolid descendants of the Montezumas are getting their eyes open. It is well, for they have made no progress for centuries until recently, and even yet they cling tenaciously to the customs and ideas of the long ago.

On this occasion an incident occurred which illustrates one peculiar phase of the Mexican character. The postmaster thought he would celebrate the event by sending the mail to the United States on this first train as an experiment. He accordingly issued a bulletin, advising those who had communications to send to avail themselves of this privilege, and to have their letters at the post-office by ten o'clock in the morning, as the train would leave at three in the afternoon. This would allow him five hours to arrange the packages and deliver them at the station, time enough surely. Of course we Americans were anxious to be participants in an event of so much importance. At three o'clock sharp the train pulled out of the depot for the North; but alas! the mail-bags had not been delivered. They came about fifteen minutes too late. "Just like a Mexican," said all the Americans.

In this strange old land all things tend to remain as they were from the beginning. The farmer breaks up the soil with a plow modeled like those used in Egypt three thousand years ago. It is made of a stick of wood, with an iron point, and a single rear handle to guide it. Then a pole is extended from the middle of the ground-piece with a cross-bar on its end, which is fastened with leather straps to the horns of cattle. With this instrument the ground is merely scratched. The sweeping is done with a bunch of straw or stiff grass. The house servant takes slowly to a handled broom, and will not use one if it can possibly be avoided. A blacksmith will work in his shop in an atmosphere dense with the smoke of the furnace for want of a chimney, which might be built of adobe brick in a few hours at almost no expense. The skins of animals are used every-where for carrying and storing liquids, precisely as was done in the Orient in the days of the Pharaohs. Threshing is done by driving a number of animals over the grain in the field threshing-floor, and then the chaff is winnowed from the grain by throwing it up, that the wind may blow though it; hence the expression, "like the chaff which the wind driveth away."

The Mexican character is a compound of Indian stolidity and Castilian haughtiness. With him change is slow. Time has no meaning to him. We Americans are in the habit of saying, "Time is money," not so the descendants of the Aztec. He is never in any hurry, and as a rule never does to-day what he can possibly put off till to-morrow. He opens his place of business at nine o'clock in the morning, and closes it in time to drive through the paseo, or walk in the plaza or alemada. The merchant is willing you should buy of him if you will, but does not seem very eager about the matter. The word *mañana*—to-morrow—expresses his way of not doing things on time.

This is a land of extremes. It contains the loftiest mountains and the deepest of valleys. In some parts the soil is so poor as to be almost entirely unproductive, and in other sections its richness is fabulous. Here the different varieties of cactus grow right out of the burning sands, and there the earth carries on her bosom the luxuriousness of the tropics. Now you are down where oranges, lemons, figs, bananas, pine-apples, and other tropical fruits hang on the trees, and then you are away up in the region where the snows whiten the mountain summit the whole year through.

The *tierra caliente, tierra templada*, and *tierra fria* may all be passed through in twenty-four to thirty-six hours. The same extremes exist in the social life of the people. On one hand you are greeted with a coarse hilarity, on the other by a stilted Castilian politeness, which has been imported from the mother country of the Spaniard.

One must learn in Mexico not to take too much for granted, especially when a man meets you, and makes you a present of his residence. He will grasp your hand with ardent cordiality, and assure you that his house is yours, or that it is "always at the command of your grace." The very next man you meet may tell you that your house is number so and so, and he will be offended if you do not come and occupy it. It is a little burdensome to be the owner of so much real estate all of a sudden. One English traveler said that he had thirteen houses presented to him on the same evening. This is only the Mexican way of saying, "I am pleased to see you." They are kind, and yet they seem to be cruel. They live in rudest huts and survive on cheapest, coarsest food, yet are fond of music, and cultivate it to a high degree. Rich and poor meet together in the plazas, in the churches, and every-where else. In the cities there are no aristocratic quarters. One-story adobe houses stand beside the mansions of the rich, and often a millionaire will live on the second or third floor, while a grocery, a pulqueria, or a meat-shop occupies the ground floor. The most elegant private residence in all Mexico has a railway ticket office on one side of the entrance, and a cigar shop on the other. Such were my observations and experiences as I wandered along these old paths.

CHAPTER XVII.

FROM TOLTEC TO SPANIARD.

Ancient ruins—Pyramids—Egypt outdone—Mexican Noah—Roving tribes—Hideous images—Worship and blood—Whence came the Toltecs—Who were the Aztecs—Thieving *versus* praying—"Nine points of the law"—Mixture of races—Dusky aristocrats—Marriage and mestizos—Cortez and his religion—Ignorance not bliss—Tricks of the trade.

ALL over Central and Southern Mexico there are relics of a departed race whose annals antedate even those of the Aztecs. Antiquaries have endeavored to read their history in the stones of Tula, which was the old Toltec capital, now a place of ruins. Even modern Tula presents no special attraction. Old Tula is now overgrown and half-hidden from sight. San Juan Teotihuacan, also, is famous for its two great earthen pyramids, which stand out on the plain half a mile apart. One of them was dedicated to the sun, the other to the moon. The earth for miles around is filled with small images—*caritas*—insomuch that it seems as if these ancient people spent most of their time in making them.

The greatest, however, of all these earth pyramids is at Cholula, near Puebla, which may well take rank among the "wonders of the world." It has been claimed by some that it is only a natural hill faced in spots with adobe. I climbed up one of its ragged and sloping sides myself to a height thirty feet or more, and could trace the lines between the bricks as clearly as one can see the outlines of the books in a library. That enormous structure stands out in a level plain distinct from any hill or chain of hills. It is irregular in form, resembling far more a broken hill than a four-sided pyramid. It rises in clear view of Popocatepetl, and only about five miles from the outermost rim of its base. That pyramid is a miniature of the volcano, and it seemed to me, as I stood there, that it must have been constructed by the Toltecs when the volcano was yet at least partially active, and was designed to be an altar of sun worship, an effort of man to imitate the works of the divinity in which he believed. It is not built of stone, like those of Egypt, nor is it so lofty, but its base covers about forty-five acres, and its altitude is two hundred feet. The curling smoke of Popocatepetl rose to heaven like that of Sinai, which "burned with fire," and close beside it men offered some sort of devotions to their gods, on the summit of this *toscalli*.

Nearly all nations trace their origin away back into the dim and shadowy past, the region of myths and fables. The native Mexicans do this. They have a tradition tinctured a good deal with Scripture, and yet that tradition was there before any Mexican ever saw or heard of the Bible. According to that account, in the age of water a great flood completely covered the face of the whole earth, and all men were transformed into fishes. But there was an exception made to this by the great Deity in the case of one man and his wife, who were permitted to escape the universal fate by means of the hollow trunk of a cypress-tree. The name of the man was Coxcox, that of his wife Xochiquetzal. In course of time the waters abated a little, and their canoe grounded on the peak of Colhuacan, a high elevation of land. Here children were born to them, and greatly multiplied in numbers, but were all born dumb. Then a dove was sent from heaven, which gave them tongues, and many languages were the result. Fifteen of these sons and daughters, who were thus miraculously gifted with speech, became the heads of different tribes of people. From these descended the Toltecs, the Aztecs, and the Acolhuans.

One can see here a very marked resemblance to the Bible account of Noah and the flood. Another tradition has been preserved also among the natives, in which a man named Tezpi figures. If the first one is the genuine story the other is the apocrypha. Tezpi's fortune was better than that of Coxcox, for he was able to save, in a spacious vessel, himself and wife, besides his children and some animals, and food for their use. When the waters began to subside he sent out a vulture, that it might go to and fro over the whole country and bring him word when the dry land began to appear again. But the vulture never returned to Tezpi. It fed upon the carcasses which it found scattered over every part. Tezpi then sent out a humming-bird, among some others. After a day the humming-bird returned, bearing in its mouth a green leaf, which showed Tezpi that new verdure had come upon the earth. Then Tezpi saw that his vessel was aground on the mountain of Colhuacan, and he landed there and began the work of rebuilding cities and founding families.

It is most likely these stories are one and the same, with variations. They have been read from the Aztec picture-writings which had fortunately escaped the flames of Zumarraga. These pictures represent a boat drifting over the waters, containing a man and a woman. It must be that this Mexican tradition, confirmed by those of some other nations, is founded upon a great historical fact.

The history of Mexico reaches far back into the past, and shows that at least three distinct powers have ruled upon her soil : first, the old Toltec, which has left such wonderful ruins as those found, especially in the extreme south. The Toltec race may have included a number of aboriginal tribes. Some indications point to an Asiatic origin of these people, which is the most plausible theory. But, be this as it may, they worked out a civilization of no mean character, as their remains testify. They were also possessed of a degree of wealth that was in keeping with their architectural designs. Whatever power or grandeur the Aztec people could command had its origin in that of the Toltecs, who laid the first foundation. The Aztec empire gave way before the arms of the Spaniard, and the rule of the latter, after three hundred years, died out from its inherent corruption. Then to-day the Aztecs, somewhat modernized, are not only the most numerous class of the population, but their representative men are among the foremost citizens of the republic.

As I wandered about viewing the symbols of the ancient faith, I could not help thinking of the savage spirit which animated the breasts of these people, degrading them far below the level of the North American Indians. The ancient Hebrew bard said, " They that make them are like unto them, so is every one that trusteth in them." Go and look upon one of those ancient Aztec or Toltec idols, and you will form a low opinion of the people who worshiped at their shrines. Their deities were represented by ill-shapen images of serpents coiled upon themselves, and other hideous-looking things. These images could only have been born out of the darkest of human passions—terror, hatred, revenge, cruelty. Theirs was, indeed, a religion of blood, and thousands of human beings were annually immolated upon their altars, especially among the Aztecs, if the stories which have come to us be true.

I judge there was a descent, in both religious ideas and practices, in passing from Toltec to Aztec dominion. The Toltecs were probably sun or fire worshipers. Their numerous pyramids would seem to indicate it. If so, then theirs was a pure worship compared with their Aztec successors. The following is from the pen of Rev. Mr. Dobbins, who has made a study of this phase of Aztec life :

"The places of worship, called *Teocallis*, were pyramids composed of terraces placed one above another, like the temple of Belus, at Babylon. These were built of clay, or of alternate layers of clay and unburnt bricks, but, in some cases, faced with slabs of polished stone, on which figures of animals were sculptured in relief. One or two small chapels stood upon the summit, inclosing images of their deities. The largest known Teocalli contains four stories of terraces, and has a breadth of four hundred and eighty yards at the base and a height of fifty-five yards. These structures served as temples, tombs, and observatories.

"The Aztecs believed in one supreme, invisible creator of all things, the ruler of the universe, named Taotl—a belief, it is conjectured, not native to them, but derived from their predecessors, the Toltecs. Under this supreme being stood thirteen chief and two hundred inferior deities, each of whom had his sacred day and festival. At their head was the patron god of the Aztecs, the frightful Huitzilopochtli, the Mexican Mars. His temples were the most splendid and imposing. In every city of the empire his altars were drenched with the blood of human sacrifice.

"Cortez and his companions were permitted by Montezuma to enter his temple in the city of Mexico, and to behold the god himself. ·He had a broad face, wide mouth, and terrible eyes. He was covered with gold, pearls, and precious stones, and was girt about with golden serpents. On his neck, a fitting ornament, were the faces of men wrought in silver, and their hearts in gold. Close by were braziers with incense, and on the braziers three real hearts of men who had that day been sacrificed. The smell of the place, we are told, was like that of a slaughter-house.

"To supply victims for the sacrifices, the emperors made war on all the neighboring and subsidiary States, or in case of revolt, in any city of their dominions, and levied a certain number of men, women, and children by way of indemnity. The victims were borne in triumphal processions and to the sound of music to the summit of the great temples, where the priests, in sight of assembled crowds, bound them to the sacrificial stone, and opening the breast, tore from it the bleeding heart, which was either laid before the image of the god, or eaten by the worshipers, after having been carefully cut up and mixed with maize. In the years immediately preceding the Spanish conquest, not less than twenty thousand victims were annually immolated."

When Cortez, with his Spanish cohorts, invaded and conquered the Aztec people, Zumarraga, as before stated, destroyed all the records he could lay his hands upon. Charity requires us to admit that the act was well meant, but love of truth compels us to brand it as an outrage against history. Nevertheless, some ancient records in stone and some picture writings on a species of cloth made from the fibers of the maguey plant, fortunately escaped destruction. From these it is learned that the Toltecs appeared about the sixth century of the Christian era, but whence they came must ever remain an enigma. From the few monuments left us it seems as if they were Egyptian in character.

There also came peoples known as the Chichemecs, Nahualtecs, and Acolhuans, all of whom doubtless were varying types of the Toltec character The Aztecs appeared in the twelfth century, and remained masters of the territory until the Spanish invasion, in 1519. The latter, with their fire-arms, were too powerful for the former, and so, in 1520, the reigning Montezuma fell, and his people were left in the grasp of the invaders. With the conquest came the religion of Rome, which has held sway ever since. Spanish Catholic civilization in Mexico was an improvement on that of the ancient Aztec. Spanish thieving was better than Aztec praying, for the Aztec religion was one of blood, not of bulls or goats, but human blood. The story recorded by the early chroniclers is a strain on one's credulity. If history can be believed, from twenty to seventy thousand human beings were annually offered in sacrifice to the Aztec deities, who, if they had existed and had demanded such oblations, far more merited the title of devil than deity. By some writers these figures are made even larger. At the dedication of one great temple seventy thousand human victims are said to have been offered. When Cortez took possession of the capital, his officers reported the finding of one hundred and thirty-six thousand human skulls in one edifice! On these great dedicatory occasions the mutilated bodies of the sacrificial victims were given out for cannibal feastings. Wretched as Spanish rule has been, it was well to put an end to such butchery.

While the less numerous Spaniard even to-day dominates over the more numerous native in the best portions of the republic, yet there are places in the remote ranges of the mountains and in the low and unhealthy coast regions of Southern Mexico where native Aztecs are in the ascendency.

At the time of the conquest the land in the high, healthy regions of the country became the property of the conquerors, but in the other and less favored portions, where the foreigner feared to settle or had no inclination to do so, the Indian obtained possession of the soil and used it for raising his maize and pulque plant.

The Spanish conquerors claimed the ownership of all the territory of the Aztecs on the selfish principle that "might makes right." But there were some sections which they could never wrest from their lawful occupants. The Aztec held his ground on a principle also probably not formulated; namely, that "possession is nine points of the law." In time a reactionary law was enacted in Spain, granting to each Indian village a free possession extending about six hundred yards from the church in all directions, and in addition to this a square tract of twelve hundred yards base line. These they still own and can cultivate in common, though many prefer to work on the ranches and in the mines.

The population, especially in the capital, is greatly mixed. The census in Mexico is not taken and cannot be with any thing like the accuracy which characterizes the work in our own country. Nevertheless, rough estimates are made which approximate the truth. The Indians in many places preserve, in a degree, the habits and manners and speak the language of their ancestors. They deem it a departure from the customs of the past to wear shoes, and either go barefoot or protect their feet with leather sandals. Every thing that is purely Mexican can be seen in the capital. All the types of men are there, and all the peculiarities appear upon its streets. The conquest has entailed upon Mexico a great variety of people.

In another place I have spoken of the *leperos*, who are the descendants of the worst Spanish with the worst

Aztec blood. Recent statisticians estimate the population of the republic at ten million five hundred thousand people, of which fully one half are natives, who come under the general term of Indians. Then come the *creoles—criollos*—a people of Spanish descent, numbering one million five hundred thousand; next the *mestizos*, a mixture of white and Aztec blood, including the *leperos*, three millions. The balance of the population is made up of various nationalities, Europeans, Americans, and Africans.

The creoles are thus described by a recent writer:

"The race, which was imposed upon the country at the coming of the Spaniards, is the result of a union of these with the natives, and are to-day the representative Mexicans. They are of European parentage in part.

"At the time of the revolution, 1810-21, a term of contempt was used in speaking of the Spaniards; they were called Gachupines. The creoles were at one time the gentry, the aristocracy of Mexico, and even have aspirations in that direction now. In them we recognize the features of the Spaniard of the South, the conquerors and first colonists having been Andalusians. They are gentle and refined, yet vain and passionate, excellent hosts, delightful companions, addicted to gaming, and passionate admirers of the fair sex. The latter number among them many exceedingly lovely women, with dark complexions, large, languishing eyes, lithe and delicate forms, and dainty feet and hands.

"In their dress the creoles differ in no important particular from the French, the ladies especially conforming to the latest fashion plates from Paris, with this exception, that at morning mass, and in making unceremonious calls, they wear that graceful Spanish headdress, the *mantilla*; and the gentlemen, when on horseback, or in the country, adopt the picturesque riding costume of the mestizos. They have many lovable traits; their goodness of heart, their cheerful endurance of the petty ills of life, the respect and courtesy paid by children to their parents, and the frankness with which a stranger is received by the family, who will combine to please and entertain him—these are but few of their amiable qualities."

The creoles do not differ from Europeans or Americans in any particular appearance. The men wear stove-pipe hats, and garments to correspond. Kid-gloved hands sport gold-headed canes, and diamond studs sparkle on the bosom and flash from the fingers. The wealthier of this population live in well-furnished houses, and ride in carriages drawn by blooded horses.

The women adorn themselves in costly fabrics and expensive jewelry. Paint and powder are used so freely by many as to be very noticeable. Away back in the interior, in adobe huts, I have seen little girls with their hair "banged," and was led to wonder whether the idiotic fashion had been imported to the United States from Mexico, or whether the Aztecs had so far fallen from their former reputed greatness as to observe such a ridiculous custom.

Señor Don Garcia Cubas, a learned native Mexican, says:

"The difference of dress, customs, and language makes known the heterogeneousness of the population. . . . The habits and customs of the individuals who compose the creole division conform in general to European civilization, particularly to the fashions of the French, with reminiscences of the Spanish. Their national language is Spanish; French is much in vogue, while English, German, and Italian are receiving increasing attention. The nearest descendants of the

Spaniards, and those less mixed up with the native race in Mexico, belong, by their complexion, to the white race. The natural inclination of the mixed race to the habits and customs of their white brethren, as well as their estrangement from those of the natives, is the reason that many of them figure in the most important associations of the country, by their learning and intelligence, including in this large number the worthy members of the middle classes. From this powerful coalition the force of an energetic development naturally results, which is inimical to the increase of the indigenous race (the Indian), not a few of the natives themselves contributing to this fatal consequence, who, by their enlightenment, have joined the body I have referred to, thereby founding new families with the habits and customs of the upper classes.

"From this we may infer the gradual extinction of the native Indian race by gradual absorption into the more powerful mixed class; yet, although they are slowly melting away in the north, in the south they are increasing in number, until the country south of the capital is to a great extent in their possession."

Now let us descend a few degrees in this social scale, and we shall find two or three millions of people who live in small quarters; walk instead of ride on their journeys; wear cheap, coarse clothing, and but little jewelry, if any; protect their feet with sandals, and work hard in shop and field. These are the before-mentioned mestizos, a term which designates a large mixed population. They are the descendents of Spanish invaders who intermarried with Aztec women three centuries ago and less. The latter were baptized by the priests of the Church of Rome, who came over with Cortez, and hence the marriage was not considered a misalliance. The relation between Spain and Mexico had become very close. The latter had forced upon her the religion of the former. The conduct of Cortez, in Mexico, is an example of the spirit in which conversion was attempted in the New World. Having cast down and destroyed the altars in one of the Mexican temples, a new altar was erected, which was hung with rich mantles and adorned with flowers. Cortez then ordered four of the native priests to cut off their hair and to put on white robes, and placing the cross upon the altar, he committed it to their charge. They were taught to make wax candles, and Cortez enjoined them to keep some of the candles always burning on the altar. A lame old soldier was left by the conqueror to reside in the temple, to keep the native priests to their new duties. The church thus constituted was called the First Christian Church in New Spain (Mexico). Father Almedo, who accompanied Cortez in his expedition, explained to the Mexicans the mystery of the cross. He then showed them an image of the Virgin, and told them to adore it, and to put up crosses in their temples instead of their accursed images. When the Mexicans began to feel the power of the invader, some of the chiefs conciliated his favor by presents. Twenty native women were presented to him, who were baptized by one of the ecclesiastics, and Cortez gave one to each of his captains. These were the first Christian women in New Spain. The natives, both of India and the New World, soon perceived that one of the means of conciliating their conquerors was to make a profession of Christianity. In Hispaniola (St. Domingo and Hayti) many natives did this in order to oblige and conciliate Columbus.

While the higher classes of the Aztec people did intermarry with the invaders, the lower classes did not, which accounts for the large population of the original stock which still remains. The mestizos are the result.

of three centuries of social relations, not always in keeping with divine law, in which soldier, monk, and priest have each taken part. Of this class the author of *Mexico and the Mexicans* says:

"The mestizo, then, is properly the offspring (not always properly begotten) of white father and Indian mother. He has an inborn originality, and is the representative of national customs and peculiarities. He is a magnificent horseman; one might take him for an Arab, as, lance in hand, he rushes past upon his light steed. In the warmer regions he wears (on Sundays) a carefully plaited white shirt, wide trousers of white or colored drilling, fastened round the hips by a gay girdle, brown leather gaiters, and broad felt hat, with silver cord or fur band about it. The peasants, or *rancheros*, are usually distinguished by the *calzoneras*, or open trousers of leather, ornamented with silver, with white drawers showing through, a colored silk handkerchief about the neck, and the *zarape*—the blanket-shawl with slit in the center, resembling a herald's mantle. The women seldom wear stockings, though their dainty feet are often encased in satin slippers; they have loose, embroidered chemises, and woolen or calico shirts, while the *rebozo* a narrow but long-shawl, is drawn over the head and covers the otherwise exposed arms and breast."

The mestizo population has inherited in part the brown hue of the mother, and the greater energy and more vigorous mind of the father. When of good extraction, they are of medium size and pleasant countenance, swarthy, but fresh and animated.

As servants they are generally faithful and not over fond of the bath-tub. They constitute the middle grade of life, and have great power of physical endurance on the one side, and high ambition on the other. The well-to-do mestizo is inclined to disown his progenitors on the Indian side, and chooses all his associates on the white side of his family. After two generations the brown skin so greatly disappears that he can scarcely be distinguished from a creole.

The cultivated mestizo is the most promising element in Mexican society. In the professions, in mechanical industries, as well as in war, he occupies a front rank. Juarez and Diaz, the two most prominent men of modern Mexico, belong to this class, and out of it must come the emancipators of the country.

The Aztecs, or Indians, number six or seven millions, and are about as poor and abject as any people on earth; but they can scarcely be called wretched, for in fact they are not. As I looked upon them every-where, I thought of the old saying,

> "Where ignorance is bliss,
> 'Tis folly to be wise,"

but to apply it to these people would be a perversion of language. If they but realized their degradation and poverty fully, it might spur them to strive for some higher condition of existence. They do become restless and mourn at times their fate, especially when they learn how other people live, but their long subserviency to ecclesiastical power and civil misrule has dwarfed the body, the soul, and the mind.

The native Mexicans are not a scholarly people, but they are possessed of some ingenious traits. Along the Santa Anita canal women will take turnips and other succulent vegetables, and dexterously cut them into shapes, which resemble certain flowers, giving the petal and sepal forms quite true to nature. They color them with different bright pigments in a very artistic way. They are offered you by the señorita for a few centavos, with a coquettish smile thrown in. They will answer simply as curiosities for an hour. There are some other tricks which they play upon innocent tourists. A lady from New York was one day met on a street in the city of Mexico by a man carrying in his hands a cage containing some very beautiful birds. They were of the brightest and most delicate plumage, and were declared to be the finest of songsters. The lady, being rich, was regardless of the price asked, and at once purchased them. She took the feathered beauties to her hotel, and after a few days gave them a bath, when, to her astonishment, the paint all washed off, and she found herself the owner of some very ordinary birds. If 'she did not relish the joke, probably the Mexican did. These same unlettered people carry on only a few branches of industry, but have more than ordinary ability to produce objects purely ornamental, viewed from a Mexican stand-point. They are devoted to high, bold colors in every thing.

In the manufacture of "antiquities" they do a considerable business. These are sold to unsuspecting travelers, and are carried away to be placed in cabinets and museums. They manufacture, also, images in wax and clay, representing themselves in dress, color, and occupations, which are surprisingly true to nature.

CHAPTER XVIII.

A GRIP OF STEEL.

The great cathedral—The plunder—Bells, candlesticks, and diamonds—Cleaning up and *cleaning out*—High and low castes—Praying and thieving—Kissing the girdle—Shrines for the million—The *weakly* press—A scheme that succeeded—Under the *pallium*—Myths and fables—Guadalupe—Pilgrims—Too much altar—Idolatry—Two Marys—Self-scourgings—Horrid scenes—Confessionals—Bull-fights.

THE most attractive object in the Mexican capital is the fine old cathedral, which stands on the site once occupied by an Aztec *teocalli*, or temple, where pagans offered their human sacrifices to *Mexitli*, the war god of Anahuac. The Spanish invaders demolished the Aztec temple, and erected a church on its foundation in 1530. This first church of Cortez was succeeded by the present cathedral, which was completed in 1667, at a cost of nearly two millions of dollars. It has generally been regarded as the most sumptuous edifice of its class in America. The old ground occupied by the teocalli of Montezuma extended about ninety feet on each side at the base, and the structure decreased as it arose, until the top was only thirty feet square. On this summit was an altar, the great sacrificial stone, *El Piedra de los Sacrificios*, now exhibited in the patio of the National Museum. The cathedral is cruciform in shape, with a front on the eastern side of the Plaza Mayor of over four hundred feet, and extending back about the same distance. Close by its side—in fact, adjoining it—is the parish church, distinct from the former, known as the *Sagrario*. The interior of the cathedral, though it has been plundered several times in the exciting days of the revolutions, is yet magnificent after a certain style. It contains five naves, six altars, and fourteen chapels. Some of its pictures were painted by celebrated artists. A balustrade once surrounded the choir, of a metal so rich that an offer to replace it with one of solid silver of equal weight was refused. It is said to have weighed twenty-six tons, and to have been brought from China in the old days of Spanish dominion. The reader is under no obligation to believe this story. The high altar was once considered one of the richest in the world, and even yet retains much of its former splendor. This church is also said to contain candlesticks of pure gold so heavy that a single one is more than a man can lift readily—doubted. Its architecture is the Spanish Renaissance, elaborately decorated with stone and bronze. Within its towers are hung about half a hundred bells, varying in weight from those of a few score pounds to one, judging from its size, which, being eighteen feet high, must weigh a number of tons. I was informed that in this same cathedral there is a sacred vessel of some kind, two or three feet high, set with five thousand eight hundred diamonds, and another one set with two thousand five hundred emeralds and rubies, and that, besides these, there are here *chalices*, *cruets*, and *pixes* of solid gold, incrusted with precious stones; censers, crosses, and statues of the same precious metal, studded with emeralds, amethysts, rubies, and sapphires. I did not see any of them. There was once in this cathedral, so the story runs, a statue of the Assumption, made of solid gold, and set with diamonds, worth a million of dollars, but, if it ever did exist, it has disappeared probably in some revolution, and, like Napoleon's apostles, was sent out to help spread the gospel of civil liberty. Once there was a golden lamp here valued at seventy thousand dollars, which cost one thousand dollars to clean up, but which the Liberal troops *cleaned out* for nothing, for no one knows where it is now. The great glory of this edifice existed at a time when bishops, priests, and monks were masters of the country, and ruled it with a rod of iron. Well might they enrich a church with the spoils of a nation two thirds of whose property they owned.

Enter at any hour of the day or evening and you will see many kneeling figures—here a delicate señorita by the side of her mother or some other relative, acting as her chaperon, wearing the black mantilla, sign of her higher caste, and in whose veins flows purest Castilian blood. Beside them, in devotional attitude, will be an Indian woman, whose scant and filthy habiliments render her an object to be both avoided and pitied; and then, perhaps, within a few feet of them, a ragged peon, bearing on his shoulders a bundle of produce, all alike intent on paying their devotions to the image of the Virgin.

On feast days—and they are many in this land, when the churches are thronged with devotees, Spaniard and Aztec, rich and poor, clean and filthy, mingling together in an indiscriminate mass—the *leperos*, while pretending to great devotion, avail themselves of the opportunity to do a little pilfering. For instance, a señorita goes into a church to pray, and while kneeling before some image a ragged thief kneels close beside her, and while her eyes are upturned to the object of her worship, his eyes are watching for a parasol or *porte-monnaie;* or a gentleman bows before the altar with his hat on the floor beside him, and when his prayers are said he is hatless. The pilferer carries the hat to a second-hand clothing store or pawn-shop, and disposes of it at a price which enables him to pay the priest for forgiving the sin, besides leaving him quite a large margin of profit in the transaction.

The church was once every thing in this country. At Toluca, a very pretty city, I visited the principal church, which is rich and abounds in gildings, paintings, and images. On the public streets leading to it, and within three or four blocks of the main entrance, I counted thirty-two persons of both sexes, who, if they were in almost any city in our own country, would be liable to arrest for indecent exposure of person. I happened to be there when the bishop was on some mission, and as he came out to take his carriage saw over twenty women, most of them of the better class, surround him and vie with each other in trying to kiss his hand. Most of them succeeded. Some kneeled before him and kissed the brazen crucifix attached to the girdle which he wore around his waist. A number of these persons were young girls under twenty. The reader can imagine what a power such a man would have over these maidens were he disposed to use it. An awful tale of sin and cruelty connected with the history of convent life in Mexico will some day be revealed, when the secrets of all hearts shall be made known.

I have said that this is a land of churches. I never saw or expected to see so many ecclesiastical structures anywhere. There are church buildings enough in Mexico, it seemed to me, to accommodate a population of fifty millions of people. One will see three or four vast stone piles in almost every city within five or six minutes' walk of each other. In the city of Queretaro, with a population of about thirty-five thousand souls, I counted twenty-three churches, some of which were very large and expensive. There were at one time one hundred and sixty in the city of Mexico. I noted six large brick and stone edifices in one of my morning rambles, not one of which was over five minutes' walk from where I stood. Some of these are not in use, and are consequently falling into decay, while very few are being either built or repaired anywhere in the republic. It would seem as if the old Spanish priests for the last three hundred years thought there was nothing to do but to build churches and convents. These are numerous, while school-houses are few. It is a fact greatly to be lamented, that only a small portion of the Mexican people comparatively speaking are able to read and write. There being no very accurate census returns to which reference can be made, the number of illiterate persons is not definitely known, but the most reliable estimate that can be arrived at places the aggregate at six or seven millions—about two thirds of the entire population. Newspapers are not very common, though they do exist. In the city of San Luis Potosi, with a population of thirty-odd thousand, there are two small weekly papers, and they are *weakly* as well. Of the number of daily papers published in the city of Mexico, not one of them has a circulation of five hundred copies outside of the metropolis, and a very limited circulation within. There are cities of from twelve to twenty-five thousand inhabitants where not a single copy of any daily newspaper is subscribed for by the entire native population, and where not fifty newspapers of any kind are received at the post-office, except those addressed to residents and visitors of foreign birth.

In view of the illiteracy of the people, this is not to be wondered at. But if they do not patronize the newspapers, they do the confessional, which, I suppose, answers the same end. The eccentric Artemas Ward once remarked of a certain village in the West somewhere, that "there was no newspaper published in the place, but there was a ladies' sewing society, which answered the same purpose." The early Spanish priests were not ignorant men by any means. In fact, they represented the best learning of their day, and they employed that, as well as their cunning, in building up the Romish Church in the land of their adoption. We have an evidence of this in their method of planting churches.

They soon discovered that Mexico was deficient in water privileges, and hence, wherever there was any water, such as lakes, springs, or rivers, they took possession of the surrounding territory in the name and by the authority of the holy Catholic Church. In the first place, an image of the Virgin is carved out of gypsum, or made of some other material, which they would bury in the earth somewhere in the neighborhood of any spot where there was water or the outcroppings of silver. Then some priest or monk has a vision or pretended revelation from heaven, commanding him to lead the people to that place. Accordingly the church bell is rung at midnight, and the people leave their *jacals* and repair to the church, where the priest informs them of the will of the Virgin Mary—" Mother of God," as she is so commonly styled by them—which is, that they must go to such a place forthwith. The crowd knows no law but that of obedience, and so, with lighted candles, led by the *padre*, in his ecclesiastical robes, they start on a journey to the spot. The priest now begins a search for the image, which a very little excavating soon brings to light. He then assures his poor deluded followers that it is the wish of Mary that a church should be erected on that spot. The will of heaven, of course, must not be disobeyed, and so they go to work and erect a shrine into which to place the new-found image. Around this gathers a colony of Aztecs, and in time the rude structure is replaced by an edifice of better proportions. In time a large church, costing $100,000, possibly, would be erected there by the labors and contributions of these poor peons. The labor necessary to its erection would be demanded under the threat of eternal perdition, while the laborer who carried the stones of the building on his back received but the barest subsistence. In this way hundreds of churches all over Mexico were founded two hundred years ago.

On many a church front may be seen a picture, in bright colors, of two arms crossed—one in a sleeve, the other naked—the naked arm symbolizing the poor Mexican Indian of "untutored mind," the sleeved arm representing the Church which came professedly to clothe, feed, and shelter the people. In the great National Art Gallery of the capital there is a painting of a bishop taking off his own garments and bestowing them on the poor people, whom the artist has grouped about him. In the rear of the bishop is a basket of bread, and by his side stand three or four well-fed and sleek-looking priests. The picture was intended to show that the Church had come to clothe the naked and feed the hungry. What an outrage to compel even art to so falsify the truth! If ever any people on the earth were stripped of their clothing and starved to array the priesthood in rich and gaudy apparel, and to furnish them the "fat of the land," these poor Mexicans are that people. Where the churches are the richest and most numerous, as a rule, the people are the poorest. Their earnings have gone to the church, leaving them only rags, huts, and the cheapest and coarsest of food.

The time was when great and expensive pageantries were the order of the day. The archbishop, accompanied by the bishops, clergy, friars, and nuns, decked out in their long, glittering robes, were frequently seen parading themselves in public places—the archbishop walking under a rich *pallium*, wearing his bordered miter, leaning on a rod of pure gold, with a breastplate hanging on his bosom studded with costly gems worth thousands of dollars, to be gazed upon by an admiring and adoring throng, composed mostly of people clad in rags, and elevated but little above barbarians.

Mexico is a land of myths and fables. The credulity of the ignorant masses is wonderful. The story is told that in one of the old monasteries, once upon a time, an image of Christ was found in a greatly decayed state, which had been eaten in part by the rats and was otherwise sadly marred. The bishop passing through the parish one day saw it and ordered it to be buried at the same time and place with the first adult who should die in the community. For a long time death passed by all the grown-up people, but carried away many of the children. The piety of the people greatly increased about this time, but the multitude did not go and worship the image after the decree had been issued for its interment. At length disease attacked the adults, loud noises began to be heard in the church, and strange lights were seen precisely at the spot where the image was placed. Some claimed that they saw angels; others beheld the spirits of distinguished ancestors who had been buried there rising from their graves and praying before the image, performing penances and undergoing flagellation, while the *miserere* was sung by divine voices accompanied with celestial harps ; while others said the image actually wept and sweat drops of blood. At length the image appeared quite renovated ; the crowd then saw the blood which was exhibited to them by the curates and priests. Instead of the old crumbling figure, they beheld one entirely new, which the angels had repaired and varnished. The archbishop went in person with a long procession to conduct it to the city, where a temple was consecrated to it and which now bears its name. Such is the fantastical tradition of the image of St. Theresa.

I spent an afternoon in paying a visit to the shrine of Guadalupe, situated a little over three miles north-east from the capital of Mexico. The hill on which it is erected is called Tepeyac, and is destitute of nearly every species of vegetation, being a bold prophyritic rock. It overlooks a great part of a magnificent valley, which Humboldt declared to be one of the finest in the world. A curious tradition has this spot for its scene. It runs as follows:

"One morning an Indian, named Juan Diego, was passing along the brow of Tepeyac, on his way to the village afterward named Guadalupe, to get some medicine for his uncle, Juan Bernardino. The mother of the Saviour met him, dressed in a drapery of purple and gold, a blue veil with silver stars, a diadem of gold and diamonds, and a circle round her head more resplendent than the sun. The Virgin ordered him to go immediately to the archbishop, and tell him that she wished him to build her a church in that place. Juan Diego objected, saying he must go and cure his uncle, but the Virgin replied, that on his return he should find his relative restored to health. The Indian performed his mission; but nobody took notice of him in the episcopal palace, and he returned to his hut.

"The Virgin of Guadalupe afterward appeared to Juan Bernardino, and it is said restored him to health, and then urged Juan Diego to press her claim on the ecclesiastical authority. Juan Diego, therefore, went to see the archbishop again, who told him that he must show some proof or sign of the truth of what he said. The Indian informed the Virgin of this on her third appearance to him, and she then ordered him to gather some roses on the ridge of the hill, and carry them as a proof of her apparition. The Indian thought it impossible to find flowers on so barren a mountain, especially in winter, but she ordered him to entertain no doubts. He went after the roses, which he found at the distance of a few steps. He put them in his *tilma*, or mantel, and walked to the palace of the Miter, where, with much difficulty, he found admittance to the prelate. There, in the presence of the waiters and other religious servants of the archbishop, Juan Diego reached out his tilma, to present the proofs of the apparition of Mary : when, portentous wonder ! the form of the Virgin herself, as she had appeared to him on the Tepeyac, was impressed on the tilma of the Indian. That tilma has had a distinguished place since that in a very rich cathedral.* A convent of Capuchins was built on the hill ; and a chapel at the foot of it, in which is a spring of sulphur water, to which also is attributed a miraculous origin." Such is the superstious story of the founding of the great church of Guadalupe, which all good Mexican Catholics believe.

A vein of petroleum, too, is shown here, as affording blessed oil useful for all classes of maladies. The Aztec Indian believes that this spring rises when prayers are offered to the Virgin of Guadalupe, and subsides at the end of the prayers. Here the "faithful do congregate." The devoted worshipers of *Nuestra Señora de Guadalupe*, by which title the Virgin is called, actually

---

* That tilma, of San Juan Diego, with its pretended miraculous picture of the Virgin, is framed expensively in metal, and hangs in the High Altar of the Church at Guadalupe, where it is an object of worship. At the door of the church ribbons are sold on which are printed marks showing the exact length of the Virgin's face, with the motto, "*Medida Del S. Rostro De Maria.*"

go there on their knees from the city, in considerable numbers at certain seasons, as an act of great penance. Men go on their bare knees through the sand and heat, while women have attendants who spread down cloth of some kind before them to make the ground softer to the knee. They solicit money on their way to be bestowed as an offering to the Virgin at the end of the journey, and the greater the amount collected the greater the blessing. The road from the Plaza Mayor to Guadalupe is broad, straight, and hard. I walked out along it one day and counted nine prayer stations between the city and the shrine, which resemble chimneys left standing after a fire, only they are more ornamental. The church here contains many costly fixtures brought into Mexico, we are told, when the richly freighted galleons of Spain sent their cargoes overland from Acapulco to Vera Cruz on the way to the mother country from the far East. The cathedral of Guadalupe is, perhaps, the finest church in Mexico. It is built of brick, with four towers around a central dome. The interior is very grand. Tall onyx columns, highly polished, support lofty Moorish arches, while rich colors adorn the walls and ceilings. This church is noted for its solid silver railing, about three feet high, extending from the choir to the high altar. A good many churches have been stripped of their gold and silver ornaments, which were converted into coin to supply the sinews of war; but the shrine of the miraculous Virgin of Guadalupe, owing to its peculiar sacredness, has escaped the hands of the spoiler. The value of that altar may be estimated from the fact that an enterprising American offered to replace it with a silver-plated one of the same design, and pay a bonus of $300,000 for permission to do so.

The greatest feast day of Mexico occurs on the 12th

of December of each year, which is thus described by a Catholic paper:

"The beautiful day and sublime scenes of Tepeyacatl are brought to mind, the Queen of Heaven talking lovingly of our nation's prosperity with a poor Indian, despised by the world, but whose fidelity and purity of soul commended him to God, because in the sight of God not the rich and powerful, but humility and purity attract the favor of Infinite Mercy; thus the Queen of Heaven, who could only see as God sees, passing by the rich and powerful, designed to speak to an humble Indian, making him rich promises for our good. She wished that a temple should be erected wherein to honor her, and in which she could show forth mercy to such as should invoke her blessing and make known their petitions, and has left us, painted on the blanket (*ayate*) of the happy Indian, her precious image as Holy Mary of Guadalupe, in testimony of her partiality to us. Three hundred and fifty years have passed since these miracles took place, and the heavenly painting which the august mother of the Redeemer, and beloved mother of the Mexicans left with him as a memorial portrait, exists among us and is venerated in the magnificent temple which, in fulfillment of their vow, the piety of our fathers built to her memory, and copies of this beautiful picture are found in almost all our temples and in our homes. On this image are written, says a recent writer, in divine characters, the manifest destiny of Mexico, against which vainly cavil those who, without raising their eyes from the earth, consider themselves the supreme arbiters of the fate of countries, as though there were not over all their thoughts an infinitely wise and merciful providence on which our destiny depends. We doubt not, should she not lose it by her evil deeds, the manifest destiny of Mexico will be to receive without ceasing the distinguished benefits conferred by Divine Goodness and the special protection of the mother of the Most High."

The Mexican Catholic is an idolater. From one end of the land to the other the Virgin Mary is supreme. But, then, they have two virgins. In the many revolutions among themselves, one party, the monarchical and aristocratic, has marched to battle under the image of the Virgin of Remedies—*Nuestra Señora de los Remedios*—while the Liberal or progressive party has borne that of the Virgin of Guadalupe, so that in the various revolutions it has been Virgin against Virgin. In all the churches, large and small, may be seen these images, clad in all sorts of flashily colored garments, shod with sandals, and bedecked with tinselry. They are legion. God, the Father, and Christ, the Son, are put in the background, and Mary is every-where the prominent figure. The position she holds in the religious system of the Mexican people is well seen in an inscription over the door of the church erected on the summit of the great pyramid of Cholula: "Mary, the daughter of Heaven, the wife of the Holy Ghost, and the mother of God." Stories, the most silly and extravagant, about her are current among all who do not think.

A French priest, Emmanuel Domenech, thus described the Mexican religion as it appears in modern times under Catholic rule :

"The Mexican is not a Catholic; he is a Christian simply because he is baptized. I speak here of the masses, and not of numerous exceptions which are to be found in all classes of society. I affirm that Mexico is not a Catholic country, because the majority of the Indian population are semi-idolaters; because the majority carry ignorance of religion to the point of having no worship but that of form. Their worship is materialistic beyond any doubt; it does not know what it is to adore God in spirit. The idolatrous character, of Mexican Catholicism is a fact recognized by all travelers, and, above all, by our officers of the French army, who have traversed Mexico in every part. The worship of saints and madonnas absorbs the devotion of the people to such an extent that they have very little time left to think of God. It is in vain to look for good fruits from this hybrid tree, which makes of the Mexican religion a singular collection of lifeless devotions, of haughty ignorance, of unhealthy superstitions, and of horrible vices. It would take volumes to recount the idolatrous superstitions of the Indians, which are still in existence. On account of the lack of painstaking instruction, there appear in the Catholicism of the Indians numerous vestiges of the Aztec paganism.

"Sacrifices of turtles and other animals are still practiced by thousands of Indians in many places. In the State of Puebla they used to sacrifice, not many years ago, on St. Michael's Day, a small orphan child, or else an old man, who had nothing better to do than to go to the other world."

The worship of the Romish Church in Mexico is not only idolatrous and superstitious, but it contains an element of cruelty which reminds one of Oriental paganism in its lowest forms.

The following extract from a work, entitled *Life in Mexico*, written by Madame Calderon de la Barca, wife of the Spanish minister to Mexico, is strong proof of what has been said concerning the cruelty and superstition of modern Mexican worship. Alluding to the devotions of a certain season, she writes:

"All Mexicans, men and women, are engaged at present in what are called *desagravios*, a public penance performed at this season of the year in the churches during thirty-five days. The women attend church in the morning, no man being allowed to enter; and the men in the evening, when the women are not admitted. But both rules are occasionally broken. The penitence of the men is most severe, their sins being, no doubt, proportionably greater than those of the women, though it is one of the few countries where they suffer for this, or seem to act upon the principle that if all men had their desert who would escape whipping? To-day we attended the morning penitence, at six o'clock, in the church of San Francisco, the hardest part of which was their having to kneel for about ten minutes with their arms extended in the form of a cross, uttering groans— a most painful position for any length of time. It was a profane thought, but I dare say so many hundreds of beautifully formed arms and hands were seldom seen extended at the same time before. Gloves not being worn in church, and many of the women having short sleeves, they were very much seen.

"But the other night I was present at a much stranger scene at the *discipline* performed by men. Admission having been secured for us by a certain means, private but powerful. Accordingly, when it was dark, enveloped in large cloaks from head to foot, without the slightest idea of what it was, we went on foot through the streets to the church of San Augustine. When we arrived a small side-door opened, apparently of itself, and we entered, passing through long vaulted passages and up steep winding stairs, till we found ourselves in a small railed gallery looking down directly upon the church.

"The scene was curious. About one hundred and fifty men enveloped in zarapes (shawls), their faces entirely concealed, were assembled in the body of the church. A monk had just mounted the pulpit, and the church was dimly lighted except where he stood in bold relief, with his gray robes and cowl thrown back, giving a full view of his high, bold forehead and expressive face. His discourse was a rude, but very forcible and eloquent description of the torments prepared in hell for the impenitent sinners. The effect of the whole was very solemn. It seemed like a preparation for the execution of a multitude of condemned criminals. When the discourse was finished they all joined in a· prayer with much fervor and enthusiasm, beating their breasts and falling on their faces, when the monk stood up and, in a very distinct voice, read several passages of Scripture descriptive of the sufferings of Christ. The organ then struck up the *miserere*, and all of a sudden the church was plunged into profound darkness, all but a sculptured representation of the crucifixion, which seemed to hang in the air illuminated. I felt rather frightened, and would have been glad to have left the church, but it would have been impossible in the darkness.

"Suddenly a terrible voice in the darkness cried: 'My brothers! when Christ was fastened to the pillar by the Jews he was scourged.' At these words the bright figure disappeared and the darkness became total. Suddenly we heard the sound of hundreds of scourges descending upon the bare flesh. I cannot conceive of any thing more horrible. Before ten minutes had passed the sound became *splashing* from the blood that flowed. I have heard of these penitences in Italian churches, and also that half of those who go there do not really scourge themselves; but here, where there is such perfect concealment, there seems no motive for deception.

"Incredible as it may seem, this awful penance continued without intermission for half an hour. If they scourged each other their energy might be less astonishing.

"We could not leave the church, but it was perfectly sickening; and had I not been able to take hold of the señora's hand and felt something human beside me, I could have fancied myself transported into a congregation of evil spirits. Now and then, but very seldom, a suppressed groan was heard, and occasionally the voice of the monk encouraged them by ejaculations or by short passages of Scripture. Sometimes the organ struck up, and the poor wretches, with faint voices, tried to join in the *miserere*.

"The sound of the scourging is indescribable. At the end of half an hour a little bell was rung, and the voice of the monk was heard calling on them to desist; but, such was their enthusiasm, that the horrible lashing continued louder and fiercer than ever. In vain he entreated them not to kill themselves, and assured them that Heaven would now be satisfied, and that human nature could not endure beyond a certain point. No answer came back but the sound of the scourge, which are, many of them, made of iron, with sharp points that enter the flesh.* At length, as if they were perfectly exhausted, the sounds grew fainter, and, little by little, ceased altogether.

"We then got up and, with great difficulty, groped our way in the pitch darkness through the galleries and down the stairs until we reached the door, and had the pleasure of feeling the fresh air again. They say the

---

* The author purchased in the city of Mexico as curiosities a full set of *disciplines*, consisting of iron-toothed belts to be worn around the arms, legs, and other parts of the body; also a whip made of iron, with the "sharp points" described by the above-named author. They may be bought in any of the *portales* where people carry on traffic in second-hand goods.

church floor is frequently covered with blood after one of these scourgings, and that sometimes men die in consequence of the wounds."

These atrocities have not entirely passed away. A writer in the *New York Times*, of recent date, gives the following account of a scene witnessed in New Mexico, where the same form of religion largely prevails:

"Five men, naked to the waist, barefooted, and wearing black robes and hoods that completely concealed their identity, were seen to issue above the lodge-house of the sect, led by the master of ceremonies, who carried a genuine cat-o'-nine-tails. Two huge wooden crosses, weighing two hundred and fifty pounds each, were placed on the shoulders of two of the self-torturers. The sharp edges cut into the naked flesh, causing the blood to spurt out and drop on the ground. One penitent produced a sharp goad, which he thrust into the flesh of his fellow-sufferers from time to time, while the procession moved up the street, singing a wild chant in Spanish. Halting once, the crosses were transferred to the shoulders of others, the attendants meanwhile applying their raw-hide whips mercilessly, each blow taking off skin and bits of flesh. The procession again started and took its way to the goal, half a mile distant.

"During the march not a groan was heard, nor was a word spoken; but just before reaching the goal, a small adobe hut, an ordeal was encountered which tried the nerves of the boldest. For some distance from the door cactus plants had been strewn upon the ground, and as the barefooted cross-bearers approached it one hesitated. Instantly half a dozen whips descended upon his bare shoulders, and, with a bound, he sprang into the thorny plants, his every step and the footsteps of his followers being marked with blood. As the torture grew more terrible, the chant grew louder, and the thongs fell with more vigor. Reaching the door of the house, the procession was lost sight of, a sentinel guarding the entrance, and only broken whips and poles and blood bearing witness of what occurred within. Issuing from the house, the procession reformed and turned to their house of worship. And so the horrifying exercises continued, one band of penitents succeeding another until night, when a grand procession and chant wound up the exercises for the day. During these marches to and from the house of refuge, the scene at times was too sickening for description. Powerful men submitted their bodies to the most merciless flagellation, until, in some instances, the bare muscles were seen quivering at every blow. The whole proceeding was a savage attempt to honor the Easter season."

One of the interesting places in the city of Mexico is the Church of Santo Domingo, where I saw an image of the dead Christ, representing him immediately after the crucifixion, at full length, lying in a regular bed. The face was bedaubed with red paint, to give it the appearance of blood. A white cotton spread came up to his chin. The feet, also spotted with red paint, projected from under the bed-clothes at the foot. On a stand, at the head of the bed, two or three candles were burning. A couple of women, dressed in black clothing, sat by the bed-side as watchers. Near by was a box to receive the offerings of the devotees.

I sat within a few feet of this image for the space of an hour, and witnessed a motley concourse of people, old and young, rich and poor, passing by and paying to it their reverential devotion. Many of the women kissed and hugged those "bloody" feet, stroking them with their hands soothingly, as a mother would stroke the injured limb of her crying child. If this be worship, then it is the coarsest and most repulsive conceivable. Many of these persons were from the upper walks of life. They were doubtless sincere—let us be charitable—but the superstition and ignorance are most appalling.

The churches are supported mostly by the women, who dress in black. Gray and blue are badges of the lower class. As people rise in the world they don the black. Besides, the finer the material the more indicative of higher social standing. So it has come to be a proverb that the "women in black keep up the Church in Mexico." Most of these old churches would be dark and gloomy enough were it not for the many candles which the faithful keep burning. Go into one at whatever hour of the day or evening you choose, there are always many worshipers upon their knees murmuring their Spanish prayers, or pouring their heart secrets into the ears of the *padres* at the confessional gratings. One is almost amused at the fantastic colorings in the churches. The taste of these Spanish fathers ran riot along this line. The Holy Family, together with many saints held sacred in the calendar of the Church, are clad in all the colors of the rainbow. The images of the Saviour are generally bloody and lugubrious, often with blue hair and fanciful-colored legs, tissue-paper roses ornamenting the wounds in his side and hands, while from the heart of Mary protrudes a dagger.

At the risk of wearying the patience of the reader with so many pictures of degradation, I must ask, Is it to be wondered at that such appalling spectacles should present themselves under the circumstances?—a land where the Church favored despotism, and despotism in turn upheld the Inquisition, which condemned men for thinking that God ought to be obeyed before man! What should be expected from a people who for three centuries have been under such rule? A convert to the newer faith in Mexico writes:

"The political catechism of this blended tyranny taught that the king ought to be obeyed blindly, while the religious one declared that the 'pope' was infallible, and that whosoever did not obey him would be lost forever. Under that teaching men did not even dare to think, and, morally, became abject slaves. Mexico, at the end of the last century, seemed closed to the Gospel, but fifty years of independence have completely changed the situation.

"After our emancipation from Spain's tyrannical government, having to seek among ourselves for the true elements of political life, we keenly felt the sad prostration of our country, resulting from its former abject condition. Suddenly thrown upon our own strength, and not possessing the needed knowledge to enable us to act wisely, we were hardly able to move forward in the path of progress. We could realize our unfortunate condition, but knew not its cause. We wanted to progress, but would stumble and fall without knowing why. The veil of our inexperience hid from our view what ought to have been easily discerned. We longed to be free, but liberty, like a *mirage*, would vanish from us as we thought we approached it. The chains that had bound us to tyranny had not yet been wholly broken. We had achieved our independence from Spain's monarchs, but we had not yet obtained religious liberty. Rome had not yet released its prey. At last, by sad experience, we found in the Roman Church the real cause of the impotence of our efforts to be free. Then commenced a gigantic war against the dark fanaticism caused by the errors of the Church of Rome. Multitudes among us wished to free Mexico from that Roman tyranny that in the course of three centuries had taken such deep root in our soil. We freed ourselves from Spain's monarchs after eleven years of war, but it has needed fifty years of contests, of heroism, and an army of martyrs, to shatter the political power of the Roman Church in Mexico."

Mexico has no Sabbath. Her priests have taught the people that the pope has the right and power to declare that the sanctification of the Lord's day shall continue only for a few hours, and that any servile work may be done on that day. But where did the Roman pontiff obtain power to do away with God's law?

In the confessional the priests are instructed to ask whether any 'work is done on fast or feast days, but no inquiry is made about work on the Sabbath. The latter may be violated because it is only a law of God, but the former must be kept sacred because it is a law of the Church. The poor Mexican has been taught that to work for churches and monasteries was not forbidden by divine law, for almost all the churches and convents claim to be poor; therefore, men could lawfully work for them on the Lord's day—*domingo*—or they could reap their grain, or plow and till the earth, providing the fruits were given to the Church. Under such instructions, it is not to be wondered at that the seamstress could sew, the butcher slaughter his animals, the baker make his bread, the hunter hunt, and the fisher fish. Their religion does not interdict any sort of business or amusement, however hilarious, on that sacred day. Long ago it was decreed by the Church that upon the entrance of a prince or nobleman into a Spanish city it was lawful on Sundays to exhibit the bull-fights, because such marks of joy are morally necessary for the public weal. As New Spain, the former title of Mexico, was a copy of old Spain, the bull-fight has ever been popular. This brutal amusement always

occurs either on a gala day or on Sunday afternoon. One can imagine the unsacredness of the day when such a scene as the following is the principal attraction. A recent writer, from a personal view of one of these hilarious sports on a hacienda, says:
"A bull-fight costs no more than a ball, although the best *toro* on the place be sacrificed, and the pay of professional fighters is about the same that skilled musicians would receive for dancing music. Usually a horse or two is also killed in the encounter, but these are the aged and worthless ones, selected for the purpose because their days of usefulness are over. After the *matadors*, in their Spanish doublets and circus spangles, have distinguished themselves by first tormenting the bull to rampant fury and then dexterously killing him, the dead beast is turned over to the rabble, who proceed to roast him whole, having already dug a hole in the ground and built a fire in it, enjoying a grand barbecue under the open sky, while their betters are feasting on more dainty viands in the great hall of the mansion. On the evening after a bull-fight a ball is always confidently expected to come off in the same 'ancestral hall' where the dinner was held, which the peons have made haste to decorate with green branches and garlands of flowers, till it looks like an immense arbor. The whole motley crowd of the day-time grace the festive scene by their presence—the peons squatted upon the floor, wrapped in their blankets, too placidly happy even for speech; agents of the hacienda; *dipendientes*, house servants, coachmen, bull-fighters, and the priest of the establishment, while guests and family occupy one end of the hall in the capacity of audience to their numerous entertainers. The servants and peons perform the dances peculiar to their class and country, interspersed with quaint folk-songs, and, after each effort,

make the most respectful salaam to the 'audience,' entreating the aristocrats to accept thanks for the honor of their attention."

At Orizaba, while I was there, a bull-fight was held on the Sabbath for the purpose of raising money with which to pay for the altar-railing of a new church. Bulls, horses, and services were all donated for the occasion!

The blazing summit of Mount Orizaba once shone like a star through the darkness of the night, gaining for it the Aztec name Citlaltepetl—" The Mountain of the Star."

May another Star yet shine more effulgently on this land so long held in darkness and superstition as in a grip of steel!

CHAPTER XIX.

THE MARCH OF SCOTT'S ARMY.

Feasts and flowers—Tomb of the brave—From mountain to sea—The hero of Chippewa—The grim castle—Doomed city—Rain of death—A sad wail—On to victory—Cerro Gordo and Perote—Town of the angels—Pathway of conquest—Flanking the foe—Battle after battle—Molino del Rey—Storming of Chapultepec—Entrance into the capital—A weak foe—A mistake—Cruel fate.

THE festival days in Mexico are very numerous, and are particularly observed in the larger cities. It is almost impossible for one not a native to keep track of them. There were several *fête* days in honor of somebody or something during my stay in the capital. One of them occurred on the 5th of April, when the whole population seemed to be given up to hilarity. The streets and plazas were crowded with all sorts of people in gala costumes. The great display of flowers offered for sale at almost every corner was a noticeable feature of the day, especially so in the markets. This is a land of flowers, and they are surprisingly cheap, as any one will learn who enters a *zócalo* to make a purchase. The soil, the climate, as well as the popular taste, are alike favorable to their culture. Think of purchasing a bouquet composed of thirty or forty common blush and white roses for twenty-five cents! Here you will see lilies with leaves a foot or more in length, and breadth to correspond.

The natives not only understand the science of floriculture, but they display great taste in the arrangement of flowers for vases and baskets. The brown-skinned señora is rather handsome, too, when her ebon tresses are adorned with richly-colored tropical blossoms. On gala days, or at their special social and religious festivals, the atmosphere is often made heavy with the odor of these choice floral beauties massed in clusters, pyramids, columns, etc. Just at that time my own patriotism was stirred, and I stepped into a *zócalo* and bought a very large and beautiful bouquet, for which I paid thirty-seven and a half cents, to take with me to the American cemetery, that I might place it on the monument erected to the memory of the soldiers who fell in the war of 1847, when General Scott took the capital.

This burying-place is tolerably well cared for—quite as much so as one might expect, seeing its owner, the United States government, is so far away from it. Of course some one is paid for looking after it, but just how much looking is done I cannot say. There are a number of other graves and tombs within the inclosure, where reposes the dust of a number of American private citizens who have died in Mexico. The chief attraction to me at this visit was the monument erected by Congress to mark the resting-place of the brave men who fell in battle, or succumbed to fatal disease, in that celebrated campaign. The following inscription tells the story. On one side it reads:

"To the Memory of the
AMERICAN SOLDIERS
Who Perished in this Valley
in 1847,
Whose Bones, Collected by
Their Country's Orders,
Are here Buried."

On the opposite side are the names of the battle-fields:

"Contreras.   Molino del Rey.
Cherubusco.   Chapultepec.
            Mexico."

While General Taylor was operating on the line of the Sierra Madre, the government of the United States ordered General Scott to attack Mexico on the east. That order was issued in November, 1846. But many months must elapse before he could put his plans into execution.

The army of Santa Anna was encamped at San Luis Potosi when a large number of Taylor's best troops were sent to join the army of General Scott in the attack on Vera Cruz. Doubtless it was this movement which emboldened the great Mexican captain to march upon Taylor at Buena Vista. Such a depletion of the forces of the latter would seemingly render a victory to Mexican arms both possible and probable, and a victory of some kind was what Mexico and Santa Anna both wanted at that time. The advance of the Mexican chieftain and the rout of his army, in 1847, have been elsewhere described. There was no prospect of any forward movement of the army under Taylor in the direction of San Luis Potosi, the expediency of which the general himself doubted, in view of the long marches through a hot and barren region which such an advance would necessitate. The wily Mexican commander was not blind to the fact, however, that his own troops could do what Taylor's could not in such a climate. Mexico now assembled her armies on the line between her capital and the principal sea-port of Vera Cruz. It was reasonable to suppose that her enemy would attack her on the front. Cortez himself had entered the dominions of the Aztecs at this very point, and fought his way to their capital along the passes of the great mountain chain which bends off toward the eastward.

General Winfield Scott was selected as the most fitting person to command this army of invasion. He had great fame as a soldier. The laurels he had won at Chippewa and Niagara had not entirely faded. So General Taylor was left on the defensive merely, while his superior in office should conduct active operations on another theater of the war. To prepare a suitable armament for this campaign was left almost wholly to General Scott. The first thing to be accomplished was the capture of the city of Vera Cruz and the renowned castle built for its defense in the harbor, if a mere roadstead can be called a harbor. Though the order was issued in November, 1846, it was not until February, 1847, that the soldiers of his command began to assemble.

The point selected for the rendezvous was the island of Lobos, about twelve miles from the eastern coast, between Tampico and the city to be assaulted. Lobos has been called one of the "gems of the Blue Gulf." It is a small coral islet, not more than three miles in circumference, a spot where grow the choicest tropical fruits, and where the climate is most delightful. Here were gathered the land forces designed to invade and complete another conquest of Mexico. Here, in these blue waters of the great gulf, were the ships of war that should take part in the struggle. That naval assemblage and outfit were not as great as General Scott desired them to be, but were the largest which the United States had ever employed in any of its wars. On the north Mexico had been humiliated by the great victory of General Taylor at Buena Vista, the tidings of which reached the army of General Scott at this particular juncture of affairs. It could not do otherwise than greatly increase their zeal. Mexico was not only humiliated, but weakened by the reverses which had overtaken her armies, and must have been dispirited when confronted at her strongest point, the castle of San Juan d'Ulloa, by a naval force of such magnitude as to dwarf her own into utter insignificance.

It was on the 5th of March, 1847, that the harbor of

THE MARCH OF SCOTT'S ARMY. 245

Vera Cruz saw assembled there a vast fleet of armed vessels, whose canvas darkened the skies. They were the frigates *Cumberland* and *Raritan*, with forty-four guns each; the sloops of war *Falmouth, John Adams,* and *St. Mary,* twenty guns each; the steamer *Mississippi,* ten guns; the *Princeton,* nine guns; brigs *Porpoise, Somers, Lawrence, Perry,* and *Truxton,* ten guns each; in all two hundred and seventeen guns, and an army of thirteen thousand men. With this combined land and naval force General Scott had come to reduce the fort and capture the city. .

The castle of San Juan d'Ulloa is a large, round, stone fortress, of a dingy yellow, built upon a small island out in the bay, about half a mile from the city. There it was that Juan de Grijalva, one of the earliest adventurers in the service of the king of Spain, is said to have landed, and where he found a temple in which human sacrifices were offered to the Aztec deities. The Spaniards understood these offerings to be made in accordance with the command of the kings of Acolhua, one of the provinces of the Aztec empire. The term Ulloa is supposed to be a corruption of the former name, Acolhua.

General Scott first reconnoitered the position, and, though he was in command of powerful war vessels for the times, he evidently thought it too much of an undertaking to begin the attack by the bombardment of the fortress. He therefore decided to sail to the southward of the city, and there, between the island of *Sacrificios* and the mainland, under cover of his guns, debark his troops, which was done without the loss of a single man. The landing was unopposed by the Mexican general in command of Vera Cruz.

The Mexican force in the city numbered only about four thousand men aside from the castle, which contained about one thousand. The castle was a proud one. It is rumored to have cost Spain $13,000,000. It mounted a great many guns of large caliber: ten eighty-four-pounders, ten sixty-four-pounders, ten fifteen-pounders, eight twelve-pounders, thirty-seven brass and twenty-five iron twenty-four-pounders; besides many mortars and a vast magazine of ammunition. That old castle had stood a great many years and had come through many a siege. In 1821 Vera Cruz, with all its boasted strength, was besieged and taken by the Revolutionists, and in the following year was retaken by the Spanish troops. From September, 1823, to November, 1825, it was bombarded three times by the Spaniards, then in possession of the city. In 1825, the castle itself was captured by the Mexican forces, and the city enjoyed a season of repose. In 1838 both castle and city were taken by the French. Poor Vera Cruz has paid dearly for the privilege of being a seaport city. Between the guns of naval squadrons and the *vomito*, which may be said to be perennial there, life is hardly worth living. Yet they do live, and take great pride in their city. The American commander was, perhaps fortunately, not compelled to test the strength of the castle. There was a better way. After landing his forces on the south side of the city, he formed them in a semicircle in its rear, at a suitable distance, so that Vera Cruz was completely girt about, with an army in the rear, and ships of war in front. Its capitulation could only be a question of time.

On the 22d of March the Mexican commander was summoned to surrender. This, like a brave man, he refused to do. Then General Scott opened his land batteries on one side, the ships opened theirs on the other, and for four days these guns belched forth their deadly fires, pouring a constant shower of shot and shell on the devoted city, causing a most fearful destruction, not only to property, but to life. In vain did the foreign consuls plead for a cessation of hostilities. Scott's only demand was surrender. On the morning of the 26th a flag of truce was sent to the American general offering terms of capitulation. It may have been foolish on the part of the Mexican general and governor, Morales, to attempt to withstand the shock of such an armament as that which assaulted him, but it was heroic. Vera Cruz fell, but was not dishonored. I will let a Mexican historian describe these terrible scenes :

"All was over with Vera Cruz. In vain had four or five hundred of her inhabitants perished. In vain had six hundred soldiers shed their blood, and four hundred of them been killed. The graves of those brave men were not to be dishonored by the conqueror! ... In vain had the city suffered the ravages of six thousand seven hundred projectiles of the weight of four hundred and sixty-three thousand pounds thrown into it by the enemy. Day dawned on the 29th. At eight in the morning the artillery saluted the national flag, which was displayed at Ulloa and on the land batteries, with the last honors which the unfortunate but gallant garrison would be able to pay to their standard. The fatal hour arrived. The soldiers, in tears, divested themselves of their accouterments; and while stacking their arms some broke them in pieces to avoid surrendering them to the enemy.

"The sacrifice was consummated, but the soldiers of Vera Cruz received the honor due to their valor and misfortunes—the respect of the conqueror."

That the picture may not be deemed overdrawn, let one of our historians speak :

"Within the city the effect of the American fire was terrible and destructive in the extreme. The earth shook at every discharge. Broad sheets of flame appeared to leap forth from the batteries of the assailants. Smoking ruins, crashing roofs and buildings, attested the severity of the bombardment. The firm pavements were thrown up in masses, and deep ridges plowed the streets. The iron gratings of the balconies were torn from their fastenings, and casements and lattices shivered in pieces. Wailing and lamentation were heard in every part of the town. Fathers were stricken down upon their own thresholds, and mothers smitten at the fireside as they leaned over the helpless offspring, who clung to them in vain for protection. Stout manhood and decrepit age, the weak and the strong, fell dead together."*

The objective point of Scott's movement was the city of Mexico, and as soon as possible the victorious column was headed toward the capital, about three hundred miles distant. The Mexicans were "cast down, but not destroyed." They had the advantage of defending themselves in their own mountain passes, and on grounds with which they were familiar. An army of thirteen thousand men occupied the heights of *Cerro Gordo*, seventy miles from the coast. Santa Anna was in command in person of the national forces at this stronghold. But the attack was made on the 18th of April, the heights were stormed and carried, and once more the Mexicans were forced to surrender. Their position was a strong one, fortified, as they were, on hills of considerable elevation, the principal one being Cerro Gordo, which towered far above the others, rendering the attack exceedingly hazardous. The struggle was severe and determined on both sides, continuing through two days. In this action General Scott lost, in killed and wounded, four hundred and thirty-one men, of which number thirty-one were officers. The

* Jenkins's " Hist. Mex. War."

THE MARCH OF SCOTT'S ARMY. 249

Mexican loss was great. Whèn the battle was nearly at an end, and the result certain, Santa Anna fled on the back of a mule, leaving behind a part of himself, his cork-leg, and a chest containing $16,000 in silver coin.

The city of Jalapa next surrendered, to a division of the army under General Twiggs, without firing a gun. Jalapa knew she had had, and could continue to have, her revenge on the world in the use of her old-fashioned drug, jalap, which is produced there from a native root. If the soldiers who composed the invading army had all been compelled to *take jalap* when they were boys, certainly they were ready to take it now, that they were men, without compulsion. The city is on the old stage-route between Vera Cruz and the capital, about sixty miles north-westerly from the former, and is a favorite resort for health and pleasure seekers in this part of the republic. It is now connected by rail with the sea-port. Next followed, in quick succession, the fall of Perote, a walled city, with its great stone castle, said to be one of the strongest in the country at the time. The spirit of resistance was now so weak that Perote was also given up without an effort at defense. This point is about four thousand feet above the level of the gulf. The invading army had to feel its way through a hostile country, whose mountain passes were the natural hiding-places of guerrilla bands, so that it moved slowly. On the 15th of May, General Worth's division entered Puebla, a city of sixty thousand inhabitants, without meeting any appreciable opposition. Here, in Puebla—*La Puebla de los Angeles*—the "town of the angels," sometimes called the "City of a Hundred Churches," where its ranks were re-enforced by fresh troops from the coast, the army rested for many weeks. Puebla is an old city, founded in 1531. It lies in plain sight of Popocatepetl, which rises in majesty south-westerly of the city, towering above it in solemn grandeur. It is the capital of the State of the same name, and lies in a beautiful valley over seven thousand feet above the level of the sea. Puebla is fair to look upon. The population is now about seventy-five thousand. It is the seat of a famous college, and has a museum of considerable note. Among its industries may be mentioned factories for making cotton cloth, porcelain, and glass. It also has an iron foundry and flouring mills. The Mexican onyx works, too, are famed. It is the second city, in point of wealth and importance, in the republic. The streets are broad and well-paved, the churches numerous, grand, and imposing. Its plaza and alameda have an air of brightness which renders them inviting. I visited the college, and wandered for hours through its halls, corridors, library, and garden, impressed with the scenery and associations of the place. Cholula, with its great pyramid, the largest in the world, is only ten miles from Puebla.

In August the army marched toward the capital. The route selected by General Scott was that followed by Cortez, which lay between the two great snow mountains, Popocatepetl and Iztaccihuatl. The first point of importance was at Pennon, less than a dozen miles from the city of Mexico. The place was strongly fortified by Santa Anna. General Scott might have taken it at a great loss of life, but concluded to pass it on the right. He took a direction south of Lake Chalco, and thus compelled the Mexican army to evacuate Pennon. At Contreras a severe battle was fought on the 19th of August, in which the rout of Santa Anna's army was complete. His loss in killed and wounded was estimated at two thousand men; many prisoners were taken, with arms and munitions of war. Among them two pieces of artillery were found, which had been captured from

THE MARCH OF SCOTT'S ARMY. 251

General Taylor on the field of Buena Vista. About four thousand five hundred men of Scott's army were engaged in this conflict, only sixty of whom were killed. The Mexican loss was unknown. Thus another defeat was added to the long list. Still they were as determined as soldiers could be under the circumstances. The battle of Cherubusco followed the next day, and again these defenders of their soil were put to flight before Scott's victorious troops. This was a hard-fought battle, in which more than a thousand Americans, including seventy-six officers, were killed and wounded. The Mexican loss was reported at seven thousand in killed and wounded.

The American general had now reached his objective point—his army was in the vicinity of the capital. The scenes were exciting. That army was being rapidly depleted under the influence of disease and the bullets of the Mexicans, and he was forced to press forward rapidly to final victory. Just then an armistice was requested by the Mexican commander, which was granted. Scott's whole effective force was now reduced to eight thousand five hundred men. He was in the midst of a hostile people. But it came to the knowledge of the American commander that Santa Anna only wanted an armistice for the purpose of strengthening his works and recruiting his army, and not for peace, and hence, on the 8th of September, General Scott issued orders to advance to the capture of Chapultepec. Near the castle stood Molino del Rey (king's mill), then used as a manufactory of arms, and where the Mexicans were in great force. A battle followed, in which the Americans lost nearly a thousand of the rank and file, and fifty-nine commissioned officers. The Mexicans lost in this engagement, in killed and wounded, three thousand men. The battle of Molino del Rey, next to Buena Vista, is said to have been the severest and bloodiest engagement of the war. Here it was that General Worth lost a quarter of his entire division. About three thousand five hundred Americans engaged in terrific combat more than ten thousand of the enemy. Of the fifty-nine officers who fell, eighteen died on the field. The Mexican loss in killed and wounded was reported at two thousand, besides losing a thousand who were taken prisoners. The war was approaching its close—both armies realized the fact—and hence the terrible onslaught of the one and the heroic resistance of the other.

The principal obstacle now to be overcome was Chapultepec, the Gibraltar of Mexico—"Grasshopper Hill," in plain English. The castle is built upon a rocky eminence about one hundred and fifty feet in height, and is to Mexico what the famous rock castle is to old Edinburgh, and reminds one of it. Within its fortifications once stood the palace of the viceroys, under the old Spanish *régime*. The only practicable ascent to the castle was on the west and south-west sides, which were very rugged and steep. Within its defenses were said to be six thousand men, under command of General Bravo, a distinguished officer. On the 12th of September General Scott determined to begin an assault. Up to this hour the Mexicans had lost every battle, from Palo Alto, on the Rio Grande, to Buena Vista, on the line of the Sierra Madre, and from the capture of Vera Cruz to Molino del Rey.

General Twiggs was sent to the south of the city to make a feint and draw attention to that quarter, while early in the morning the batteries opened their fire on the castle, continuing the bombardment throughout the day. On the morning of the 13th, storming parties advanced to the attack. General Pillow began the ascent on the west side, in the face of a deadly fire of cannon and musketry. Slowly over rocks and chasms the advance was made. Mines had been laid, but so hard pressed were the defenders by the assaulting column that they had no time to spring them. Their works were strong, but the day to them was lost. Scott's troops were within the walls—Chapultepec had fallen! This lost, all was lost, for the castle commanded the city. On the night of the 13th, after the fall of this stronghold, Santa Anna's army evacuated the capital, and on the following day, the 14th of September, 1847, General Scott entered it with his army. The bands played "Hail Columbia" in the Plaza Mayor, and the flag of the United States floated over the "Halls of the Montezumas." At the storming of Chapultepec the Mexican loss was severe—1,000 were killed, 1,500 wounded, and 800 prisoners were taken. The American loss was 130 killed and 704 wounded.

The war was ended. Our troops held the position they had gained until in time the commissioners of the two governments met at Guadalupe de Hidalgo, and signed the treaty by which the United States came into possession of what is now our great South-west.

As I stood on the heights of Chapultepec and looked down on the surrounding plain, it seemed almost marvelous that it could have been taken by a force so small as that which assaulted it. The explanation lies in the fact that the Mexicans were inherently weak, the soldiers were poorly disciplined, and the people behind the army were not united. Their generals were jealous of each other, thinking far more of themselves than of their country, and on almost every battle-field they were rivals for place and power. The rank and file were poorly armed, poorly clothed, poorly fed, and worse paid. It was a victory to the American arms, but a victory over a weak antagonist.

General Grant, who learned his first lessons of war in Scott's campaign in Mexico, is reported to have stated, when standing on the parapet at Chapultepec, in one of his visits to that country, that General Scott made a mistake in his march upon the capital. Had he carried Pennon, and gone around the city to the northward, he could have captured Chapultepec as easily as he did, and at the same time avoided the series of battles at Contreras, Cherubusco, and Molino del Rey, thus saving the lives of thousands of his troops. The chief point was to gain the castle, for with that in his possession the country would be conquered and the war ended.

Now that forty years have passed away since the victories of Scott and Taylor, it is no reflection upon American patriotism to ask, For what purpose was all this bloodshed? The answer is mainly that American slavery might have more soil in which to take root and grow strong. Does it not seem strange that these people of a sister republic should be slaughtered on their own territory, that helpless women and innocent children should be made to feed the flames of war by laying down their lives thus to fasten the chains of slavery more securely on the limbs of American Negroes? Such is fate.

I placed the bouquet on the broad base of the monument directly under the names, "Contreras," "Cherubusco," "Molino del Rey," "Chapultepec," "Mexico," for however unrighteous that war the brave men of the army who marched with General Scott from Vera Cruz to Chapultepec were not its authors, but merely its agents. I could, with equal sympathy, have placed another on the monument erected in the grounds of the castle in honor of the equally brave men who fell in its defense at this battle, which virtually terminated the march of Scott's army.

CHAPTER XX.

FROM SEA-COAST TO MOUNTAIN CREST.

Variety and change—Flowers and birds—Beauty and death—Yawning chasms—Perpetual snow—Toward the crest—Popocatepetl—Silver and gold—Agave plantations — Plains of Salazar—Strange meeting—The maguey and its uses — A city on a hill—A curse—How I was treated—Markets and marketing — Religion and sport — "Doing the bear," or courting under difficulties — A fatal meeting of two lovers—Home life.

MEXICO is noted for its extensive table-lands—the most remarkable of all the tropical plateaus on the globe. They stretch from the sixteenth degree of north latitude, with a varying breadth, to the limits of the tropical zone.

I have elsewhere spoken of this land as being one of great extremes in its population. Considered geographically it is pre-eminently so. When the traveler approaches Mexico from the ocean, he first comes to the low hot lands which border it, where the climate is tropical. These are the *tierras calientes* in Mexican physical geography. Extensive sandy plains, on which grow only the mimosa and prickly-pear, stretch away before you in one part, while broad savannas, darkened with the shade of palm groves, lie before you in another. Along the water-courses the landscape fairly glows with the exuberant splendor of equinoctial vegetation. The high, steep banks of the streams approach near to each other, and the graceful branches of the cotton-wood, the fan-like leaves of the palmetto, the velvet foliage of the magnolia, together with the long, trailing moss which hangs from their boughs, unite to form one splendid picture of nature which is often beautifully mirrored in the still, clear waters beneath them. Away from these the soil in many sections is parched and quite barren. Vines and creepers of various orders festoon the branches of stately trees; brilliant-hued flowers give color to the landscape, and wild roses, honeysuckle, and jasmine impart their delicate fragrance to the air. Amid this dense foliage of leaf, bud, and flower, humming-birds of gorgeous plumage and butterflies of resplendent wing find their paradise. Here is heard the notes of the *clarine*, not the handsomest, but the sweetest, of all the feathered songsters of this tropical clime. But, alas! this region confirms the couplet in the old hymn,

"We should suspect some danger nigh
Where we possess delight."

Along with this beauty of color, richness of fragrance, and sweetness of song, malarial influences are generated by the decomposition of the rank vegetation, which renders the *tierras calientes* the most unwholesome sections of the globe. From vernal to autumnal equinox this part of Mexico is the home of fevers, which are most destructive to human life.

Here the season is perpetual, flowers are ever in bloom, green fruits and ripe hang on the tree boughs the year through, and the farmers' crops follow each other in endless succession. The hot lands have their limit at about sixty or seventy miles back from the coast, where the traveler begins to ascend into a region of purer and healthier atmosphere. Now the vegetation changes its character continually. The fig, the broad-leaved banana, the sugar-cane, the vanilla, indigo, and other plants belonging to the low hot lands disappear. An elevation of four or five thousand feet is soon attained, where tropical verdure has given place to the flora of the *tierra templada*, or temperate land. The malarial influences of the coast cannot rise into this region of mists and clouds. The oak, the cypress, the camphor and the coffee tree have come into the field of vision now. The railroad sweeps around the base of mighty mountains, which a thousand years ago poured their fires in vast deluges on the plains below. Now on your right and then on your left great chasms yawn, adown whose precipitous sides one may look a thousand feet. Still upward you go to where fields, waving with the golden wheat or glossy-leaved corn, are interchanged with plantations of the agave, which attains its greatest perfection on these table-lands. In this zone the thermometer indicates a temperature of about seventy to eighty degrees during the day in the summer, but sinks to about fifty or sixty degrees in the night-time. Our course is onward and upward. There is a region still higher and colder, called the *tierra fria*, or cold land. This is the last and highest of the terraces of Mexico.

The line of perpetual snow is reached at about fifteen thousand feet, but at ten thousand the temperature becomes almost too cool for comfort. If the tourist chooses to continue his journey on upward toward the summits of the mountains he will pass through every variety of climate and every zone, from that of tropical heat to the regions of perpetual snow and ice—from where the palm-tree waves its banners in the sultry breeze to the lichen-covered rocks whose jagged outlines fret the southern skies.

I felt that I could not leave Mexico until I had placed my feet on the highest accessible point short of the summit of her greatest snow mountain. The latter I did

17

not wish to ascend, for good and sufficient reasons. An opportunity was offered to go west over the National Railway, in a special train, toward Morelia, to spend a few days on the western Sierras. Leaving the Colonia station at the capital in the early morning, we passed the castle of Chapultepec, on our left, just as the signal-gun was fired, and in a very short time were well out of the valley of Mexico, and were beginning to ascend the slope toward the Pacific Ocean. The grade soon grew very steep, and the iron horse had to labor hard to overcome the influence of the earth's gravitation. When we had reached the Rio Hondo we were a couple of hundred feet above the domes of the city, and had entered the foot-hills that bound the Vale of ancient Anahuac. The first stopping-place was Huisquelucan, which they pronounced "whisky-lookin'." The scenery here is very fine. The railway track crossed great ravines, which are spanned by massive iron bridges, with roaring brooks below you. But up we climb from point to point, sometimes traveling many miles around the head of a barranca too wide and deep to bridge, and then coming back around a great curve to the starting-point again—a railroad above you, a railroad below you, but all the same railroad, so that it has been said, playfully, the passenger on the platform of the rear coach in the train can light a cigar from the fire of the engine as it sweeps by him.

From these high points one can look down on the valleys below, where many small farms, divided by long hedges of the maguey, dot the landscape. These Aztec people raise corn and vegetables for the city market, and cultivate the maguey plant for the pulque which it produces. The land in the valleys and deep gulches is rich enough, but the mountain sides are exceedingly barren. As in other mountainous regions before described, little is seen beside the stunted nopal-cactus, mesquite, and some species of dwarfed pine. The view of the distant valley of Mexico, with its lakes, is simply grand, made all the more so from the blue mountain ridges far to the eastward in the dim distance. At last we reached the summit, which is about ten thousand feet above the gulf level. In ascending the eastern side the barrenness is marked, but almost the instant you approach the edge of the plains of Salazar the whole aspect changes. The sterility, the stunted growths, the desolate look, are gone, and greenness and thrift have come in their stead. Why? Because after crossing the summit we enter a region touched by the moisture-laden breezes of the Pacific Ocean. At this point we were nearly three thousand feet above the capital, and were beginning to descend toward the valley of the Rio Lerma. Our party remained for twenty-four hours on the *Llanos de Salazar*. This is one of the highest railroad stations in the world. That of Leadville, on the Union Pacific, and Arroyo, in Peru, are higher, the latter being at an elevation of more than eleven thousand feet. The train was a special, sent out by the railway company for the accommodation of some artists and newspaper correspondents, whose business it was to make sketches of the scenery and write up the road. We could stop at any point we chose. We were one day on the summit of the Sierras, seated around our table at twelve o'clock, noon. Sitting there at dinner I felt impressed with the strange coming together of people and things. The dining-room car was built in York, Pennsylvania. Our colored cook, "Jimmie," was from Jamaica. The gentlemen composing the party were from Mexico, England, Australia, and the United States. Soup was served made of oysters from Baltimore. The canned corned beef was from Chicago. The bread was

Mexican. The canned butter came from Copenhagen, Denmark. The crackers we ate bore the stamp of "Oswego." The mustard was put up in Paris. The cheese was from England. The coffee was native. The only thing that seemed lacking was something to breathe, the atmosphere at this elevation being so rare. One of the Englishmen of our party provoked considerable laughter when he said, solemnly, that he did wish he could have a "good mouthful of fresh Hinglish hair."

Mexico is a land of mountains and valleys. The mountains are a continuation of the Cordilleras of South America. In the extreme south they are mere hills, but soon begin to rise, and in latitude 19° reach a mean elevation of nine thousand feet above the level of the sea. Their direction through Mexico, from Tehuantepec, is to the north-eastward. When they reach 20° north latitude they divide into three ranges. The eastern bears off toward the Atlantic, in the valleys of which are nestled the beautiful and prosperous cities of Monterey, Saltillo, and San Luis Potosi. The western range traverses the States of Jaslisco and Sinaloa, and then disappears in northern Mexico.

The central range runs through the States of Durango and Chihuahua, decreasing in altitude as it extends northward. I crossed two of these ranges, the first in passing from Monterey to Lagos. For many hours we climbed skyward, until we gained an elevation of eight or nine thousand feet, where the air was greatly attenuated. The middle range was crossed on the way toward Morelia.

No account of this magnificent natural scenery which comes into view as one passes from sea-coast to mountain-crest would be at all complete that did not include some reference, at least, to the great mountain peaks, Orizaba, the Cofre de Perote, Iztaccihuatl, Popocatepetl,

Nevado de Toluca, Ajusco, and Colimo. All of these have altitudes of more than 11,000 feet, and, lying along a vent in the earth's crust running nearly east and west, some of them were formerly active volcanos. But the greatest of all these great mountains is Popocatepetl, which, by the earlier measurements, was given an altitude of 17,884 feet above sea-level, but is, by more recent barometrical observations, believed to be much higher. Taking in the *Pico del Fraile*, the upper rim of the crater which no human foot has ever yet pressed, or ever will, quite likely, and allowing for it 2,000 feet, Popocatepetl has an altitude of nearly 20,000 feet.

Few travelers care to ascend into this region, and when they do so it is generally for the purpose of being able to boast of a feat involving great courage and powers of endurance. The labor required to gain even the highest accessible point is quite too great to justify the undertaking by the ordinary tourist. Besides, at that elevation the atmosphere is exceedingly rare, and consequently there is always a liability to hemorrhage of the lungs, or sudden death from heart derangements. As the ascent is mostly undertaken simply from motives of ambition or curiosity, only such as are perfectly sound in body should attempt it. At that great elevation the temperature is very low, which is also quite trying to the system.

Though possessed of perfect health, I did not attempt the ascent of any of these peaks, notwithstanding I was urged to do so. It was full enough for me to see them and learn how to pronounce their names. Take, for example, Iztaccihuatl, the White Woman. Does the reader desire to know how to pronounce that terrible Aztec word? Here is the prescription. First seat yourself in a good stout chair. If you have false teeth in your mouth, remove them, so they may not drop down your throat and interfere with your digestion. Take firm hold of the arms of the chair. If possible, brace your feet well against the wall, throw your head back against the chair, fill your lungs, and let drive! If it comes out Iz-tack-sea-watl, with the accent on the "sea," it will be sufficiently correct for all practical purposes.

But one can poorly conceive of the magnitude of Popocatepetl by reading about it, or viewing it from a distance. Go in any direction you may in the valley of Mexico, that vast irregular cone is in sight, standing out before you in silent and awful grandeur. What must it have been some thousands of years ago, when it poured its fiery lava over all the region round about. From its lofty summit the two oceans that wash America may be seen when conditions are favorable.

The crater is elliptical in form, and, according to M. Boscovitz, an eminent authority, is 5,000 feet in its longest diameter. The gullet of this giant has never been disturbed since the discovery of the New World; but in former times it must have thrown out molten matter abundantly, for thick beds of ashes and scoria are found for more than twenty leagues beyond its base. Wherever it has been possible for them to accumulate their mass in some places displays a depth of 150 feet and over.

The top of the volcano is covered with snow at all seasons, and, by a strange contrast, says the writer above quoted, "its once blazing summit, now extinct, has become an emblem of the alliance between the regions of winter and the empire of fire."

The crater of this grand mountain is about one thousand feet deep. The descent was formerly accomplished by means of a windlass and rope, and was made for the purpose of procuring sulphur. At the bottom were found great deposits of snow, while long stalactites of ice were hanging from the projecting rocks, where the sun never strikes, or where they are not molested by the jets of heated vapor that even now are emitted from the crevices of the earth. It is commonly believed that Cortez obtained sulphur for the manufacture of powder in this crater, but that may only be a tradition.

The silver mines of Mexico are not in these particular giant mountains, though it is more than likely that within them, and far beyond the possible reach of man, infinite quantities of the precious metals lie concealed. The silver mines of Mexico are mostly between 18° and 24° north latitude, and are generally found on the west side of the Sierra Madre.

Guanajuato, Catorce, Zacatecas, and Pachuca are the most noted centers of silver production. The *Real del Monte*, at the latter place, is one of the richest in the republic. It was there I saw silver bars piled up in the hacienda like cord-wood. The Count de Regla took from this rich vein $5,000,000 in twelve years. It has been stated by good authority that two thirds of all the silver in the world has come from the mines of Mexico. Up to 1880 they have yielded the precious metal to the value of *twelve billions of dollars*. There are probably three thousand mines in that land of mineral wealth, but only a few comparatively are valuable in a high degree. The yield now is about $25,000,000 a year of silver, and $3,000,000 of gold. Mexico produces ten times as much silver as is furnished by all the mines of Europe. But O the people! the people! the extreme poverty of the people! The mountains are full of silver and gold and copper and zinc, etc., yet most of these people you meet throughout the country are barefooted, and have scarcely clothing enough to cover their nakedness. They hew the silver ore out of the mountains by the ton every day, and yet are the owners of nothing; verily their fate is pitiable.

Through all this up-land region the maguey plant, the American agave, sometimes called the "century plant," is one of the chief productions, and, like many other good things, may be abused. Its heart is the source of the national beverage—*pulque*—the curse of the people. But, in fairness, it may be stated that this plant is not wholly evil. The uses to which it is put are numerous. For instance, the fiber of the leaf is a thread in common use for sewing coarse cloth. The thorn on the point of the long leaf can so be cut as to remain connected with the fibers, thus forming a natural needle and thread. A very good quality of paper is made from the bark of the leaf. The leaves, being very large and thick, are frequently used for thatch on the huts of the poor. The plants are arranged in rows, and make excellent fences. The material of the maguey is wrought into baskets, hats, fans, hammocks, curtains, etc. When young it is fed to the cattle, and when old and dried can be used for fuel. When the plant has attained the age of about seven years there flows from the base of the central stem a sap at the rate of two or three gallons per day for half the year; this is the juice which furnishes the before-mentioned pulque, regarded by the natives as drink, food, and medicine. There is a little romance about almost every thing; even the pulque plant is not destitute of it. I have read the following fable concerning it:

"A noble Toltec, named Papantzin, found out the method of extracting the juice from the maguey, and sent some of it to his sovereign, Tecpancaltzin, as a present by his daughter, the beautiful Xochitl, the flower of Tollan.

"Enamored alike of the drink and the maiden, the king, wishing to monopolize both, retained the lovely girl a willing prisoner, and in after years placed their son upon the throne. This was the beginning of the troubles of the Toltecs, who had then enjoyed peace for many years. That alliance led to their eventual dispersion and extinction, all brought about by the hand of woman and through the means of strong drink." The old story of "wine and women."

Through all his disasters, however, the Indian has clung to his pulque, each generation adding to the acres of maguey planted by their ancestors, and at the present time its consumption has reached enormous proportions. That which, in our own country, comes nearest the maguey plant in point of usefulness, without any of its bad qualities, is petroleum, which furnishes a good many substances that enter into our daily life. For example : it yields a volatile gas, that illuminates our dwellings; a lubricating oil, for machinery; naphtha, used for mixing paints and dissolving gutta-percha; asphaltum, for making varnish to brighten up our furniture, as well as for roofing our houses and paving our streets; paraffine, for candles and chewing gum; carbolic acid, for disinfecting purposes; and various aniline dyes, employed in giving the richest colorings to silk fabrics; besides, in its combustion, it serves for cooking our food and heating our dwellings.

The valley of Toluca is famous for its pulque, as one can readily learn from the extent to which the maguey plant is grown. The city of Toluca, with one exception, is the highest city in the republic. From the main plaza the famous mountain Nevado de Toluca is in plain sight. A professor in the college here informed me that the Pacific Ocean, one hundred and sixty miles distant, can be seen from the summit of the mountain, and that the Gulf of Mexico can also be seen with a good glass. The mountain is snow-crowned during most of the year. I was pleased with the city of Toluca, for it presented a cleaner appearance than some others through whose streets I had wandered. But, like the capital, it is cursed with *pulquerias*—the ubiquitous Mexican gin-mill. There is a great deal of drunkenness in Mexico, but very little quarreling and fighting. This universal beverage of the people is plenty and cheap, costing only a penny a glass, or three cents a quart. When drank freely it produces stupor. A native informed me that when a growing boy commences the use of it his mental powers begin to wane, and he rapidly becomes stupid. The ancient Aztecs, long before the days of Cortez, employed it to produce intoxication. Other stimulants are used as well—mescal aguardiente, "fire-water," brandy, whisky, wine, beer, etc. It is claimed that drinking pulque does not cause headache, nor does it fire the brain, like mescal or whisky. So much of it is consumed in the metropolis that there is a train on the Mexican railway which comes in every day from the gulf region, called the "pulque train," whose earnings are a thousand dollars a day from that traffic alone. I saw one morning, in front of a market-place, a huge and clumsy cart, drawn by a yoke of oxen, on which there was a great, black-looking sack of very curious shape, out of which an animal of some kind had been extracted, which was filled with pulque. This was the "bottle" of the Scriptures, and it was a huge one. It was not a "wine-skin," as the Revised Version has it, but a pulque-skin. This drink is said, by some persons, to be a very wholesome and nourishing beverage, and is declared to be a specific for dyspepsia and kidney affections. All classes use it, and regard it as the Irishman does his whisky, as a " good creature of God." I tasted it one day, on advice of a friend, when in a region where water was scarce and unwholesome, but did not relish it. One must learn to like it by continued use, as he learns to like garlic, tortillas, and chilé. That pulque tasted to me about like a mixture of sour milk, Dutch cheese, pickle-brine, soap-suds, and petroleum ! The little which I sipped, as an experiment, on that occasion treated me very meanly before morning.

To get a fine view of the rich valley of Toluca, I ascended the cupola of the college with one of our party, and was not only delighted with the panorama before me, but was fortunate enough to meet a professor who could converse in broken English. There were about two hundred students in the institution and a dozen professors.

It was gratifying to visit a college in Mexico. She needs modern schools more than any thing else; schools which teach science, language, art, criticism, etc., instead of so much catechism. They have had the latter for centuries, and the result is very apparent. Dr. Ellingwood says:

"Popular education has been hitherto unknown. Until recently the great mass of the people have been kept in entire ignorance. Within a few years several States have established primary schools, and private schools have been opened in the cities. The facilities for acquiring an education are being rapidly increased, and it is reasonably hoped will soon become universal."

One of the professors in the college at Toluca informed me that primary education has been declared compulsory, but he admitted that the law in this case, as in a good many others, is largely a dead letter. There are at present in the whole republic about 9,000 public elementary schools, attended by 300,000 pupils, and 138 schools of higher grade for professional education, attended by about 15,000 students. The school fund has reached as high as $3,000,000 a year, all of which is a promising sign.

The market-place at Toluca was the cleanest and most orderly of any I saw. The main market in the capital is very large, the throng is generally very dense, the sights curious, and the odors, as one pushes about among the motley crowd, not the most agreeable to the olfactories of a sensitive mortal. There are plazas especially devoted to marketing where every thing in the form of a commodity is sold. Here you can purchase vegetables and fruit to your stomach's content. There are stands where all kinds of beverages are for sale, patronized, alas! too freely by the populace. If your taste runs to jewelry, the venders of cheap trinkets are on hand to ask large prices, and then take small ones. If dry goods are wanted, they are abundant. Pigs, poultry, and pottery, or any thing else you want or don't want, you will be urged to buy. In some places the municipal governments have erected buildings, which shield the heads of both buyers and sellers from the scorching sun, but in the smaller villages generally the market vender must make his own booth, which he does by putting up two or three poles, and spreading his blanket over them. In all these market places the sights are odd enough. The sellers, whatever their sex, usually sit on the ground, with their goods—fruits, vegetables, candies, toys, etc., etc.—piled up in front of them in little heaps on straw mats, or bits of manilla cloth, or perchance on the bare ground. The men sit silent and taciturn under their broad-brimmed sombreros, while the women are generally garrulous and at times not a little coquettish. They are not at all particular about hiding their forms from view. The buyer can depend upon it that either sex will get the best of the bargain if possible.

The market-places often have wells and fountains, where the water-carriers congregate, and where mischievous boys take great delight in playing their pranks on each other—for boys are boys the world over. A good many people deal in second or some other hand articles in all the market-places and about the *portales*. One can find a great variety here. A man will spread out his old piece of cloth on the pavement or ground and cover it over with rusty nails, screws, files, old pistols, swords, fragments of iron, door keys, photographs torn from old albums, crucifixes, cheap pictures of saints, and sets of false teeth that show signs of long use in somebody's mouth.

Only servants and sight-seers go to market. A lady or gentleman of position would not think of such a thing. A native woman of social standing is seldom seen on the streets, and never unattended. She may walk to church in broad daylight accompanied by a friend or relative, or if a servant follows close behind her. By the social customs she cannot even ride in her own carriage with only the coachman in front. She certainly would not go to market and mingle with the rabble. Sabbath is the great market-day of the week, and is spent between business and pleasure. On Saturday afternoon the roads leading to the cities are thronged with men, women, and even children, carrying on their shoulders great bundles of vegetable produce, charcoal, poultry, crockery, and every marketable thing, or driving donkeys laden with these same articles, to be sold on Sunday. At break of day the work of selling begins, and there is more bartering on that day than any other in the week. Then comes mass in the churches, when they pay their devotions to Mary. Marketing over and prayers said, the *Plaza de Toros*, or Bull-Pen, is the next to receive attention. The bull-fight is the event of the day, and usually begins at four o'clock in the afternoon, continuing two or three hours. The more brutal and bloody the better. Then follow drunkenness and revelry the rest of the day, when the sensual crowd find their way home only to repeat this the next Sunday. I was credibly informed that in the interior of the country even the priests, in some instances, take a lively interest in these wild sports. They have been known to hurry through the mass, and then, with their game birds under their arms, enter the lists at the cock-pit, and bet as freely as any of the crowd.

Young people in Mexico do their courting at a great disadvantage. The young men usually pass up and down the streets, between the hours of five and eight o'clock in the afternoon, where reside the objects of their admiration.

A young señor fixes his eyes on the balcony or window of a young señorita's residence, that she may recognize him by some sign, if she, like Barkis, " is willin'," or decline his overtures by turning abruptly away. Right here in Toluca, two years ago, a couple of young gentlemen were both interested in the same señorita, and by accident met simultaneously in front of her residence to " do the bear "—*hacer el oso*, as they call it—that is, court the fair young lady. Of course they quarreled, and one of them drew a knife and stabbed the other fatally. Whether she regarded the survivor all the more as a hero and married him or not I did not learn. Perhaps she was sensible, and discarded him. A story is related of a young lady who had three admirers, two of whom pressed their suits so persistently that she went to sea to escape their attentions, and, lo! they both followed her on the same vessel. What to do she did not know—the dilemma was great. However, she consulted the captain, who advised her to leap into the ocean, and then choose the one who had courage enough to come to her rescue. So she plunged in and both her lovers leaped heroically after her. If her dilemma was great before, it was greater now. She could not marry both of them, and so wedded the one who remained at home and attended to his business.

The young man can get a glimpse of his lady-love when she walks with an attendant in the plaza, or he can follow her to church, and, while she is worshiping a dead saint, he can be watching a living one. But keep at a respectful distance he must until some third party intercedes in his behalf. If she drives out shopping in the evening he will be very likely to perambulate along the sidewalk after her carriage. He does not expect to speak to her, unless by the merest accident. If she casts one single smile on him he is restful. Then he promenades regularly before her residence, walks under her window, or signals to her from a door-way across the street. Besides, they have a language of flowers and of the fan and the cigarette; all alike are made to do Love's errands. A few gracious smiles from her embolden him to write a note, which he incloses in a bouquet and throws upon the balcony, or places it in her hands by some trusty servant of the household. But all is uncertain yet; he may fail in his enterprise, for even Mexican damsels are sometimes coquettish. If he belongs to an influential family, he can easily procure the kind offices of some one who will propose him as a *fiancé* for the young lady. If he is accepted, then he can pay his addresses in person and converse with her, but even then only in the presence of the relatives.

It must require a deal of love, and no less of patience, to be compelled to walk up and down in the hot sun or descending rain, stand for hours in some friendly doorway, and do one's courting at long-range for months, and sometimes years. But this is the price the señorita demands for her heart and hand.

There is far too little home-life among these people. Marriage by the priest involves a cost of about a dozen dollars, and by the alcalde, or magistrate, two dollars. But the devout Catholic would rather live without marriage, and in violation of God's law, than to have his matrimonial bonds executed by a civil officer. So, being too poor to pay the priest, and too religious to be married by a civil magistrate, he lives in a state forbidden by divine law. This sin is prevalent through all this land, from sea-coast to mountain crest.

CHAPTER XXI.

SONGS IN THE NIGHT.

The departure—Town of the angels—Cholula and its great pyramid—Down the mountain slopes—Wild scenery—Fearful chasms—The plains below—City of the "True Cross"—On ship-board—Home—After-thoughts—From Montezuma to Wesley—Sale of the shrines—Outlook from an azotea—The "Southern Cross"—Motley crowds—The two civilizations—The Bible in Mexico—New ideas—Possible reaction—Signs which follow—Telephones, railroads, etc.—Growl of the priest—A land for invalids—Patience—Progress.

THE dream of my boyhood days was at last fulfiled—the long-cherished hope had become a reality. I had, at the least, taken a hurried glance at old Mexico with its unequaled natural scenery and its strange and tragic history, and now the time had arrived for my departure. It was in the gray of the morning, when matin bells were clanging in the towers of a hundred churches, that I started on my way toward the blue gulf. The journey lay over the Mexican Railway. A whole chapter might be written descriptive of that route and the scenery through which it passes. The road, which is a masterly stroke of engineering skill, was the conception of some English capitalists half a century ago, and is, consequently, through a portion of the distance, one of the oldest railways on the continent of North America.

Owing to the numerous revolutions which have characterized the history of Mexico, it has been under the rule of forty different presidencies, and has proved the financial ruin of a great many people in consequence of the fluctuations in the price of its stock. Alas for
18

human ventures! Though of only moderate length, such was the difficulty in climbing the mountains, that it was nearly forty years in building, costing not far from $50,000,000.

I looked forward to the trip coastward with pleasurable anticipations. After wandering for some weeks over the table-lands amid clouds of dust, groves of cactus, and plantations of maguey, the thought of going down once more where the normal atmospheric pressure of fifteen pounds to the square inch prevails was refreshing.

Our train, that morning, was off on time. The road passes out of the valley of Mexico in a north-easterly direction, close under the dome of Guadalupe, and thence on through the narrow space between Lakes Texcoco and Xaltocan, soon coming in sight of the famous pyramids of San Juan Teotihuacan. Thence it bends to the south-east. In a few hours we were in the country of the Tlaxcalans—a people who were made to figure conspicuously as the rivals of the Aztecs in the days of the conquest. The first objective point was *Puebla de los Angeles*—town of the angels—to reach which a change of cars was made at Apizaco. Puebla lies in a broad plain, with the great snow mountains in full view, distant about thirty miles to the south-west, while Mount Malinche, named in honor of a woman, Cortez's interpreter, lifts its frowning head in the east. Puebla is one of the finest cities in the republic. I could only tarry there a couple of days, during which time, after visiting the great cathedral, the onyx works, the college—*Colegio del Estado*—and strolling through the Paseo Nuevo, taking a look at the new prison, then in course of erection, and visiting the mission of the Methodist Episcopal Church, a detour was made to the far-famed pyramid of Cholula. Gladly would I have tarried longer in such a place. Think of a pyramid covering forty-five acres at its base, and rising to a height of two hundred feet. Some say it is a natural hill faced with adobe. Even if that be true, great was the devotion of the people to their gods when so much hard work was done in their honor. Christianity has a lesson to learn even from pagans.

Returning to Apizaco, on the main line of the Mexican Railway, the journey was pursued over broad plains covered with fields of maize and wheat and plantations of the maguey plant ; and anon down, down, down fearful grades, around enormous bends, the road often skirting the borders of huge barrancas thousands of feet in depth, rocks piled on rocks, twisted and contorted in wild confusion ; mountain peaks towering far above peaks of less altitude, plains spread out before you in the dim distance! On the left are the glittering summits of Orizaba and San Andres, farther away still the great Cofre de Perote, outlined against the blue sky.

Passing the cities of Orizaba and Cordoba—the latter in a famous coffee-growing region—we were soon whirling along over the dusty plains of the *tierra caliente,* which extend from the base of the mountains to the gulf—now over vast stretches of sandy waste, and now amid palm groves, banana and pine-apple gardens, interspersed with clumps of orange and lemon-trees and other tropical fruits, whose names are difficult to spell, and even far more difficult to pronounce. Besides, the voice of the mosquito was heard in the land !

A few more hours of dust and heat and we were landed in Vera Cruz, a city without a carriage or coach of any kind, public or private, for there are no driveways within its borders ; not like old Venice either, with its gondolas—a city without even the smallest suburb, in fact—a walled city, built of stone and brick on about one or two hundred acres of land, the port of entry for a nation of more than ten millions of people, where nine tenths of all its foreign commerce pays duty, and, alas! the perpetual home of the much-dreaded *vomito*.

I remained there only a day, and not without some risk at that. I had been on the mountains and over the table-lands, but was now on the sea-coast, and the change was delightful. The temptation to wander about the old city could hardly be resisted. I visited one or two antique churches, adorned with the usual assortment of gaudily arrayed Marys and grotesque images of saints seen every-where else in this country. I sauntered out along her main paseo, sat down under the shade of her cocoa-palms, watched her far-famed zopilotes sitting on the corners of the towers—a crow-like bird that does the street-cleaning without getting up rings and jobs. I was soon on board the steamer, which was lying close under the walls of the dilapidated old castle of San Juan d'Ulloa, which is said to have cost the Spanish sovereign $13,000,000 to build, and which would crumble into ruins before a dozen modern rifled cannon in twenty-four hours. Our steamer took her course along the gulf coast, halting at the different ports of southern Mexico to load and unload freight of various sorts, principally *Jeniquen*, or hemp, until she reached the *Ultima Thule* of Mexico—far-away Yucatan. Thence she steamed across to Cuba, and, after three days of tropical sweltering in the spacious harbor of Havana, and perambulating through her narrow and filthy streets—not forgetting to visit what is claimed to be the tomb of the great Columbo—we passed out under the guns of Moro Castle and pursued our way northward around the coast of Florida, coming in sight of Key West. Then we felt that we were, indeed, homeward bound.

Fourteen days after waving our adios to Vera Cruz I landed in New York, having journeyed in all about eight thousand miles by land and sea without serious accident or permanent hinderance of any kind, arriving at my home within seven hours of the time designated for the return before setting out upon the journey; and such are the facilities for travel in this age of the world that I could have reached it on the very train and at the precise hour named had it been absolutely necessary to do so.

Now hear the conclusion of the whole matter. The question is not, What has been seen? Where have I traveled? but what has been learned of our sister republic? What are her relations to the great family of nations? What the hinderances to her progress? What the signs of her redemption? What are her chief wants? How can the "United States of the North" serve to the best advantage the "United States of the South?"

What if, for centuries past, Mexico has been groping her way in the dark? What if her people have been literally crushed under the heels of political and religious despotism? Shall the great Protestant world turn from her and feel no sense of pity, nor reach out a helping hand in the time of her greatest need?

The traveler in this land, though confronted on every side with symbols of the old *régime,* will not fail to note that a very decided change is coming over the face of society. Like the cloud on Mount Carmel, it is not yet much "larger than a man's hand," but it betokens a shower of blessings yet to fall on poor, bleeding Mexico. The change is necessarily slow, but then all great social and religious reforms are essentially slow in their movement.

During my sojourn in the city of Mexico I was favorably situated for observing men and things. Through the great kindness of our resident missionaries I was allowed the use of what my lady hostess called her "sky parlor"—a comfortable room built on the azotea—the flat roof of what was once known as the Church and Convent of San Francisco—then the greatest of its kind in all Mexico, but now the property, in part, of the Methodist Episcopal Church. In the days of its ancient glory it covered several blocks of land, a massive stone and brick structure, and, but for its great central dome, resembled far more a fortress than a church. On several Sabbaths I worshiped in this old pile with a good congregation, composed mostly of converted Mexicans. We were led in our singing by two native boys, not much, if any, over sixteen years old. One of them presided at the organ, the other played a cornet creditably. Thus led, we sang the familiar hymns, translated into Spanish, which we sing at home, set to music we have known from childhood. A strange feeling came over me as I first sat on the platform in that beautiful auditorium, once the court, or patio, of the convent, large and elaborately designed, erected on the very spot, it is said, where some hundreds of years ago there stood one of the old Montezuman pagan temples.

This building was one of the many sequestrated by the government, under the leadership of Juarez, in 1859, when the new order of things began, up to which time the Church owned, directly or indirectly, nearly every thing in the country worth owning. The Liberal party saw that this vast ecclesiastical power must be broken, and, with a mighty and fearless stroke, dealt the blow. The convents and nunneries were broken up, and monks and nuns were banished the country, or compelled to live some other sort of life.

Hundreds of these churches and convents were taken possession of by the civil authorities all over the land. Many of them, like this one, were sold to the highest bidder; others stand vacant and idle at this hour. Some of them have been converted into school buildings, or have been utilized for mechanical industries. I passed one in my rambles, on one occasion, in which I heard the sound of a buzz-saw, and could not help thinking how much more practical religion there was in that sound of industry than in the meaningless tinkling of bells and the incessant mumbling of prayers once so common within those walls.

As I stood on the azotea of this old ex-convent of San Francisco, evening after evening, when I came in from my walks, at about ten o'clock, there came into the field of vision a constellation in the heavens never seen in the North, the magnificent "Southern Cross." It was generally very bright and beautiful, and seemed to hang just a few degrees above the horizon. To me it was a symbol of Christ's reign, and, like Constantine of old, I, too, could exclaim, "*In hoc signo vinces*"—Under this sign thou shalt conquer. Mexico has had the cross as a mere symbol for ages, but she has known nothing of the real life of the Gospel, the possession of which will make her a conqueror in the end. But Christ is here in fresh, new power, let us believe, and the natives are waking up to a better life.

From this eminence I could not only look up into the brightest of tropical heavens, but could also look down upon the hundreds of acres of azoteas which stretch away before one's view. I could count the domes and towers of the almost innumerable churches which had been erected through the three centuries of Catholic supremacy, and could behold the motley crowds of men and women, in thoroughfare and plaza, intent in their pursuit of either business or pleasure. But what a change has come over Mexico, that this very building, once the stronghold of Romanism, located in the heart of this great city, on the great *Calle de San Francisco*, should now be cut up into sections, run through by streets, and be devoted to the printing of Protestant books, the preaching of the Gospel by Protestant ministers, and the education of the young in the elements of the new faith! Surely some agency has been at work to produce such a change as this. Mexico has been Catholic, but will yet be increasingly Protestant. Romanism has put forth great efforts to possess itself of the whole of the New World. She planted her colonies all around the continent of South America and through Central America, besides making a strenuous effort to get control of the whole of North America. For three centuries that effort was continued unabatingly and with vigor. The fall of the Old French power in North America gave the territory now embraced in the United States to the Protestant cause. Mexico, as a Spanish colony, fell into the grasp of Romanism, and remained there.

One hundred years before the settlement of Jamestown, in Virginia, Brazil, Hayti, Cuba, Central America, and Mexico were centers of the Catholic religion in the western hemisphere. Pizarro conquered Peru nearly one hundred years before the *Mayflower* anchored in the waters of Massachusetts Bay. Buenos Ayres, on the east coast, and Santiago, on the west coast of South America, were founded nearly two centuries before the settlement of the empire State of Georgia.

The Amazon was explored seventy-five years before the Hudson was known to civilization. As early as A. D. 1519 Ferdinand Magellan discovered and named the strait which bounds South America on the south. All these events took place a full century before our fathers laid the first foundation stones of the great Protestant republic.

Behold now the two great sections, and see the difference between them. How grandly does the Protestant civilization of the North tower above that of the Catholic in the far South! "Look at South America, with rivers that are deeper, with plains that are broader, with seasons that are longer, with a climate more temperate, with fruits more luscious, with soil that is richer, with every thing necessary for superior productions; yet South America remains to-day a country whose wealth is unpossessed, whose forces are unreduced to meet humanity's wants. Compare its railroads, its domestic commerce, its internal navigation, its foreign trade, its private and public wealth, and it dwindles almost into insignificance relatively to its territory.

"What has this civilization produced in great and striking personalities? There are names that will appear in local histories, but who has given birth to a great thought that the whole world welcomes? Whose life has entered into the life of the whole world and become a part of it? Where are the names that will stand beside those of Franklin, Fulton, and Morse? Or, on the other hand, what has this civilization produced in the elevation and culture of the masses of people?"

One of our missionaries answers these questions by declaring that the aborigines are as truly pagan now as when they were under the dominion of the Incas.

When these countries were colonized, Spain stood at the head of human governments. She should have been able to send out sturdy scions that would have developed a more than average growth. Yet the production has been, with little exception, an aggregation of unstable republics, whose histories have been but annals of revolution. They seem to lack the power to assimilate the different elements and create an organic union. There, too, is Mexico, where the same power has reigned, and though possessed of every element of national wealth, "beautiful for situation," she has yet been without either prospect, honor, or peace.

The hope of Mexico is not in her soil, her climate, or her mines. These are the bases of her physical wealth, it is true. Religion and education have to do with a people's greatness. Her old religion has depressed her spirit and dwarfed her intellect. A new one alone can redeem her; a new religion, with the improvements it brings with it along all lines of daily life.

It is only a trifle over half a century since the first Protestant Bible found its way into Mexico. Little by little has the light crept in. When the American army invaded that country in 1846, a few copies of the Holy Scriptures, along with some religious tracts in Spanish, were scattered among the people. Thus it has often happened that the sword in the hand of the warrior has prepared the way for the Prince of Peace. Some precious seeds of truth were in this way cast into Mexican soil.

Miss Rankin, a lady of piety and zeal, began her work on the lower Rio Grande in 1852. Though relatively small, it was indeed great in its results as an entering wedge. The American and Foreign Christian Union next entered the field, and was soon followed by missionaries of the American Board. In 1863 Protestantism was formally inaugurated in the beautiful city of Monterey. Then, in 1871, it was established in the capital of the republic. In 1872 the Friends Foreign Missionary Association and the Presbyterian Church both began work. In 1873 the two Methodisms occupied chosen fields, and have pushed their forces to the front. The Associate Reformed Synod followed in 1877, and the Southern Baptists in 1880. The Protestant world is surely awake to the spiritual needs of these poor people.

There are now scattered throughout the republic ninety-eight ordained and about the same number of unordained ministers of the different denominations. About one hundred and fifty colporteurs and Bible agents are engaged in evangelistic work. Every Sabbath witnesses the assemblage of more than three hundred congregations of Protestant worshipers, many of whom occupy well-built churches of their own. Church communicants number over sixteen thousand, against none in 1869, with nominal adherents of about twice that number. Six thousand Sunday-school children are enrolled in the Protestant schools. The day-schools number about three thousand children. Four theological seminaries have been established for the training of native young men for the ministry, and within ten years more than fifty millions of pages of religious literature have been issued from the different Protestant presses. These churches and religious agencies of the new order are planted in leading centers from Chihuahua and Monterey in the north to Progreso in the extreme south. In no country on the globe is there an opportunity to preach the Gospel to a greater number of willing hearers, at so small an outlay of money, as in this our sister republic. The friends of the Protestant cause, however, let it be remembered, greatly fear a reaction from liberalism through the influence of the Church party, which is possible, and, were it to take place, would not only endanger their cause, but greatly impede the progress of the new civilization. Therefore let the friends of Mexico do their whole duty in this great struggle for the redemption of a people. On this point one who has long resided there writes:

"We who have been on the ground during all these years have seen with pain and sadness this gradual relapse and the growing indifference and coldness toward

Protestantism on the part of many life-long Liberals, and the open hostility of some who were partisans of the reform. In the city of Mexico this change is not so noticeable, for the large foreign population there has a wonderfully liberalizing effect. But throughout the country at large this change has been increasingly observable during the past three years. The construction of railroads and the establishment of other enterprises under the auspices of American capital and direction have greatly alarmed the clergy and the masses, lest it should all lead to American domination in this country. As one of the results, there has been greatly increased opposition to Protestantism ; the priests have worked on the credulity of the people and aroused their religious zeal; religious festivals have grown in importance ; pilgrimages have been revived ; old churches have been repaired and new ones built ; processions forbidden by law have been freely tolerated in many places ; and outbreaks against Protestants have become alarmingly frequent."

The above was not written in any spirit of complaint, but only to show the need of a deeper devotion to a cause which must not be deserted through either fear or discouragement.

With Christianity has always gone a grander and broader civilization. Touch the brain of a people with the "truth as it is in Jesus Christ," and you stir thought out of which will come naturally all the improvements of commercial and industrial life. In Mexico things are changing. In all the cities through which one passes it is noticeable that American ideas especially are gaining the ascendency. The Yankee is abroad in the land putting in telephones by the hundred in the different cities. One cannot walk the length of any business block in any city scarcely without hearing the click of the sewing-machine, or seeing something distinctively American. Policemen and soldiers are almost invariably armed with American pistols and rifles of the most approved pattern. American organs and pianos are on sale at the great centers of trade. American mechanics are introducing planing-mills for manufacturing sashes and doors and other building material. In the principal cities street-car lines have been established, after the American method, and often by both American enterprise and capital. In the larger cities our modern system of electric lights is employed in illuminating the streets and plazas. The railroad interests, too, are largely in the hands of Americans, who not only furnish the capital, but conduct the enterprises. The thoughtful native cannot fail to see this inroad upon the ancient order of things, while the wily priest is unsparing in his denunciations of these aggressions, and would doubtless gladly banish these modern improvements and reinstate the old *régime* of popular subserviency and priestly domination.

There is a little danger, however, that the American love of money-making may crowd too many improvements upon Mexico for her own financial good. This is especially true with respect to railroads. There is not enough business at present to employ profitably all the roads built and being built. But, then, eventually they will bring in new, fresh life, which will create enterprise and capital. The Mexican Central line, from Tampico, on the gulf, across the country to San Blas, on the Pacific coast, will become naturally a highway of the nations, greatly shortening the distance between the far East and the West. The opening up of new routes of travel and the adoption of improved methods will essentially change the whole aspect of things. If the scream of the locomotive will not wake up the old Toltec and Aztec dead, it is stirring the lethargy of their living representatives.

Pleasure and health seekers in large numbers will yet find their way to the cities of Monterey, Saltillo, San Luis Potosi, and other points, to spend the winter months where the climate is simply perfect. The only or main reason why this has not already been a sanitarium for invalids has been the difficulty of getting there. This the railroads have effectually removed. And furthermore, we are likely to be a little impatient with our Mexican neighbors, and to censure them because of the seeming tardiness with which they accept the new ideas. That was a mistake we of the North all made at the close of our civil war. We expected the people of the South would in a couple of years see the error of their ways and fall into line. We forgot that for two hundred years they had been educated to believe in the divine right of slavery. A body of people changes slowly. So the Mexicans are changing slowly. We must not expect any great and sudden revolution. They have much to unlearn. Protestantism is the leaven which is hid in the three measures of meal, and in time will leaven the whole lump.

Mexico, though far from being really prosperous, is more so now than ever before. The revenue comes nearer meeting the expenditures of the government. It has in operation not far from three thousand miles of railroad, against almost none ten years ago. The only line in existence then was that from Vera Cruz to the capital, which was begun in 1837 and completed in 1873. Her army is larger and better equipped than formerly. Emigration, for almost the first time in her history, is being talked of with encouragement. The mines are producing more native silver, and the mints are coining more dollars, than in previous years. Cotton-mills are manufacturing more fabrics for home use, while agriculture, the basis of a nation's thrift, is taking on new forms wherever modern methods have been adopted.

Is Mexico making substantial progress? Let the reader judge. Since the overthrow of the Maximilian dynasty, in 1867, they have established a free constitution, embodying those essential guarantees of liberty which the Anglo-Saxon race regards as fundamental. The Church and State have been effectually and permanently divorced, and in that divorcement the vast and ill-gotten estates held by the Church have been largely secularized, and thus a power that could always be used in the interest of despotism was forever broken. Her free constitution guarantees the right of free speech, the freedom of the press, liberty of conscience in the worship of God, universal suffrage, trial by jury, and the subordinating of the military power to the civil. The primary-school system is, also, an outgrowth of this modern thought, and never could have been had the old priestly tyranny continued to rule in that land. In short, Mexico is a republic formed chiefly on the basis of our own.

From the smallest conceivable beginnings, less than half a century ago, have come these great changes, which must now advance, for revolutions never go backward. A writer in the *New York Evangelist* recently summed up this subject in the following pertinent language :

" Mexico is our neighbor. She has been unfortunate. The centuries of Spanish rule left her in the condition of the man who went down from Jerusalem to Jericho and fell among thieves. The Maximilian dynasty, designed to retain her in civil and religious thralldom, was the finishing blow of foreign usurpation. Since its overthrow Mexico has been returning to consciousness; has been striving to become a nation. Great changes have already been effected for the better. Greater still remain to be effected, and to secure these she appeals to us by her mute misery, and by the lips of her most patriotic and eloquent sons, for help. We are interested in her welfare. She shares the continent with us. Her destiny is ultimately to be associated, if not identified, with ours. She is a sister republic, feeble, burdened with heterogeneous and debased elements, largely a prey to ignorance and civil anarchy, yet striving on the whole nobly to assume a proper position among the nations. Her natural resources and enterprise are steadily inviting the investment of our capital and enterprise. Their importance is conceded, and sagacious statesmen cannot but recognize the claims to national sympathy which she presents. . . . The truth has been spreading. Christian institutions have been springing up. Revivals have taken place which give assurance that even Mexico may be transformed by the power of the Gospel. She is in some respects in a condition not unlike that of the nations of Europe at the dawn of the Reformation. Her own bitter past is full of instruction and warning. She is not disposed to go back to the experience of subjection to that spiritual domination which has cursed her so long. She is accessible, as never before, to the enlightenment of the age, to the enterprise of the century. The present seems the hopeful spring-time of her regeneration."

THE END.

www.ingramcontent.com/pod-product-compliance
Lightning Source LLC
Chambersburg PA
CBHW031337230426
43670CB00006B/353